THE LAST OF THE LIGHT

for Jonathan Key

> . . . facilis descensus Averno:
> noctes atque dies patet atri janua Ditis
> sed revocare gradum superasque evadere ad auras
> hoc opus, hic labor est.

The Last of the Light
About Twilight

PETER DAVIDSON

REAKTION BOOKS

Published by Reaktion Books Ltd
Unit 32, Waterside
44–48 Wharf Road
London N1 7UX, UK
www.reaktionbooks.co.uk

First published 2015, reprinted 2016
Copyright © Peter Davidson 2015

Printed and bound in China
by 1010 Printing International Ltd

A catalogue record for this book is available from the British Library

ISBN 978 1 78023 510 3

Contents

Tim Brennan, *Evening Sky*, 2007, digital image.

INTRODUCTION

We should begin by such a parting light
To write the story of all ages past
And end the same before the coming night . . .
Sir Walter Raleigh, 'The Ocean's Love to Cynthia' (*c.* 1590s)

The owl of Minerva begins to fly only at dusk.
G.W.F. Hegel, preface to *Grundlinien der Philosophie des Rechts* (1820)

Last night the storms passed over in the dark to leave this borrowed
day of stillness and bright air. The barley is harvested now and the
long slopes above the house are pale with stubble. It is cold by the
end of the afternoon, colder still in the thin wind as I climb out
above the shelter of the hawthorns, where the track bends right
towards the farm, and the mountains on the western horizon come
into view. This walk comes earlier every day, as the year hurries
down towards the dark. I press on ahead up the stubble field until
the whole broad valley lies below me, with the wider landscape
spread beyond it. The black hill above Cullen, then the receding
shadows of the greater hills that begin beyond Huntly, fading into
distances and cloud.

To the south is the outriding mountain of Bennachie, with its
row of rocky teeth that gave the ridge its Celtic name, 'The Mountain
of the Comb'. That name became the 'Graupius' of Mons Graupius,
the place where the legions were defeated, the northernmost point
that the Roman Empire reached on land. So I stand on shadowed
slopes, on the bare shoulder of the hill, outside the old boundaries
of Empire, on the far margin of Europe.

The lime-white castle of the Jacobite Hays closes the valley to the south, its woods curving about it, huge beeches washed with umber as autumn takes hold. There is a bonfire among the plantations, one straight column of rising smoke. The castle wavers and dissolves behind it. Across the tawny land, with the last rolls of straw in the fields, there is a scatter of stone farm-towns, each with its hedges and tree. Our house is invisible on its ancient site in the valley bottom, folded into the sheltering flank of the hill, lost in its grove. There is something secretive still about these remote landscapes of old rebellion – Lancashire, Aberdeenshire – the places that held out against all the revolutions, religious, industrial and glorious alike. The castle guards its own 'dark corner of the land', with the Jesuit badge still carved over the fireplace in its great hall, part of a furtive culture of codes, ciphers and allusions. To the north the slopes fold into dimness and away into cloud massing over the coast.

The sun is far into the west now: the mountains to the south have gone to flat grey and leaden blue. The farmland in the valley at my feet is sinking into the shadows. Only the western ranges hold the light. The sky above them is faint azure with a thin glaze of yellow laid over it, spreading up from the horizon. However hard I stare, shading my eyes against the sun balanced on the rim of the mountains, I can't see where gold gives way to blue. John Ruskin laboured all his life in the attempt to describe the almost indefinable colours of a clear western sky, coming in the end to rest on the beautiful form of words that fixes the thing as nearly as it can be defined: 'transparent blue passing into gold'.[1]

The sun sinks below the nearest peak. Deep in the distant hills, mountain slopes and high grasslands are flooded in gold. Looking westwards over the darkened fields towards this transient, bright kingdom, I am seized by an unreasoned longing to be there in that unreachable, temporary paradise at the frontier of the day. I know that it will fade when the sun goes below the mountains and the cold flows down with the evening wind. But, for this one moment, that last territory of the light seems to draw into itself every longing for travel that I have ever felt and every longing for home.

How little resistance we have to these longings that come with evening: the vague yearning for the place we haven't come to yet, or the place that we have left without hope of return. Belated longing for journeys in time as much as place. The melancholy of Europe evoked at the opening of Angela Carter's *Black Venus*: 'Sad; so sad those smoky-rose, smoky-mauve evenings of late autumn, sad enough to pierce the heart . . . the time of impotent yearning, the inconsolable season.'[2] Why do we respond to these words with such an emotion of recognition? Is it because we are predisposed to do so by our personal histories, our educations, the inherited cultures that we share? The great origin myth of the west is Virgil's tale of the voyage of the Trojan refugee Aeneas towards a promised home in the lands below the sunset, and the disappointments and losses that haunt him even in Hesperia. Is it the condition of the European 'evening-land' to see life itself as exile – *hoc exilium* – felt anew with the fall of every dusk?

> We turned from the rail with a sigh, aware that the light was sifting away into darkness, as casually as the plumes of smoke from the funnel of the ship that carried us. We had become, with the approach of night, once more aware of loneliness and time – those two companions without whom no journey can yield us anything.[3]

Thus Lawrence Durrell, travelling through places at the root of the European arts, on the voyage from Cyprus to Venice. Through the centuries, European culture has, to some degree, felt itself to be an after-culture, a broken culture of shadow and echo. All times after the lost, bright world of Greece and Rome are 'twilight ages'. Those who lived in the overshadowed world after the fall of the Western Empire had to look back to the full sunlight of antiquity for wisdom in every field of human endeavour – medicine, poetry, law. The great humanist endeavour of the Renaissance was in essence the piecing together of the scattered fragments of the works of the ancients, even amid an awareness that much was lost beyond recovery. For a thousand years Europe has readily accepted the old idea of the constant decay and dimming of the world. This has affected almost everything. It is only the generals and dictators who proclaimed in action and architecture that they had re-made the glories of the Romans. The age of gold declines to our age of iron, and exile and shadow are the undersong of our histories. Our own age too can readily be seen as a spoiled and darkening one, littered with a tidewrack of failing monuments to the hopes of post-war Europe.

By Christian tradition, too, Europe has seen itself as defined by twilight: the twilight of the scattered, fallen world as opposed to the ordered, sunlit garden from which humanity is exiled. The light of our brightest day is but a shadow of the sun before the fall. The Anglo-Saxon *Lives of Adam and Eve* assert that the light of the world that we humans inhabit is but one-seventh of the light of the otherworld of Eden. Like twilight, the whole human condition is thus conceived as occupying a halfway point between a greater light and a greater darkness. Throughout the long Middle Ages twilight was also a time of unease, the antechamber to the night, the time to solicit supernatural protection. In *Beowulf*, it is at nightfall that the monster Grendel emerges from the outland of the black mere, to approach the human world:

> *Sceaduhelma gesceapu scrídan cwóman Wan under wolcnum.*[4]
>
> and stealthy night-shapes came stealing forth under the cloud-mirk . . .[5]

It is on the threshold of the night that the hymn for Vespers weaves its web of protection around the threatened house:

> *Procul recedant somnia*
> *et noctium phantasmata . . .*[6]
>
> May evil dreams and the phantoms of the night be kept far away from us . . .

The word 'exile' resounds through the western liturgy, bearing the idea that the only lasting home that humanity can know is in the far garden, the celestial city.

The first lights appear far below in the windows of the scattered farmhouses. How yellow the lamplight shines in this fading world of slate-blue, smoke and umber, of the last light held in the margins of the clouds, as Ruskin remembered them, 'their edges burnished by the sun like the edges of golden shields, and their advancing march is as deliberate and majestic as the fading of the twilight itself into a darkness full of stars'.[7] Twilight can be thought of also as the time of tranquillity and return, when all things scattered by the day are drawn back to their right places. Sappho thought of the dusk, of the benign evening star as a guardian of the homeward way:

> Bringing the flocks homeward,
> Bringing the child home to its mother.[8]

Evening paradises can be located on earth in the southern European imagination: slanting sunlight on groves of orange trees. The evening heavens of the north have to be elsewheres, like the slopes that have now darkened among the mountains to the west: imagined in far hills or in the sunset clouds.

In the south of Europe, any clement evening draws forth whole populations to thread familiar routes through streets, squares and cafes; to stroll together, greeting colleagues and friends, tracing patterns of connection under those colonnades, those avenues of palms or bitter oranges that seem barely imaginable to me now, alone in the cold on this Scottish hillside, as the day dwindles to a yellow line on the western horizon.

Yet only a month ago, I was standing on another hill, in dusty warmth of late summer. Late August thunderstorms had broken the suffocating heat of the Veneto, although the chestnut trees along the slopes were brown from long drought. The afternoon was still hot during the walk up the slope to the Villa Valmarana, fallen figs in the dust underfoot, hazelnuts and chestnuts ripening along the road. But the heat had faded while we had been in the main villa, and I had paused for a moment in the box garden at the end of the detached guest wing to look across to the sanctuary of Monte Berico.

The gravel and walls were still hot in the evening sun; the tunnels of hornbeams between villa and guest wing were turning shabby, withering for lack of rain. The fountain in front of Neptune in his great niche was dry.

The view out over the valley with its olives and vines below was still of the Italy of Ruskin, even of Goethe, for all the prosperous modern villas hidden discreetly amongst the trees. Slopes of hanging woodland, the ilexes amongst them still inky green. The dome and bell-tower of the sanctuary clear against the softening light. Smoke from a garden fire hanging against azure fading to white, blurring the sharp outlines of the cypresses along the ridges of the hills.

I was trying to make sense of the frescoes by the Tiepolo family in villa and guest house, when three strokes of the bell sounded three times across the valley. It is hard to account for the choices of subject for these wonderful painted rooms. The frescoes in the *pallazina* (the villa itself) are by the eighteenth-century Venetian painter Giambattista Tiepolo. They are justly celebrated for their uncanny virtuosity, for the painted cloud hovering in front of the feigned columns in the entrance hall, defying sight and reason it its apparent reality. The four ground-floor rooms are painted with scenes from European epic – *Iliad* and *Aeneid*, Ariosto's *Orlando Furioso*, Tasso's crusading epic *Jerusalem Liberated* – yet the cumulative effect of a thoughtful visit is a kind of disquieted melancholy. A puzzled sense lingers that something is wrong despite the accomplishment and beauty of the paintings themselves, their palette so fine that it is as though the figures and the architectures and landscapes through which they move were shaped out of late-afternoon sunlight, rather than simply being lit by it. It is very difficult to follow the choice of episodes to be depicted – the series is possibly linked by the theme of the greatest heroes conquered by love, conquered by desire. But the result seems to convey an insistence on the idea of decline, to show great heroes at their moments of greatest weakness.

The bell had started a train of thought of its own, moving below the conscious surface of the mind, surfacing only as the words 'now and at the hour of our death' formed on my lips. The Angelus bell sounds out of the deep time of Europe, the ancient divisions of the day. The ringing of the bell at six is not only a call to brief prayer and recollection of the Annunciation, it is also a pivot between afternoon and evening, the point where the mind turns to the liberty after the day's work, to the cooler hours after the heat of afternoon. It is an echo turned outwards to secular society of the intense reckoning and marking of the hours of the day in the lives of the religious orders. Their daily pattern of observance – the prayer of the hours in matins, vespers, compline – is a time-capsule preserving the human day as it was perceived in the first millennium. Public time in the Middle Ages and Renaissance was communal, marked by church bells, and later by public sundials and clocks. Much of that ended when the pocket watch became widely affordable and, at least in the north of Europe, one of the consequences of modernity is that there is barely a sense of shared progress through the day. Rush hours are left as the only markers of common humanity. Time is now privatized and specific to the individual. In the south, the Angelus bell and the later *passeggiata*, that spontaneous and universal movement into the central streets of the town, keeping the visible fabric of society in repair by weaving through the crowds of friends and connections, look back in different ways to coherent and communal uses of evening.

Six o'clock, so they will be closing the great gates of the villa in a moment. But it strikes me, at this end of afternoon in the box garden between the *palazzina* and the *foresteria*, that I am also standing within a historical perception of twilight. Between the failing heroes in the villa and the elegant transience of the contemporary scenes painted in the guest-wing by Tiepolo's son Giandomenico is what we could call 'Horatian' time, the Roman poet Horace's sombre perception of a world declining into evening as each generation goes down one further degree on its long slope. *We are worse than our parents and the next generation will be worse still.*

Did Count Giustino Valmarana, who commissioned both sequences of frescoes in the last year of his life, feel a public or civic decline from the brightness of the heroic world to the deepening twilight of his own day? *Nos nequiores* – certainly, the Venice of 1756 was not the Venice of 1571. Perhaps it was he who chose the subjects for the painted rooms: in the hall on the axis of the house Agamemnon hides his face, weak enough to sacrifice his daughter for a favourable wind. Achilles sits shadowed in the feigned architecture of the first room, sulking over the distribution of slaves, turning his back on his goddess mother rising from her native sea. Aeneas weeps and covers his eyes as Mercury orders him to set destiny before love. After too long, Tasso's hero Rinaldo says farewell to the enchantress Armida, in a composition dominated by dust-rose and purple draperies against powdery grey cliffs, the very colours of the Mediterranean twilight. Overall, there is a post-baroque sense that it is late in the day, late in everybody's day, and even the heroes of the dawn of the world and the paladins of the crusades had already within them the seeds of the decline. Everything is old, everything is complicated. However beautiful it all is, it is moving to evening and its end.

A different kind of disquiet attends the rooms in the guest house, the *foresteria*, a sense of the passing moment of the eighteenth century caught in paint, of the transience of fairground and carnival, even of the pathos of fashion considered as a marker of the passage of time, when there are no larger events to mark it. So many figures turn away from the spectator. A great evening cloud overshadows the landscape behind the rustic lovers. The last room has fairground scenes in feigned picture frames. Here, almost all the figures have their backs to us and those that turn towards us are masked. They are crowding round something that we cannot see – a peepshow in a box, in the speech of the time, a *new world*. We can only imagine what they see in this *Mondo nuovo* – the title itself is at once sad and faintly menacing in this context of a crowd in disguise under a chalky evening sky, whose minimal washes also suggest sands at low tide and an empty sea. Is the new world in the box geographical or temporal? Does it offer a hint of the world that comes after the old world has run to its end?

As the great gates close behind us, and we walk past the statue-crowned gateposts opposite the villa with a tangled, deep-shadowed grove behind them, I think that everything that we have just seen

Detail from Giandomenico Tiepolo, *The New World*, 1791, fresco formerly in the
Villa Zianigo in the Veneto.

belongs to the last years before the wars of Empire and the neoclassical
revival resulted in a conformist seriousness about antiquity and
enforced, for a time at least, the outward expression of belief in a
new dawn.

Hazels and chestnut trees, limewashed walls giving out heat as
the air cools. Maize fields and drainage ditches, olives and vines.
Sky dust-white, then purple for ten minutes, then dark.

HOW DIFFERENT FROM the abrupt, purple dusk of Italy the slow
death of the northern daylight is, with its whitish-yellow light now
faded behind the western mountains. No wonder that the long
twilight is the particular obsession of the north of Europe. One of
the surest ways of defining the mind of the north is to define it in
terms of light: prodigality of light in the white nights of summer,
paucity of light in the dark of the year. And the slow blues of the
twilights between them with the lamps coming on one by one.

The 60th parallel takes on an importance here as the meridian of those latitudes that experience a distinctly northern pattern of light. Territories lying ten degrees to either side of the 60th parallel, to a greater or lesser degree, know those extremes of light and dark and, crucially, those twilights that shape and define the north of Europe. Long evenings and protracted sunsets stretch from about 50 degrees to 70 degrees. Northern winter days that end in damp and frozen air: ash and rose and crimson over the cities, grey and gold over the remote provinces.

Beyond 70 degrees the north is the frontline in the battle of the light and the dark. Thinking about the arts of the north, the 60th parallel is nearly a centre-line: from 50 to 74 degrees might be said to encompass the inhabited north, all places where awareness of light is not only essential and formative, but the foundation of modes of feeling that find expression in all the arts, but most especially the visual arts.

These latitudes are the realms of the twilight: all these territories have some degree of twilight rather than darkness all through the night at midsummer. *The white nights* – a wonderfully precise phrase, evoking the lighted but colourless sky of the evenings when the summer sun is setting almost due north, before the cobalt midnight and the dawn out of the north. To the north of all this (north across the skerries and the islands, far beyond the reflected *simmer dim* of the Shetlands and the Faeroes) are the lucid midnights of Tromsø and their dark opposite, snow falling through lightless air through the murk-tide of winter. Arctic north, absolute north, is simply defined in the absolute of light and dark.

South of the 50th parallel are the territories of true darkness at midsummer, the year-round equipoise of night and day, short twilights, the noonday demon of the August sun. Heat and light are the enemy here in the malign brilliance of high summer, and the cooler hours of darkness – *la madrugada* – are the time of release and pleasure. So the history of twilight has also a geography focused on those places where twilight is inevitably a mode of feeling as well as a natural phenomenon. 'No twilight', said Coleridge, 'within the courts of the sun'.

The words for twilight – dusk, half-light and crepuscule – should concern us too:

> Dusk. In Greek, the dusk is metaphorically *lykóphŏs*, 'wolf-light', which I have also heard in Austria (*Wolflicht*). In French it is *entre chien et loup* (between dog and wolf) – the dogs have knocked off barking for the day: the wolves are about to start howling. There was an English saying 'dark as a wolf's mouth', where 'mouth' may originally have been the wolf's *month*, the perpetual dusk of January.

In French, dusk is also *l'heure du berger*, the shepherd's hour, when *l'Étoile du berger*, the shepherd's, or evening star, Venus, steals into the sky. It sounds 'romantic' (and the 'shepherd's hour' is held to be auspicious for lovers), but of course dusk, when the wolves were about, was exactly when the shepherd (with his dog) had to be at his most watchful, and when all things were 'between dog and wolf' in another sense.[9] In the northern latitudes of twilight, where midwinter can feel like something near to victory for the dark, the fall of the long night is a time of anxiety:

> It is, all in all, an edgy time of day. In Latin it is *crepusculum*, and in English once was 'crepuscle'. It and other derivatives – like the adjective 'crepuscular' – have now fallen largely out of use, as has 'the gloaming', a word of Scandinavian origin corresponding in literal meaning, though not in richness of association, to the French-Canadian *la brunante*, which sounds like something from cookery. 'Crepuscle', to English ears, is a bit creepy, and 'the gloaming' has echoes of doom and glumness.
> *Crepusculum* also carries a sense of doubt. *Creperae*, in Latin, were 'doubtful matters', 'because dusk', Varro tells us in one of his strongest etymologies, 'is a time when to many it is doubtful whether it is even yet day or is already night'.[10]

And always *shade* and *shadow* are ambiguous, however much they may be words of refuge and consolation in the heat of the south. And *overshadowed* is always attended by undertones of menace and defeat, from an individual under suspicion to a whole community living as internal exiles, or mistrusted second-class citizens.[11]

The last brightness has moved far west beyond the Cairngorms. As I make my way down the hill, glad to move out of the wind into the shelter of the hawthorns, a purpose grows clear in my mind: to follow the longings of the 'evening lands' through history and trace their twilight arts. If I do this – if it can be done – I will also gather together, out of those shadows, the scattered recollections of my own paradoxical education as a European in both the Scottish north and the Mediterranean south.

The noise of water is on my left in the gloom under the thorn hedge – the little burn running off the hill. In upland northern places you are seldom out of earshot of moving water, a sure guide down a slope in fading light. From halfway down the track, I can see into the farmyard along the valley. A tractor must have switched on its headlights to move a few bales into the big shed, the last job of the day. It is so far into the evening now that artificial light shines with an intense gold, yellowed by contrast, against the colourless fields and the greys and blues that linger in the sky.

As the tractor shifts about, different parts of the farmyard are lit up by the warm light, as clear as a stage seen from high up in the gallery. Light catches eighteenth-century rough stone from when there was a linen mill on the site and the big pond at the bottom of our garden held the head of water to power it. The headlights move across nineteenth-century dressed ashlar from the days of model farming as the recreation of the man who planted these beeches and ash trees to shelter and hide his new-built house. Light rests on worn textures – the scoured paint of the big corrugated iron sheds that were added in the twentieth century, when the whole valley went back to small-scale farming. Colours of the post-war years: rust-flaked Indian red, unkempt Brunswick green. Glimpses into the workshop shed with its wooden bench and oil drums against limewashed stone. There are still leaves on the trees, more brown than green, with the light striking up to their undersides. The ragged farmyard takes on a real beauty in golden light, with its dim fields folded around it. It is a dimmed, trans-figured moment of the everyday, of the kind that the English painter John Sell Cotman loved and captured in watercolour in the early nineteenth century. The engine cuts out: the light goes off and the eye is thrown upwards again into the vastness of the shifting clouds above, to glimmers in the depths of the sky.

How strange and how comparatively recent are these artificial lights by which people can work and travel as easily as by daylight. The candle and the simple lamp wick are the only defences against the dark until the late eighteenth century when brighter and more effective oil lamps come into use,[12] and even then for the majority of people, daily experience would have included the slow fall of the light, an awareness of the slow process of twilight, which, paradoxic-ally, has been banished by the brilliance of our effective artificial light. For the majority of people, with the exception of a few evening walkers and workers, the gradations of the dusk are rarely experienced, and lives are lived in a stark contrast of dark and bright. There are now comparatively few who experience Nabokov's

George Reid, *Evening*, 1873, oil on canvas.

> . . . gradual and dual blue
> As night unites the viewer with the view.[13]

By the time I come down amongst the trees around the house, the last reflected daylight in the west has faded to uniform grey beyond their branches, and the stream that feeds the big pond is loud over the stones. Still air, dimming and thickening. The light has gone completely where the boughs of the trees hang down to the grass by the water, where the pine branches brush the surface of the pond. This depth of twilight, when the one unseasonable white flower hanging on an elder bush jumps forward a hundred yards to meet the eye, is the solitary domain of those whose eyes have practice in navigating it.

Turning off the farm track onto the grass walk by the pond, I pause a moment as the lighted windows of our house come into view. But I turn, moving away from them, a manoeuvre that takes little thought once the eye has learned to work in the lowest light. Darkness is rarely absolute, particularly out of doors, and the merest outline or reflection is enough to show the way. One light bulb behind a half-open door will spill usable light from one end of a house to the other. What takes a lifetime's practice is the move away from company into solitude.

My education has been, in part, the study of this manoeuvre: as a child moving into the scented dark of the formal garden, past the fountain, away from the barbed formalities of adult conversation on the terrace. Moving away from lighted Gothic windows as a student, down lanes leading to the river, moving away across water meadows navigable by diffused light sparking on frozen grasses. Or in the blue-grey evenings of European cities, as the crowd ebb and flow in the streets as the lamps come on in the windows before their curtains are drawn. Or, ever since, on the Scottish hills, watching the sunset, perhaps, from the ridge beyond Glenlivet and the first lights coming on below in Tomintoul (startlingly clear, startlingly far) and turning belatedly eastwards, skirting the pinewoods with the light at my back, and picking a way down the stony, heathery path in the dark.

Or the same feeling of belatedness can come from the lighted world itself moving away. Like the Shetland boat, the *Hamnavoe*, putting out from Aberdeen at seven of a spring evening, moving with its portholes bright in the twilight, past the pier where I stand, past the lighthouse, past the headland and heading north out into the open sea. Such a moment becomes an epitome of all partings, all embarkations, all lighted ships or trains pulling away into the dusk.

As I stand by the pond dam, the two lighted windows of our house are reflected in dark water, and the lamplight is lying in long stripes over the grass. Nocturnes and nostalgias of Victorian England: lighted windows in late dusk. I have a recurrent dream-image not unlike the scene before me – a synthesis of scenes from nineteenth-century journals, verses, fictions. A nineteenth-century rectory, a veranda hung with creeper turned orange with autumn, last light, a lawn sloping to a river. And as I turn away from our house, its yellow lights seem stronger as the sky fades to deepest grey. Autumn and winter England open in memory: Victorian loneliness, seashores at low tide. Eliot's 'draughty church at smokefall'.[14] Northern England, Lowland Scotland: the streets of stone villas in their own grounds, the scatter of lit windows, the spectrum of industrial sunsets at the end of the hillside streets.

That feeling of sadness at dusk that is characteristic of Victorian England was already observed in early sixteenth-century Japan, with its aesthetic of *wabi*, tranquil beauty found in loneliness, simplicity, even in poverty:

Takeno Jōō (1502–55) cited with satisfaction a poem by Fujiwara no Teika . . . as containing the essence of *wabi*:

As I look afar I see neither cherry blossoms
nor tinted leaves;
Only a modest hut on the coast in the
Dusk of autumn nightfall.

The poet, surveying the scene, chooses not the pink
and festive cherry nor the bright red maple, two favorite
if *hade* [bright/loud] seasonal sights. Rather, he chooses
deep autumn, conventionally the darkest of the seasons,
and dusk, that time of day when all that is brilliant
disappears into the monochrome of twilight.[15]

As I walk on into the 'viridian darkness' under the trees, guided
by a glimmer on the water, hanging willow branches catching
borrowed light, I think of my correspondence with a friend who is,
among many things, a climber and a naturalist. I think of our shared
concern that people don't have time any more to allow their eyes
to learn the skills of half-light and the near-night. What they miss
by confinement to the hours of daylight, lighted places. The water
sounding in this still autumn air, the shuffle of a deer feeding in
the plantations of rowans further upstream, the smell of dry pine
needles. I know the rough steps up the bank into the wood by heart,
as I know the grass walk through the trees. I feel absolutely content
to be out here in the last of the light, to be able to offer this hour
to the ending day. All walks that begin by going out in the daylight
and end with return in the dark have an extra emotional dimension.
An important part of the progress of any individual can only take
place when moving through the landscape or townscape alone.

I have come up the steps at the end of the garden. One of
the upstairs rooms is lit and I can see bookshelves in the lamplight
across the dark grass. As well to start at once on the task of sketch-
ing the history of twilight, tracing Europe's arts of evening. And
as well to start by trying to focus on the central problem – how
to define twilight. It is easily defined in personal terms as a
response, mood or memory. It is easy enough to think of the most
celebrated works in different media that have responded to it –
Gray's *Elegy*, the piano *Nocturnes* of Chopin and John Field, the
paintings of failing light that suddenly became universal in northern
Europe at the turn of the nineteenth century – but what is the
twilight itself?

Some of the definitions, indeed the word itself could, of course, also apply to the slow rising and gathering of the light towards dawn – the daily reverse of the falling light of evening – but already I know that that is an entirely different investigation. The whole morning world implied by the Victorian critic John Ruskin having himself called before dawn, when travelling in the Alps, so that he might walk up the ridge above the glacier to see the dawn breaking over the peaks, is the antithesis of the evening world of melancholy, peace and regret that is the territory of this book. Some lives are defined by mornings, some by evenings – mine unequivocally the latter. Reading and writing that is the product of working late by lamplight, working when the light has gone over the garden outside the window. A habitual sense of *belatedness*: missed chances in the short morning; afternoon work unfinished; the compulsion to be out, wandering and observing, as soon as the light begins to fall. Then trying to catch up by wringing the last hours out of the evening and night. Also, perhaps, although this is more elusive and will need more thought, a sense of belatedness in time underlies my fascination with evenings, a sense that I am personally content with remoteness and slowness, moving away from a dominant culture of immediacy and speed. And that there are many others in Europe who have felt this same lateness as a condition of life and that it has shaped the ways in which generations have thought and painted and written.

There is a science that defines the twilight of evening in three stages: when the sun has just dipped below the horizon, up to six degrees below, and when the first stars are just visible, it is 'civil twilight'. This is the 'blue hour' beloved of nineteenth-century French writers and painters. This is the time when the white flowers in a summer garden jump forward to the eye, when a whitewashed house on a distant winter hill shines out of the dimness. (Although the term is not free from ambiguity, this is also sometimes defined as the 'magic hour' of the film-maker, the 'golden hour' for the photographer.)

When the sun is six to twelve degrees below the horizon, it is 'nautical twilight', deepening cobalt on a clear night, at the end of which time the horizon line is no longer defined by visible brightness. On a summer night a remarkable amount of colour will linger surprisingly late in such a twilight sky. On a misty evening or if the light has been low throughout the day, this will seem as good as dark to an eye that has just come out of a lighted building. The end of nautical twilight has its place in military strategies of surprise, the level of darkness where movement will not be immediately apparent even to a watchful sentry. What the eye sees moves from the perception of colour by the *cones* in the retina to the perception of monochrome and some movement by the *rods* in the eye. These visual receptors report, as it were, to very different areas of the brain – so the perception of full daylight is physically an activity that is wholly distinct from the perception of the dimmest lights. And in any case what the human eye sees as the day dies, far from what the camera sees, is often a filtered and adapted version of what is there: this is explored scientifically by Aden and Marjorie Meinel in their remarkable book *Sunsets, Twilights and Evening Skies*[16] in which they remind us that the extraordinary capacity that the human eye has to impose memory and expectation on light conditions can often cancel the actual hue of an evening sky and substitute one closer to expectations, often filtering and reducing perception of red colour-ation in the west. Similarly, the absolute adjustment of the eye to all phenomena of light can compensate and adjust what is perceived to a remarkable extent – an idea that sets up a tension between the claims of paintings and photographs of twilight to represent justly what is *seen* as opposed to what may objectively be *present*:

> Astronomers, navigators and civilians all have their own way of looking at twilight . . . For the photographer there is the added complication that photographic film distorts any image produced in that almost dark period . . . While our eyes and brain are able to make quick adjustments, photographic film is not . . . at twilight the light levels are changing constantly, so getting the film just right (or compensating with filters) is almost impossible.[17]

There are other mirages and delusions of the evening sky: refraction in air thickened by water droplets or dust enable an observer to glimpse 'sunlight' while the sun is in fact far below the horizon. Rich scientific paradoxes to add to the old perception of the twilight of the time of visual uncertainty: dog and wolf, bush and bear.

From twelve to eighteen degrees below the horizon, it is 'astronomical twilight', apparently dark to the casual observer, to whom the constellations are as bright as they would be in full darkness.

This defines the twilight of evening considered simply as a time of an average day, but geography is the factor that shapes and alters the twilight and all perceptions of it. Those defining twilights of the north manifest themselves not only as long evenings, the absence of complete darkness at night, but also as states of lowered light that can last for days or even weeks. Because twilight lasts longer the further north (or, of course, south) you are, Polar twilight can go on for a whole fortnight, at the beginning and end of the murk-tide, the blackout at midwinter. In the territories ten degrees either side of the 60th parallel, south of the absolute extremes of light and dark, the twilights of midsummer and midwinter are at their longest.

Civil twilight lasts all night at midsummer at 60 degrees – that glimmer of redness in the northern sky seen from the north of Scotland is the faint reflection of the 'simmer dim' over the Northern Isles. *Nautical twilight* lasts throughout the midsummer night at 54 degrees north, *astronomical twilight* at 48 degrees north. *Civil twilight* over Shetland; *nautical twilight* over Newcastle and the Scottish Borders; when the sky grows dark on midsummer night over London, it is actually *astronomical twilight*.

The degree to which inhabitants of these regions of the twilight are conditioned by the long waning of the light is hard to overestimate. It strikes me suddenly that I have an example on the desk beside me: a mineral specimen, a slice of 'figured stone' taken out of the cabinet earlier in the day. Only in the latitudes of the twilight would its figurations be read as representative, would this stone be thought of as 'landscape marble' at all.

It is in fact a limestone (there is no true marble in England) found in Rhaetic beds in the West Country, particularly at Cotham in Bristol, hence its name 'Cotham marble'. The strata of mud are broken by darker bubbles pushing upwards, which are petrified into the forms of trees, bushes and clouds, while the dun-coloured horizontal strata of mud suggest the lines of ploughed fields, or sometimes (in the larger pieces) a river valley with cliffs and rocks. Always seen against a grey, fading sky.

The phenomenon of the recognition of the landscape within the stone is complex and hard to date precisely: certainly the baroque cabinets of curiosities throughout Europe are full of examples of figured marble interpreted as landscape, often with details added in oil paint to enhance the illusion. To my eye, the landscapes in Cotham marble associate powerfully with the years around 1800: to the time when the Napoleonic wars turned cultivated interest inwards onto the landscapes and phenomena of the British Islands. The grey and brown landscapes of the marble are not unlike the monochrome vignettes on late eighteenth-century porcelain, not unlike the thumbprint whorls of the trees in Thomas Bewick's engraved tailpieces, and very like the crude but haunting landscape murals in blue monochrome (an improvised, imaginary world of evening) at Llanfyllin, near Welshpool, painted there by a French prisoner of war.[18]

The recognition of the landscape in the split stone is conditioned by eighteenth-century focus on landscape parks and landscape paint-ing. But the essential factor is the romantic celebration of fading light: evening walks and painted night-pieces are both phenomena of the turn of the nineteenth century, and it is a dimmed landscape of mist or twilight that emerges from the stones. It is only as a landscape of evening (or of autumnal mist) that it can be recognized as landscape at all.

There are two examples of landscape marble in the room in which I write: one of mist, one of twilight. The first is an uncom-monly long piece, perhaps half a metre, with a continuous row of faint trees in the foreground and, in the middle-ground, streaks

of dark in light grey seem to form themselves into a continuous
river-landscape with cliffs seen in fog or half-light.

The smaller piece that lies on the desk beside me is more startlingly pictorial, in a style that seems more Victorian than Regency.
The configuration of field, hedgerow and trees is unmistakably
English. The coloration is that of autumn, late in the day: ploughed
fields of yellowish clay rise towards a shadowy hedgerow whose trees
are still in leaf, some darkened, some still brown. Pale light is fading
at the horizon, although the wide sky is filled with darkening, wind-
blown clouds. The landscape is insistently sad with the sadness of
the nineteenth century. It is late in autumn, the wind that blows
the trees and clouds will soon scatter the leaves and it will be winter.
Tennyson or Matthew Arnold: *In memoriam* or 'Rugby Chapel'.
Both poems where the speaker is out in the darkening air and the
lit houses are closed to him. What makes this random piece of stone
the counterpart of mid-Victorian poetry of lonely twilights is that a
figure is perceptible at the right of the hedgerow, cloak or ulster held
across the body, leaning against the wind that threshes in the trees.
Like the solitary twilight speakers of Tennyson's and Arnold's poems,
here is a figure walking in a landscape otherwise unpeopled.

The other association that comes to mind at once is with the
ghost stories that were a particular minor art form in England in
the late nineteenth century and earlier twentieth century. This would
make the figure in the stone less of a solitary walker and more of
a revenant, one of the number of the injured dead who lurk and
approach slowly in these fictions, until they take their vengeance on
the living at their climaxes. In this mode, it might be that the figure
might move within the marble, stalking the living, moving from
right to left, appearing in a different gap between the trees every time
that the stone is taken from its place in the cabinet to be inspected.

Yet it is not the supernatural that dominates the landscape in
the stone, rather an implied mood of the fathomless sorrow of
Victorian England: twilight, loneliness, mists rising from ploughland.
The earliest discoveries of figures in split stones were held to be talismanic, rather than aesthetic: in a very different way this arrangement

of mud strata petrified into limestone is a post-Romantic talisman in that it can invoke at a glance a season, a world, a century. Most of all it evokes a time of day, the fading of light. It calls to mind the spontaneous, sad poetry of English fishermen's words for the watches of the night at sea: light moon flood, light moon ebb, dark moon flood, dark moon ebb.[19]

The landscape outside my window is like the landscape in the marble now. Dun and shade and all detail gone. There is barely a scratch of grey on the western horizon, and I have to turn the desk lamp off to see it. There is almost no light in the rooms, as I move through the silent house, save a faint spill of light from the one lit doorway downstairs. Away from this there are only the faintest reflections – on a picture frame, on the moulding of a skirting board. All that remains is this last monochrome: afterlight at the windows seen from the darkness inside.

There is a curious poem by Browning ('Love in a Life'), surely based in part on an experience in a dream, about the unknowability of a lover, even of a spouse. This is expressed allegorically as a search through a strangely animate, seemingly infinite house for a woman who is always one room ahead of him:

> As she brushed it, the cornice-wreath blossomed anew.
> Yon looking-glass gleamed at the touch of her feather.

But the house is infinite and the daylight begins to fail, and what has been dreamlike becomes inexplicable and sad, a panic, a race against the fading light.

> . . . she goes out as I enter.

> . . .

> But 'tis twilight, you see, – with such suites to explore,
> Such closets to search, such alcoves to importune!

In the visual arts, the great virtuoso of the last of the light was the Danish painter Vilhelm Hammershøi, who is most celebrated for his depictions of the interiors of the Copenhagen flats in which he and his family lived. Occasionally he shows a bright morning throwing sunlight across Biedermeier furniture and grey-painted panelling. But the vast majority of his works are evening pictures, haunting depictions of the northern light and its fall. They are often extraordinary experiments with the very last of the light, the final ebbing of definition from grey things, the catching of a sliver of belated reflection on the moulding of a panel or a window mirrored in a polished floorboard.

He also painted subtle and persuasive images of the monochrome of winter London in the early years of the twentieth century: in these, the absolute restraint of his palette renders the absence of light present, expresses that northern light which is itself a gap or a lack. He captures alike the wonderful sculptural quality of the great black iron railings and the cold in the damp air – tending to mist, tending to dusk. And the poignancy of the gaslight in the shops, lit so early in the afternoon.

Sometimes, in his Copenhagen interior paintings, it has grown so late that the only light in the room comes from the streetlight outside, caught on the glazing bars of the window, faintly reflected on the bevel of a mirror. And, almost always, if the painting is inhabited at all, the figure of his wife has her back to us, eluding us like the woman in Browning's poem, turned away from us like the figures in Giandomenico Tiepolo's sad carnivals. Enfilades of doors standing open, each room dimmer as it recedes. Calm, silence, and the lingering arrival of evening. The light gone over the quay below the windows and the inlets of the Baltic.

My cartography of dusk can, I know, only be a European one: otherwise, the scope grows impossible, the latitudes and lights too diffuse. If this excludes the popular encounters on film of the teenage citizens of day and night, it also removes the authentic, Hoffmannesque strangeness of Rod Serling's *Twilight Zone*, beguiling, almost allegorical television films from 1959 to 1964 in America. It removes the archaic north American metaphorical uses of 'twilight' and 'shadow' to refer to the gay community,[20] 'twilight zone' as a

specific description of an area of urban transition. With regret, it
sets at a distance the visual refinement of Terrence Malick's pastoral
tragedy *Days of Heaven* (1978), shot under the dust-filtered strata
of the dusks of north America: smoke-orange, purple-yellow, cloud
blue and lilac. It also removes the otherworldly brilliance of the
meticulously staged photographs of Gregory Crewdson (b. 1962).
His works are all images of twilight in familiar, usually American
suburban, settings, but so carefully posed, lit and processed as to
render the familiar unfamiliar and uncertain. Homecomings to lit
bungalows become episodes of revenance; hinted narratives of the
magical and inexplicable. The transformative quality of twilight is
developed in single images to imply some of the narrative power of
a full-length film, and the sum of the work is to hint at a vast hidden
narrative of nightfall in which the prosaic and quotidian is transformed into something both poetic and disquieting.[21] For the
American Auden, twilight recurs as a time when the shores of
the Europe he had left behind grow most real in memory:

> Quiet falls the dusk at this queasy juncture
>> Of water and earth,
> And lamps are lit on the long esplanade . . .[22]

Indeed he associates twilight with the guiltless and cultivated citizens
of Europe, hopelessly vulnerable to each new wave of barbarians:

> . . . By lakes at twilight
> They sang of swans and separations,
> Mild, unmilitant, as the moon rose . . .[23]

The focus on Europe distances us also from a notable school of
artists of twilight in the twentieth century, the Japanese painters and
woodblock-print designers of the early century of whom the most
celebrated is Hasui Kawase (1883–1957). These woodblock designers
assimilated European conventions for the depiction of conditions of
darkness and failing light in the late nineteenth century,[24] initially as

part of the expressive anxiety in their work during the period of the Pacific War. Later they made consistent use of *azuri-e*, of the Prussian blue pigment introduced to Japan in the 1800s, in the expansion of the repertory of prints of landscape to include scenes of night and twilight. These go beyond earlier depictions of places celebrated for their beauty to include scenes of drifting evening crowds in modest urban streets, or to show haunting images of forgotten corners, small quotidian scenes from provincial life at nightfall. As the century progresses these become increasingly nostalgic, in a parallel to the serial nostalgias of the contemporary west.

A typical example of many twilight woodblock prints by Hasui is his 'Omori Beach at Night' from the *Twelve Scenes of Tokyo* (1919–21): four colours, dominated by a rich, late-twilight blue, achieve a depiction both realistic and nostalgic of a row of wooden houses by a creek, with the bright spots of lighted windows sending trails of light across the water.

My own reflection appears in the glass of the window as I switch the lamp on again, conceding victory to the dark at last. A reminder that the exploration of the history of twilight can also be an exploration of memory. And that there will be twilights to be found that will be metaphorical or allusive – I have one already in the mainstream dismissal of the kind of counter-cultural backwater in which I live as a 'dark corner'.

And many historical epochs are identified, even by contemporaries, sometimes inexplicably (or at least in an enigma that requires investigation) as 'twilights'. There is a ceaseless process from the meridian of the eighteenth century, which sees each epoch, each passing decade, each war or revolution as a twilight, as an ending, as a further step in the diminution of Europe. Victor Hugo's *Chants du crépuscule*, published in the 1830s, express a typically haunted conviction that it is already hopelessly late in the day:

> Everything today, in ideas as much as in things, in society as with the individual, is in the condition of twilight. What is the nature of this twilight? What will come after it?

. . . this strange twilight state of the soul and of society in the
century where we live: it is this fog outside, this uncertainty within;
it is I know not what that is born of the half-light that surrounds us
. . . this tranquillity shot through with sorrow.[25]

And yet in the years during and after the First World War, how
much more were civilizations and institutions seen as entering the
twilight, before the nights of destruction that ended the Second,
the Baedeker raids and the obliteration of European cities. And even
now, the atmosphere is of belatedness, of inexplicable, unaccount-
able shiftings of power in the half-light, the end and abandonment
of the projects of reconstruction.

Now, if ever, is the time to map the territories of the dusk: the
territory defined as stretching from the moment when the sun drops
completely below the horizon until the night comes – *Blanche, Vénus
émerge, et c'est la Nuit*[26] – the pale evening star comes forth, and it
is night. That is my subject and the region in which I will move is
evening with its ivory and rose, smoke grey and washed yellow,
cobalt and diamond, until the lights come on in the windows. These
are the territories of melancholy and revenants, longings and regrets,
'tranquillity shot through with sorrow', homecomings and serenities.

Now is the time to begin, as Hesperus brightens in the southern
sky. In the hour that opens the gates of memory, under dark towers
of cloud which are the gates of Europe.

I

ABOUT SHADOWS
AND GARDENS

Dama de noche, night-blooming jessamine, stand at the gate of the
darkening garden. Sweetness of jasmine, syrup in the mouth; black
Havana tobacco, fog in the throat. The scented air is thickened
beyond bearing, dense with thunder on the August evening that
rises in memory. The days of murderous heat before the feast of the
Assumption, before the first crack in the hideous summer. Not a
breath of wind off the Mediterranean, insects thronging under the
burdened olive trees beyond the garden walls. The echo of a shot,
of shots, from the foothills to the north. A momentary silence in
the conversation on the terrace, and then the fountain loud out
of the dimness of the cypresses. Pulses of sound, pauses in the fall
of water from the lion's mouth into the pool between the mirroring
curves of the stairs, dropping in the cadence of Lorca's lines:

> *Agua y sombra, sombra y agua,*
> *por Jerez de la Frontera.*[1]

Shadow and water, water and shadow, at Jerez de la Frontera.

The conversation resumes, a weighty silver lighter rasps and
flares, and more smoke from black tobacco drifts up to where I stand
alone on the roof terrace watching the advance of the twilight over
the clifftop olive groves and the sea. Already the mountains to the
north are darkening on their eastern sides, blurred by the heat of the
day. The garden of the villa is in shadow, the last sunlight shooting
rays through the red-earthed olive groves beyond. Beyond the whitewashed garden wall to the west lies the unknown territory of the
other garden: an abandoned parterre of straggling once-clipped trees

33

and stagnant canals behind iron gates locked by my grandfather's orders before I was born. His study (which I entered only once in my life, on sufferance and under supervision) takes up the whole of the tower at the eastern end of the villa. Questions are neither encouraged nor answered in this shuttered house.

I turn back to the south to look over the sea, hearing again the fountain below the terrace falling in counterpoint with the single jet in the long pool at the dead centre of the villa garden.

El día se va despacio,
la tarde colgada a un hombro,
dando una larga torera
sobre el mar y los arroyos.[2]

Day goes out slowly, Evening hangs on the shoulder of the hill, Sweeping a long feint of its cloak Over sea and rivers.

The rivers are dry in this terrible August. I walked out with my father on some days, after my five o'clock bread and chocolate, over the thymy scrubland behind the house, walked in migraine heat as far as the gully of sand, which is a watercourse in winter. Bright oleanders with their rattling leaves grow in the parched riverbed. My father's mind travelled then, I think, to his cold mountains, plumes of slow-drifting mist over pine trees, fast brown torrents pitted by rain. Standing on the arid bank, his right hand sketched the cast of a fishing line over the dust then, slowly and silently, we went back together to the locked villa. Purple dusk advances through the haze:

Las aceitunas aguardan
la noche de Capricornio,
y una corta brisa, ecuestre,
salta los montes de plomo.[3]

The olive trees wait the night of Capricorn, and a small breeze, mounted, jumps the hills of lead like a horseman.

But in these days before the first August thunder, nothing can stir the leaden air. Everything is locked down, everything is hot and immobile until the first storm breaks after the feast of the Assumption. The memory of these breathless days runs them together into one continual stifling twilight, a memory of roaming the villa and gardens, bored and apprehensive and alone: cellars smelling of oil and vine must, ink-shadowed cypress avenues paved with white dust, dark ramparts of clipped trees, moon-white boundary walls. And under everything ran the stress of season and evening and weather and history. This was an era that was itself an infinitely protracted twilight, lasting through many unnatural years. Before the resorts were developed on the coastal scrub and olive groves, Andalusia was locked in the modes and beliefs of the late 1930s by the fiat of the dictator.

That southern society of the 1960s would still have been recognizable to the early twentieth-century novelist Ronald Firbank (1886–1926), whose last completed fiction, *Concerning the Eccentricities of Cardinal Pirelli*, published in the year of his death, is set in 'white Andalucia'. Firbank is a complex and virtuosic writer, infinitely skilled in omission, elision and allusion; pointed indirection; sparse evocation. His fictions were issued in small editions, half-privately, with the bold discretion born of a prudent flamboyance. Their influence has been, and is, remarkable. One of Firbank's crucial areas of indirection is a camp focus on the extravagant externals of Catholicism, the religion to which he had converted in his early twenties. This serves to some degree to divert the casual reader: as is so often the case, camp coexists with absolute seriousness, with disquiet, even with despair. The essence of Firbank's fiction is relentlessly crepuscular, not only in many scenes set at nightfall and at summer evening parties, but also in its weary sophistication, its undertow of menace and apprehension, its sense of the hovering presence of (sometimes literal) demons. In this world at nightfall, the Church is a constant and paradoxical element – at once a cabaret of outrageous grandeurs and the only source of hope or light in the approaching darkness.

This all comes to focus in his last book, which, behind veils of indirection and exoticism, is acute in its observations of southern Spain and its Church. *Concerning the Eccentricities of Cardinal Pirelli* conveys Firbank's hard and weary sense of evil in the world – the only counterpoise being the Catholic Church, which is depicted in a twilight condition, in painfully fragile hands, like those of the eponymous hero, with his stark conflict of mystical piety and devouring sensuality.

The book is remarkably clear and accurate on Spain, its evocations going far beyond the well-worn *espagnolisme* of the nineteenth century. It is precise in its summoning of the terrible evenings of the ripening summer of the far south. The second chapter is an epitome of the whole, covering a broad range of experience and narration in its sure-footed, impressionistic progress through one hot twilight in the hanging garden of the Cardinal's palace overlooking the city:

> From the Calle de la Pasion, beneath the blue-tiled mirador of the garden wall, came the soft brooding sound of a seguidilla. It was a twilight planned for wooing, unbending, consent . . . pacing a cloistered walk, laden with the odour of sun-tired flowers, the Cardinal could not but feel the insidious influences astir.[4]

At once the struggle that is the sombre undercurrent of the apparently luxuriant camp of the Cardinal's surroundings becomes apparent,

> Morality. Poise! For without temperance and equilibrium – The Cardinal halted. But in the shifting underlight about him the flushed camellias and the sweet night-jasmines suggested none; neither did the shape of a garden-Eros pointing radiantly the dusk.
> 'For unless we have balance –' the Cardinal murmured, distraught, admiring against the elusive nuances of the afterglow the cupid's voluptuous hams.[5]

As so often in Firbank, the aspirations of his characters, expressed when they are alone, are sombre and authentic, but aestheticism, the sensual beauty of things, is omnipresent and powerful. The Cardinal's housekeeper comes forth with a silver stole to enwrap and imprison him as the twilight gives way to moonlight. Outside the voluptuous garden, the city is darkened by sepsis, epidemic disease, and the suggestion of malign influences, stirrings of evil magic practised by the very bored, be they grandees or ecclesiastics:

> 'Such nights breed fever, Don Alvaro, and there is mischief in the air.'
>> 'Mischief?'
> 'In certain quarters of the city, you would take almost it for some sortilege.' . . .
> The tones of the seguidilla had deepened and from the remote recesses of the garden arose a bedlam of nightingales and frogs.
> It was certainly incredible how he felt immured.[6]

And the Cardinal's sad recourse is to put the oppression of season and evil from his mind by sensual diversion, by setting forth from his scented prison in disguise, perhaps in drag, and to go out into the hot, infected city, to cruise for a lover of either sex. The Cardinal's passionate regrets are themselves enactments of Firbank's own sombre dilemma about the apparent freedoms of the south, social and devotional. Later in the novel (the final scenes of the Cardinal's exile, disgrace and death are strangely interspersed with what seem moments of mystical visitation, authentic illumination) once more in a twilight garden, Pirelli is shown resisting, or trying to resist, the temptation to go down into the infected city:

> Already the blue pushing shadows were beguiling from the shelter of the cloister eaves the rueful owls. A few flittermice, too, were revolving around the long apricot chimneys of the Palace . . .
> Kneeling before an altar raised to the cult of Our Lady of Dew, Cardinal Pirelli was plunged in prayer.

'Salve. Salve Regina . . .' Above the tree-tops a bird was
singing.[7]

A more innocent and tender evocation of the evening villas of
the south and their gardens is found in the works of the short-lived
Turin poet Guido Gozzano (1883–1916), who found his solace in
unfashionable things, provincial elegances, forgotten but beloved
places. He was drawn inevitably to the evening, to dim stillness, to
quiet and humble things and people, in sharp contrast to the bright
audacity of his contemporary D'Annunzio. He was associated with a
group of poets – the Crepuscolari, or 'Twilightists' – who were, like
him, elegists for things lost and superseded in the modernizations
of the new century, a group who would have wished only to prolong
the lingering evening of the past. His description of his native Turin
makes it most real at nightfall, with the streets and valleys in shadow
and all the sunlight gone to the high hills:

vedo al tramonto, il cielo subalpino . . .
. . .
ardono l'Alpi tra le nube accese . . .[8]

I see at evening, the sky between the Alps . . . Shining mountains
between blazing clouds

A trope that will reappear, desolatingly, at the end of his longest
work, 'La Signorina Felicita', is that of his living contemporaries seen
at one particular moment as if they were figures in an engraving of
the mid-nineteenth century – distanced and aestheticized, the present
(in this case an aristocratic evening party) perceived as though it were
an illustration to a long-forgotten album:

Ed il poeta, tacito ed assente
si gode quell'accolita di gente
ch'à la tristezza d'una stampa antica[9]

And the poet, silent and absent-minded, enjoys this assembly of people,
which has the sadness of an old print.

The only real moments of pleasure in these poems are those in
which he can imagine his sickly twentieth-century self safe in hiding
in the past, perhaps the past of two generations back in time, safe
in the half-light, the time out of time, of an old engraving or sepia
photograph. Gozzano's school were identified as *crepuscolari* because
of a contemporary perception that Italian literature was fading away
into a gentle and infinitely extended twilight.[10] The morning of
Dante and Petrarch, the noontide of Tasso and Ariosto, the bright
day of the eighteenth century, followed by the mellowing late afternoon of the romantics, Foscolo and Leopardi, had all given way,
or so it seemed at that moment, to a retrospective poetic of evening
and regret:

> *Signorina Felicita, a quest'ora*
> *scende la sera nel giardino antico*
> *della tua casa. Nel mio cuore amico*
> *scende il ricordo. E ti rivedo ancora,*
> *e Ivrea rivedo e la cerulea Dora*
> *e quel dolce paese che non dico.*[11]

Signorina Felicita, at this hour, evening is falling on the ancient garden
of your house; and memories descend also into my affectionate heart.
And I see you again, and I see Ivrea and the blue waters of the Dora
and the sweet landscape which I do not name.

Gozzano's long poem 'La Signorina Felicita, ovvero la felicità'
(Miss Felicity, or Happiness) is a complete, even an extreme, work
of the twilight school, of retreat from the present day, of longing for
the refuge of a crepuscular life in provincial obscurity as though in
a dream-world of the mid-nineteenth century. Most of all, it is a
work that traces the compelling development of an escapist fantasy,
at the same time as it is a savage self-reproof to the fantasist author.
His dream of escape into the past conflicts with the truth of his
life, which his failing health places him under sentences of exile
and death. He is condemned to far southern travel in winter, to
try to secure a few more years of life in the dry air far from the

foothills of Piedmonte, where he is spending his last summer in *villegiatura*.

The obsessive theme of escape into an imagined past is very close to that of Gozzano's other extended poem – 'L'amica di nonna Speranza' (The Friend of my Grandmother Speranza) – desperate in its longings for the safety of the world of the mid-nineteenth century. A sequence of scenes of *villegiatura* are lovingly reconstructed from one fragile talisman – one sepia photograph with a sentimental inscription from the summer of 1850, pasted into an album. Gozzano imagines an opulent villa with a park in the English style, the rooms full of 'fine things in terrible taste' – '*le buon cose di pessimo gusto*'. Two beautiful young women have just returned from their convent school, dreaming by the lake as the day ends (Gozzano yet again freezes and aestheticizes the scene as a mid-century engraving):

> *Non vuole morire, non langue il giorno. S'accende più ancora*
> *di porpora: come un aurora stigmattizata di sangue;*
>
> *si spenge infine, ma lento. I monti s'abbrunano in coro:*
> *il Sole si sveste dell'oro, la Luna si veste d'argento.*[12]

The daylight does not want to die, it does not weaken, it flares in purple like a dawn wounded with blood. It goes eventually, but slowly. At once the mountains turn dim, the sun takes off gold, the moon puts on silver.

This poem is modern beyond its era in its dislocation of feeling and the strangeness of its subject: the erotic intensity of the evocation of the provincial summer of 1850 – the cry of desolation with which it ends – the final line of passionate longing for the woman glimpsed only in the fading photograph.

Perhaps the appeal of these twilights of the past for Gozzano is that their inhabitants are dead, it is all finished except in imagination, and the passage of time has already worked all its harm. A Mediterranean seriousness governs these poems. At no time does Gozzano mock the nineteenth-century past, as a British poet of the early twentieth century would almost certainly have done. There is no hint of camp or of retrospective superiority: the stolid surroundings of the beautiful young women in both these poems evoke only an intensely desired safety and peace. Indeed, in 'La Signorina Felicita' the remote villa where nothing has changed becomes at evening a threshold of an alternative reality – Gozzano's territory of retreat from time, even though the daughter of the villa and her feelings remain real, present, temporal. Thoughout, he is painfully aware of this disjunction, and of the suffering that his escapist fantasy will eventually cause to the reticent woman whose name is almost the word for happiness.

'La Signorina Felicita' is a sadly tender account of this compromised love, the longing to be absorbed into the sequestered world of this young woman. It reports with honesty her innocent and uncalculating love for the poet, all enacted against the passing of the summer vacation and his awareness of imperatives of his dormant illness. The poet is truly in love with the future that he imagines for himself with her, but it is a future of the imagination and inevitably his complexities deceive Felicita's optimistic directness. The more that he allows himself to be aware that his infected lungs deprive him of any future at all save that of a migratory invalid, the more he intensifies the fantasy. Obscurity and twilight are the only regions in which the regretful balances and evasions of the poem can be sustained.

Sometimes the love that the poet expresses is for the place itself, for its quality of *pastness*, an aching litany of details of a grand house grown shabby and silent, grown too large so that the formal rooms of the *piano nobile* are deserted.

> *Bell'edificio triste inabitato!*
> *Grate panciute, logore, contorte!*
> *Silenzio! Fuga delle stanze morte!*

> Fine villa, sadly empty! Swell-moulded gratings bent and worn out!
> Silence! Enfilade of dead rooms!

Until the litany reaches the purely magical conjuration of the imagined scents of shadow and past times, which associate further with the spectral grandeurs of the frescoed walls.

> *Odore d'ombra! Odore di passato!*
> *Odore d'abbandono desolato!*
> *Fiabe defunte delle sovrapporte!*[13]

Smell of shadows! Smell of the past! Smell of sadness and desertion! Dead mythologies painted in the overdoors!

The authenticities of the place are echoed in the emotional directness of the daughter of the house. It is characteristic of the poem's ambiguous correlation of pastness with love that the nearest thing to a conventional love scene is enacted as a search for a deeper layer of past time in the villa, as the poet and Felicita explore the attic, happy in the shadows amidst the palpable remainders of history, looking out through old glass over the plain, out into the evening:

> *disparve il sole fra le nube rotte;*
> *a poco a poco s'annunciò la notte*
> *sulla serenità canavesana . . .*
>
> *'Una stella! . . . ' 'Tre stelle! . . .' 'Quattro stelle! . . .'*
> *'Cinque stelle!' – 'Non sembra di sognare? . . . '*
> *Ma ti levasti su quasi rebelle*
> *Alla perplessità crepuscolare:*
> *'Scendiamo! é tardi . . .'*[14]

The sun disappeared from the torn clouds, very gradually the night showed itself over the serenity of the Canavese . . . 'A star!' 'Three stars!' 'Four stars!' 'Five stars!' 'Don't you feel as though you were dreaming?' But you got up as though resisting the irresolution of the twilight, 'Let's go down, it's late . . .'

The conventional image of the departure of the swallows at the end of summer is deepened here: like them the poet is bound to travel south. The tone of the poem's ending is poised and very difficult to capture: as Gozzano describes Felicita's genuine sorrow for his departure, he also fictionalizes it and judges himself for so doing. His satisfaction and dissatisfaction both find expression in his habitual trope of the moment captured and distanced as if it were an illustration to a mid-Victorian poem.

> *Giunse il distacco, amaro senza fine,*
> *e fu il distacco d'altri tempi, quando*
> *le amate in bande lisce e in crinoline,*
> *protese da un giardino venerando,*
> *singhiozzavano forte, salutando*
> *diligenze che andavano al confine . . .*[15]

The parting came, bitter without end, and it was like a parting in the old days, when beloved ones with hooped skirts and crinolines, leaned out from an ancient garden, sobbing violently, saying farewell to coaches travelling towards the frontier . . .

In such a narrative he would be living his prolonged life of fantasy as the young romantic looking towards a future that would culminate in his return:

> *ed io fui l'uomo d'altri tempi, un buono*
> *sentimentale giovine romantico . . .*
> *Quello che fingo d'essere e non sono!*[16]

and I was a man of those old days, a good, sentimental young romantic . . . Which I pretend to be, and cannot be!

The poised last line is intensely sad – the poet has sought escape and has known it all along for escapism. This unnatural prolongation – living in an artificially extended past – has only hurt and confused the woman who he has, in one hopeless sense, loved sincerely. The reality of overgrown formal gardens at evening is clearly evoked but it is a setting in which he has in reality no future at all. It is only another twilight unnaturally prolonged.

A PAIR OF EASEL PAINTINGS, executed while Giambattista Tiepolo
was working on the great decorative schemes in the palace of the
Prince-Bishop at Würzburg, also treat of escapist fantasy in an
evening garden, a place where time moves at a different pace to its
movement in the reality beyond the walls. Tiepolo here returns to
one of the subjects already treated at the Villa Valmarana – Rinaldo
and Armida, a deluded lover's withdrawal into the garden that is
the fruit of the malign enchantments of the sorceress. Her illusory
realm is imagined in visual terms of remarkable atmospheric invention: uncertain depths of foliage, the manipulation of contrasting
qualities of light.

At Vicenza, the Valmarana frescoes show the same episodes
of heroic weakness from *La Gerisalemme liberata*: in those rooms,
Tiepolo imagined them in the greys and purples of the Mediterranean dusk, the magic garden as a dusty region of late summer
afternoon.[17] The contrasting pair of easel pictures, in the collection
of the Würzburg Residenz, develop the ambiguous and disquieting
nature of the episode to the full. The first, *Rinaldo under Armida's
Spell* (c. 1752–3), shows an evening garden, a curious and improvisatory combination of rough ground with highly sculptured walls
and gates. The sorceress Armida, an expression of cold detachment
on her beautiful face, holds the enchanted dark mirror, which faces
out of the picture towards the viewer, showing the viewer only
darkness. The armoured Rinaldo, distracted from the Crusade, is
sprawled at her side. A leering sculpture of a faun, a caryatid of the
garden wall, offers a dark counterpoint to the conventional *amorino*
at the feet of the lovers. Within the garden, the place of illusion,
inexistent light falls as if on an operatic stage of the eighteenth
century – a high light source from the left casts firm shadows
on the figures and on the steps of the fountain. But this light is
absolutely contained within the garden walls – Tiepolo emphasizes
this with the fine ambiguity with which the overhanging cypress on
the left is darkened and shadowed.

The most extraordinary invention of the painting is the contrast
between this fictive light and the meticulous observation of the dimmed

evening landscape beyond the garden, a distant snowy peak lit by refracted after-sunset light. Rinaldo's armed companions are uncertain figures in the deep shadows outside the walls and railings that mark the boundary of the delusive garden. The light outside has withdrawn to the distances and the fountain in the foreground is a barely modelled mass of darkness, lit by neither true nor false illuminations. Altogether, it is a remarkable visualization of deception, beauty and illusion, imagined in terms of light and its movement, as though the whole deception were being played out in an uneasily bright region of halted time, whereas outside the deception it is already evening, and light itself is on the verge of becoming too faint to be reliable. The tall trees beyond the garden wall are sketches, shadows, broadly and wonderfully painted. Despite the bright elegance of the enchantress's clothes, the firm shadows at her feet, the whole effect is disquieting and unstable, although less overtly menacing than the stormy twilight of Michiel Sweerts's *Couple and a Boy in a Garden*.

Giambattista Tiepolo, *Rinaldo under Armida's Spell*, c. 1752–3, oil on canvas.

In Tiepolo's companion piece in the Würzburg collection, which
shows the enchantment broken and Rinaldo recalled to his duty,
the hero is led away by comrades who have momentarily taken on
the aspect of guards or gaolers. The dissolution of Armida's illusory
garden is represented literally in tumbled blocks of ruined masonry
scattered amidst tussocks of rough grass. She weeps dishevelled, her
bright scarf fallen from her shoulders, in the muted and level daylight that has replaced the 'magic hour' lighting of her fictive garden.

AT THE END of the cypress walk with its pavement of still-warm
dust, there was a bolted gate in my grandfather's garden wall. There
was an olive grove on the cliff-top beyond, loud with cicadas in
the hot, dimming evening. There were no bright resorts on that
Mediterranean coast in those days. Only darkness under motionless
trees and the faint, intermittent noise of the sea. The Greeks and
Romans were, in those years, very present in the school curriculum,
and the half-lights of the ancients already dominated the imagination as territories of alienation and fear. This brooding grove was
infested with the terrors of antiquity, the abrupt nightfall in the
Iliad that catches the broken King of Troy when he has gone
beyond retreat into the enemy camp. Even more, this dark grove
near the sea brought to mind the brusque evocation of the darkling
place where Odysseus goes to speak with the dead. It is a wooded
coast in a territory of perpetual mist and darkness, a beach near
the mouths of two rivers. The instructions of the goddess Circe
are ambiguous,

> Let the blast of the North wind carry you
> But when you have crossed with your ship the stream of the Ocean,
>   you will
> Find there a thickly wooded shore, and the groves of Persephone[18]

suggesting, as they do, a rapid southward voyage to the point where
the worlds of living and dead touch each other. But when Odysseus

and his companions set forth the next day their course seems to run, in so far as it is indicated, to the west and north – towards sunset and clouded skies:

> All day long her sails were filled as she went through the water,
> and the sun set, and all the journeying-ways were darkened.
>   She made the limit, which is of the deep-running Ocean.
> There lie the community and city of Kimmerian people,
> hidden in fog and cloud, nor does Helios, the radiant
> sun, ever break through the dark . . .[19]

That is all: there is a seashore in dim light, a place to dig a pit and summon ghosts to drink blood. It is somewhere to the west of the known world, towards the regions of sunset and night, nothing is explained except the terrible disjunction between the states of the living and the dead.

Shadow and darkness under trees also define the otherworld to which the hero of Virgil's *Aeneid* makes his lonely pilgrimage. This underworld is a desolate and desolating place, for the most part, but the devastation and horror are instilled in the reader not by the stark, unbridgeable gulf between Homer's living and dead, but by the fear, self-doubt and desperation that Aeneas himself feels as he sets forth as a legate from the living to the prophetic dead, for the good of his exiled people.

The approach to this otherworld also lies through the twilight of thick woodlands, the place where the golden bough is hidden in the shadowy branches of the ilex. With this talisman and the guidance of the Cumean Sybil, Aeneas can approach the threshold of the underworld: Virgil offers the detailed description, which Homer withholds, of an approach by night to a cave mouth by a black lake, rendered darker by the enfolding shadow of the trees: '*tuta lacu nigro nemorumque tenebris*'[20] (with the dark lake folded in shadowy trees). At the moment when Aeneas and his guide plunge into the cave that their sacrifice has opened, Virgil's narrating voice utters a prayer that he may speak of the otherworld without impiety, the prayer addressed to the custodians of the places of shadows, silences and the shadowy dead:

> *Di, quibus imperium est animarum, umbraeque silentes*
> *et Chaos et Phlegethon, loca nocte tacentia late,*
> *sit mihi fas audita loqui . . .*[21]

You gods, who hold the domain of spirits; you voiceless shades! You, Chaos and Phlegethon, and broad tracts of silent night! Allow me to tell what I have heard . . .

All the experience that follows is governed by Virgil's imagination of a kind of barely definable half-light, an unearthly, lucent darkness somewhere between the latest nautical twilight and a kind of forest-shadowed moon-twilight, evoked in five intense lines, the first of which pivots on the desolation and alienation that the hero feels under this 'lonely night':

> *Ibant obscuri sola sub nocte per umbram*
> *perque domos Ditis vacuas et inania regna,*
> *quale per incertam lunam sub luce maligna*
> *est iter in silvis, ubi caelum condidit umbra*
> *Iuppiter, et rebus nox abstulit atra colorem.*

They went forward in dim light, under the lonely night under the shadow, through the empty halls of Dis and his deserted kingdoms, as when a path through a forest lies under the untrustworthy illumination of intermittent moonlight, when Jupiter has hidden the sky in shadows and dark night has taken the colour out of the world.

This sense that the experience of the otherworld is one of personal suffering as well as the terror of crossing such a boundary is emphasized by the personified emotions – grief and anxiety – that throng the forecourt of the underworld, along with personifications of those things – disease and war – that bring humans to their deaths, and thus to the world of the dead. And the spreading tree that further darkens this forecourt is itself the dwelling of shadowy terrors and monsters.

48

The very words 'shadow' and 'dream' shape the texture of
this underworld journey, as in Charon's echoing warning that the
regions beyond the Styx are the homelands of shadows and dreams:
'*Umbrarum hic locus est, Somni Noctisque soporae*'[22] (This is the land
of shadows, of Sleep and drowsy Night). Before Aeneas can come to
the Elysian Fields, and thus to the purpose of his journey, which is
to hear prophecies of the future of his people from the shades of
their ancestors, he has to pass through yet another twilight grove,
the Fields of Regret – hidden pathways through groves of myrtle –
which is the place assigned to those who died for love, including his
own lost lover Dido. All we are told of them is that death has not
relieved them of any suffering – '*Curae non ipsa in morte relinquunt*'[23]
– and the shade of Dido, who offers no forgiveness in response to
his stammered apologies, is herself as faint as the new moon lost in
the clouds:

> qualem primo qui surgere mense
> Aut videt aut vidisse putat per nubila lunem[24]

> As in the early month, one sees or thinks
> one has seen the moon amidst the clouds

It is only when Aeneas finally comes to the Elysian fields, which are
either the place of reward for the virtuous dead or the threshold of
rebirth, that the lifting of his own burden is paralleled by light like
sunlight, brightness on water, grass underfoot. Even so, even though
he has elicited reassurances for the future of his people, he and the
Sybil have to return to the world, ambiguously, by the ivory gate of
the false dreams.

As with his evocation of the light after the summer sunset in his
pastoral poems,[25] Virgil's sombre evocation of twilights and shadows
in his otherworld has had an unquantifiable influence on subsequent
writing, almost all subsequent narrative that uses light expressively
being indebted to him, consciously or unconsciously.

Virgil's underworld is half-parodied in the referential otherworld
of the fourth-century poet Ausonius' *Love Crucified*, a narrative of the

grieving shades of lovers taking revenge on Cupid. Ausonius extends the disquieting landscape in Virgil to describe a marsh where soporific poppies grow and where absence of sound matches a 'cloudy' light:

> *. . . sub luce maligna*
> *inter harundineasque comas gravidumque papaver*
> *et tacitos sine labe lacus, sine murmure rivos*[26]

> . . . lit by meagre light, amidst tufts of reeds and heavy poppies, still pools without a ripple and silent streams

For the Christian centuries after Ausonius, twilight and night associate only with horror and fear, the need for divine protection against natural and supernatural enemies, as in the evening hymn *Te lucis ante terminum*:

> *Procul recedant somnia*
> *Et noctium fantasmata,*
> *Hostemque nostrum comprime*
> *Ne polluantur corpora*[27]

> Let the dreams and illusions of the night draw far away, and crush our enemy that our bodies be not soiled

Sheer gratitude for any light at all, even for little sparks of light – *nostris igniculis* – in the great darkness, is expressed in the rapt, dancing energy of Prudentius' hymn for the lighting of the lamp, *Hymnus ad incensum lucernae*, dating from the early fifth century:

> *Inventor rutili, dux bone, luminis,*
> *Qui certis vicibus tempora dividis,*
> *Merso sole chaos ingruit horridum,*
> *Lucem redde tuis, Christe, fidelibus.*[28]

> Creator of the radiant light, our good guide, you who divide time in a fixed order, now the sun has set and terrible chaos rushes upon us, give your light, O Christ, to your faithful.

Delicate representations of twilight skies appear in first-millennium mosaics in churches in Italy. In the fifth-century mosaics in the Basilica of S Maria Maggiore in Rome, the stylized Annunciation to an enthroned and crowned Virgin shows the angel and dove hovering above her in a blue-purple evening sky scattered with bright clouds coloured yellow and scarlet by the setting sun. In the sixth-century mosaics at S Vitale in Ravenna, Christ, with victor's wreath and closed book, is enthroned on the orb of the world, against a background of noctilucent clouds in grey and pink against a golden sky. In the seventh-century mosaics in the Basilica of SS Cosma e Damiano in Rome, the Second Coming of Christ is depicted in the apse, the stern figure of Christ with scroll and outstretched hand standing on a formal pattern of clouds, orange and yellow below, greyish blue above, against a deep cobalt sky. This is direct representation of biblical texts describing the Second Coming, a morning in the evening of the world – '*et tunc videbunt filium hominis venientem in nube cum potestate magna*' (Luke 21:27, the words mirrored in Mark 13:26) – in the only words put into the mouth of the beaten, otherwise-silent Christ in the Wakefield play of the torture,

> For after this shall thou se when that I do com downe
> In brightnes on he in clowdys from abone.[29]

Against the background of the first millennium's devouring fear of evening and night, the use of deliberately induced twilight and darkness in the ecclesiastical observances for the days before Easter is an enactment on the verge of the unendurable. From the Middle Ages the Tenebrae – the slow ritual extinguishing of the flames of fifteen candles during the singing of lessons and psalms at Matins and Lauds in the hours of night in the last three days of Holy Week – moved from light to dark until the church was in complete darkness and the end of the office was signified by the *strepitus* or 'great noise' of a book slammed shut.[30]

This moves in parallel to the sacred enactments of desolation culminating in the singing of the Passion of Christ on the afternoon of Good Friday in a church stripped of lights, organ music, ornaments and textiles, with Christ's own death represented by the absence of the consecrated Host from the empty tabernacle. A wooden rattle and occasional handclaps instead of bells. Only silences and gaps and absences until nightfall on the Saturday, when a fire is kindled to light the Paschal candle from which illumination slowly spreads again throughout the church.

The lessons for the first division of Matins are the desolate, night-haunted *Lamentations* of the prophet Jeremiah, reflecting on the punishments visited on Jerusalem. To these are added the refrain '*Ierusalem, Ierusalem, convertere ad Dominum Deum tuum*' (Jerusalem, turn to the Lord your God) from the prophet Hosea, all of which are sung to a chant reserved for these words alone. The sombre words that begin the *Lamentations*, '*Quomodo sedet sola civitas plena populo*' (How desolate the city is, which was once full of people), move rapidly to the people weeping in the night – '*Plorans ploravit in nocte*'[31] – all of which resonates back and forth in time from one time of suffering and darkness to another: the siege of Jerusalem echoing the Jerusalem of Christ's passion five centuries later.

The English writer Evelyn Waugh finds yet further resonance in the *Tenebrae*, as lamentation and ritual applicable to the darkening of Europe in the 1930s, which he traces in his crypto-baroque wartime novel *Brideshead Revisited*, first published in 1945. In that book the '*Quomodo sedet sola civitas*' recurs three times, punctuating the narrative of the decline of a family, a house and a civilization: the desolation of the emptied Good Friday church is paralleled with the de-consecration of the family chapel; the desolation of Jerusalem gives voice to the protagonist's revulsion against the thin transatlantic luxuries 'where wealth is no longer gorgeous, and power has no dignity'. Finally, in the deep winter of the war, he meditates on fallenness in the chapel of the requisitioned house: 'Year by year the great harvest of timber in the park grew to ripeness; until, in sudden frost . . . the place was desolate and the work all brought to nothing; *Quomodo sedet sola civitas*.'[32]

The arts of twilight extend into extraordinary musical dimensions in the setting of the *Leçons de ténèbres* by French composers around the turn of the eighteenth century, culminating in the penitential luxuriance of Marc-Antoine Charpentier's settings published in 1714. In some respects this twilight music is stripped bare – the forces are minimal – a solo voice or at most three voices with basso continuo. Charpentier specifies that these are not to be powerful voices but intimate singers, able to execute complex music at moderate volume.[33] The Latin text that Charpentier sets retains the names of the Hebrew letters that marked the divisions of the original text and these syllables are set to extraordinary, stark and protracted melismata, the ornaments circling and extending in patterns of complex abstraction. The gradual extinguishing of the candle flames, the deepening twilight, the mounting despair of the text, punctuated only by rising phrases for the *Convertere* of the antiphon, are reflected by ever more refined musical austerity, austerity which is tense in anticipation of the stark flourishes that mark the settings of the initial letters, until the whole seems an anticipation of the complex, violent sound world of later centuries.

Sparse lights in shuttered, twilight churches remain one of the most powerful memories of the Spain of the past: constellations of votive lights sparking reflected in the metallic threads with which the robes of the statues were embroidered. Six altar candles catching and reflecting points of light from the spiral columns of the carved reredos, the towering wall of gold behind the altar. Small flames behind red glass in the hanging lamps. This was observed by Théophile Gautier during his Spanish journey of 1840: '*Quelques petites lampes tremblotaient sinistrement jaunes et enfumées comme des étoiles dans du brouillard*'[34] (Some little lamps which were trembling in a sinister way, yellow and smoky as stars in a fog). Otherwise, high darkness, few windows, and the doors guarded by heavy curtains against the white dust and the fierce heat outside. It was a rare survival of the evening grandeurs of the baroque centuries: an aesthetic of richness in dim light, of glimmering metallic thread, of reflected points of spangled light.

In the eras when the strength of artificial light was limited, even on the greatest occasions, to the brightness of candles and reflectors, and when most church ceremonies would have taken place by the light of half a dozen candles, the play of moving and diffused reflection assumes an infinitely greater importance. The use of bullion thread, jewels and metal spangles on ecclesiastical vestments would have had a wholly different effect in the half-light, with the moving flames catching changing reflections and starry points of light as the priests moved.

This aesthetic of multiple small points of reflection in low light would also have been crucial to the effect of the indoor theatre, especially the court theatre. The masque costumes designed for the English court of the early seventeenth century consistently specify gilded armour, headdresses covered in reflective metallic paint or leaf and the extensive use of cloth of gold and silver. *Tempe Restored*, the Shrovetide masque for 1632, culminated in the descent of the Queen as Divine Beauty, with her attendant ladies representing stars, 'The Queen's majesty was in a garment of watchet satin with stars of silver embroidered and embossed from the ground, and on her head a crown of stars'.[35] Some of the effect of these performances can be imagined from the account given by the Venetian Ambassador of the Christmas season of 1618–19:

> The most distinguished of the masques is performed on the day
> after the feast of the Three Wise Men, in accordance with an
> ancient custom of this royal palace, in a large hall arranged like
> a theatre . . . there were two rows of lights which were to be lit at
> the proper time . . . at first, when there was little light, as if it were
> the twilight of dusk or dawn, the splendour of the diamonds and
> other jewels was so brilliant that they [the ladies] appeared so
> many stars.[36]

Domestic rooms in the Spain of the mid-twentieth century were also shuttered all day against the heat, women in black clothes moving slowly through perpetual twilight, a ring or a pearl earring glimmering as they moved, until the doors were opened after sunset and the life of the house moved onto a terrace, into a courtyard. This languid, sunless life seemed to belong to an earlier time, continuous with shuttered rooms throughout the Iberian world from the Americas to the Spanish Netherlands, an oblique after-echo of the twilight rooms of the aesthetes of the end of the nineteenth century. Twilight is a recurring theme for the artists and writers of the 1890s: twilight is much favoured by the painters of the era and it is only at twilight that the erotic otherworld will open to admit the hero of Aubrey Beardsley's one semi-pornographic novel *Under the Hill* (1896). The characters of *fin de siècle* fiction create rooms and houses for themselves that prolong the twilight of evening throughout their waking hours, attempting to prolong the dimmed lights of the past into the gaslit present, and so they too play games with time that are neither safe nor innocent.

These silences and half-lights possess the contemporary elegist for the 1890s, John Ash, in the second of his 'Portraits' poems in the evening sequence *Casino*. In a few lines, he summons up the epitome (and victim) of an era that deliberately dimmed rooms in a kind of perverse extravagance, a defiance of the realities of light and time, an era that was obsessed with illness and shadowy games with time that end in early death:

> the determination to die young,
> exquisitely on a private income –
> Vivian our Jacobean heroine in her Art Nouveau dress.[37]

The figure evoked echoes the rooms cluttered with antiquities, inhabited by night by the reclusive protagonist of Joris-Karl Huysman's *À rebours* (1884), another character who tries to deny the passage of time, the round of seasons and days, through the manipulation of his environment into the perpetual rich dimness that John Ash evokes for his heroine:

> Living in her perpetual twilight
> In the perpetual odour of a successful banker's funeral
> Among lilies always white and violets Sappho's flower . . .[38]

In Huysmans also, this withdrawal is fraught with danger and in the end a physician orders the protagonist to return to the realities of the nineteenth century before the unrealities of his unnatural suspension of light and time kill him.

It is in darkening rooms in Brussels that Joseph Conrad's *Heart of Darkness*, written in the last year of the nineteenth century, plays out its last scene. In a novel that has made complex play with images of darkness for unknown places and for uncharted, inhuman capacities in the human mind, the half-lit ending draws together the sombre horrors perpetrated by the dead man, whose last papers the narrator has come to deliver to his fiancée:

> The dusk was falling. I had to wait in a lofty drawing-room with three long windows from floor to ceiling that were like three luminous and bedraped columns. The bent gilt legs and backs of the furniture shone in indistinct curves. The tall marble fireplace had a cold and monumental whiteness. A grand piano stood massively in a corner, with dark gleams on the flat surfaces like a sombre and polished sarcophagus.[39]

When the woman enters, still dressed in mourning, the shift to monochrome vision and the heightened presence of white surfaces, which come with falling light, all serve to focus on her face:

> The room seemed to have grown darker, as if all the sad light of the cloudy evening had taken refuge on her forehead. This fair hair, this pale visage, this pure brow, seemed surrounded by an ashy halo from which the dark eyes looked out at me.[40]

This crepuscular scene continues until the darkness of the room, and the darkness of her high-minded ignorance of the horrors perpetrated by her beloved, all come together as aspects of the same negation, the same spreading night:

that great and saving illusion that shone with an unearthly glow in the darkness, in the triumphant darkness from which I could not have defended her – from which I could not even defend myself . . . By the last gleams of twilight I could see the glitter of her eyes, full of tears – of tears that would not fall.

It is symbolically impossible for artificial light to be brought into this scene, where the twilight of the apartment in Brussels mirrors the dark actions done in Africa. No maid could bring a lighted lamp into such a room at such a time. The narrator tells lies to save her illusions, acutely conscious as he does so of the wrong he does, of his own failure as a witness, and he makes good his escape as night descends: 'It seemed to me that the house would collapse before I could escape, that the heavens would fall upon my head. But nothing happened. The heavens do not fall for such a trifle.'[41]

The painter Michiel Sweerts, born in Brussels in 1618, was one of the few early modern artists to specialize in depictions of twilight places and landscapes, light rendered with an accuracy unusual for the period, almost, but not quite, a transcription of reality. Certainly, twilight haunts what little we know of the strange, accomplished, liminal career that ended in his death, insane and with his hopes in ruins, in Goa in 1664. He is a painter obsessed with the evening: he draws together hints from Annibale Caracci (1560–1609) and the evening-skied paintings that he made in Rome in the early years of the seventeenth century. Such works as his *Pietà* and his *Domine, quo vadis?* show the foreground groups in full light, but the background skies are exquisitely rendered summer horizons just after the sun has set (indeed in the *Quo vadis?* the last rays of sun seem to strike up from below to cast a lustre round the ridges of the hills). From Caracci, this intense interest in depiction of fading evening light passes to Poussin (1594–1665), to his elegiac belatedness: the shepherds who mourn as early evening draws on in the celebrated *Et in Arcadia ego.* In Poussin's *Acis and Galatea* (1629), rich sunlight has retreated far into the west and the shadow of the earth lies below rags of golden air, while consonances of slate and cobalt are still calm at the farthest horizon. It seems beyond doubt that Sweerts learned much from Poussin, often stopping just short of direct allusion to his work.

Sweerts's life and the subjects of his pictures form an episode of the dark baroque: his disquiet and agitation are a counterpart to Poussin's dusks, approaching in calm, folding and settling. Sweerts was not a documented member of the counter-cultural society of Netherlandish painters in Rome, the *Benteveughels* – connoisseurs and practitioners of the grotesque, self-mocking, hard-drinking 'birds of a feather' – although some of his work has elements in common with theirs. He studied in Rome, painting scenes from the margins of society, from the edges of the city, scenes sometimes enacted in obscured or fading light, their content sometimes hinting at membership of a gay subculture. He became a missionary lay-brother on his return to the Netherlands, and died insane at a mission station in Asia.

His own self-portrait, painted in the late 1650s, itself hints at disjunctions: the elegantly dressed painter with the instruments of his art is depicted in an accomplished baroque grand manner, but the background is a desolate landscape with bare hills for all the brightness of the sky.[42] If the painting of a *Man Holding a Skull* is indeed also a self-portrait, it carries these disjunctions further: the agitated expression, wind-blown clothes and hair and the deep twilight over the wild country that forms the background produce a sense of trouble that goes beyond the overt memento mori.[43]

Although many of Sweerts's works are calm and finely observed character studies, his genre pieces seem at once more sombre and stranger than those of the other Netherlandish painters in mid-seventeenth-century Rome.

A Wrestling Match (1648–50) fought in front of a numerous crowd under a darkening twilight sky is rendered haunting almost entirely by the effect of the strong frontal light from an unexplained source, which catches the foreground fighters and the man pulling his shirt over his head – the figure of a clothed young man, hurrying out of their way, is also caught by the light, which dramatizes his gesture and expression to the point where they seem at odds with the rest of the scene, almost expressive of terror.

Similarly, the *Bathing Scene*, of which there are versions in Hanover and Strasbourg, the former dating from Rome in the late 1640s, the latter from the Netherlands in the mid-1650s, presents unresolved questions concerning subject and light.[44] Bathers are an obvious subject with which to demonstrate skill in figure-painting informed by an intense awareness of ancient sculpture, but both versions disturb the serenity of the group with the presence of a sombre, cloaked male figure. In the Hanover version, the light is also contradictory in a familiar baroque way: the foreground is lit by an unexplained illumination hardly related to the last evening light dying in the distance. In this picture the serenity is further broken by the actions of two of the figures in the water, who seem to be fighting or moving into an embrace.

A Couple Visiting Shepherds in the Campagna (late 1640s) also evokes dislocated emotion in its depiction of a golden Claudian evening that has somehow gone wrong – a finely dressed young man and woman appear to be making a pastoral or proprietorial visit to shepherds gathered round a fire in a cave – an Italian version of the popular Netherlandish theme of the elite observing the labours of the countryside.[45] Again the couple, but only the couple, are lit by an unnatural light source falling from the left in contradiction of the golden after sunset light outside the mouth of the cave. Within, the shepherds are lit more or less naturalistically by the light of their fire. Again this is a fairly conventional example of the baroque practice of lighting foregrounds as though on a candlelit theatre stage with light falling from behind flat side-wings, however dim the evening light in the background is supposed to be. Here it has again a curious effect of rendering the familiar strange, an impression that is much deepened by the considerable difficulty of deciphering the expressions of the young couple at the centre of the scene: his eyes are downcast as he leans on his sword. Her hand rests consolingly on his shoulder, but the fall of the light hoods her eyes and her expression is blank, even hostile. There is no communication between these two elegant young people and the shepherds. The picture appears to depict a troubled silence that has fallen with evening, a phenomenon which is even more palpable in Sweerts's most disturbing genre piece *A Young Couple and a Boy in a Garden* (c. 1650).[46]

This painting, in the Worcester Art Museum, Massachusetts, is genuinely disquieting in what can only be called its sinister and violent melancholy. A young man offers a seated woman grapes from the dark arbour over their heads. A storm is clearing and he is silhouetted against the troubled sky beyond the garden. A child with a sad face eats a grape in the deep shadows under the pergola – it is impossible to discern how he relates to the adults, although his attention seems more on the woman than the man. The atmosphere evokes evening more successfully than does almost any other baroque picture, although the lighting is complex and to some degree contradictory; it is in these complexities of light that much of the force and menace of the picture are held.

Some illumination is still falling from the westering sun, but there is also diffused and muted light in the rainy evening sky with its moving banks of rose-blue-grey cloud beyond the pergola. Although full light falls on the woman, on the man's shoes and on the pot holding the orange tree in the foreground, there is a subsidiary light source in the clouds behind him. This contributes a great part of the emotional charge: he is almost entirely in shade, darkened against the light, drawing darkness to him, in defiance of the movement of light in the foreground.

He carefully holds the bunch of grapes by the stalk as he advances. It has been suggested that this relates to the emblematic interpretation of grapes by the Dutch poet Jacob Cats: grapes must be held by the stalk as the fruit is too tender to touch, just as only in marriage can a woman preserve her chastity.[47] This at the least is in parallel with the narrative implied by the painting, or rather a bitter counterpoint to what appears more likely to be a narrative of seduction. The woman's clothing is hard to read for indications of her vulnerability: the russet colour of her plain dress suggests a modest position in society, her coral necklace and the coral-coloured

Michiel Sweerts, *A Young Couple and a Boy in a Garden, c.* 1650, oil on canvas.

ribbon in her hair sit awkwardly with this and with the black ribbons at her wrists, which seem rather to imply mourning. But the light denies any real reading of emotion: her eyes are hooded by the fall of the last sunlight, the young man's face is scarcely visible, even if his gesture is predatory rather than courtly, and the child's face, also shadowed, communicates only anxiety and unhappiness.

At the very best, the young widow or courtesan in this picture is being offered a bad bargain, graver than the twilight bargains – gambling or cruising – hinted in Sweerts's other works: she crumples the handkerchief in her left hand for all the impassivity of her face. There is no further narrative that can be elicited: as with the *Couple Visiting Shepherds,* Sweerts presents a strongly realized atmosphere, disjunctions of lighting, together with underplayed expressions of negative emotion that appear to hint at a dark interpretation.

A palpable feeling of menace, even of evil, attends the *Couple in a Garden* – all the details suggest this, however much the central narrative remains obscure. Perhaps, as with any successful tale of terror, the worst is simply the worst interpretation that you, the spectator, can place on the imperfect evidence. Certainly the statues in the background are a destabilizing detail. They are not depicted by that Netherlandish convention that assumes that all garden statues are limewashed, so that they stand forth white against the trees. These statues are ambiguous stone presences, silhouetted like the man, tonally neutral, sharing their muted colour with the sketchily painted architecture. It comes as a troubling thought that they will seem yet more ambiguously human when the twilight in the painting is twenty minutes deeper, when the evening evoked with such skill is passing into night.

And this shadowy, insoluble painting, whose narrative remains always just beyond reach, revives my own memory of myself as a bored, sorrowing child at a loose end in the deepening twilights of villa and garden while the adults talked endlessly on the terrace. Sweerts's picture recalls in atmosphere that unregretted Spanish garden as powerfully as does the scent of the night-blowing flowers of the south. It recalls that world of Franco's Spain, in its own lingering twilight: a closed society pretending with gin and silver and crystal, with ritual and intermittent hysteria that nothing had been changed by the wars and revolutions of the mid-century. A way of life whose every gesture enacted a lamentation for an era neither fine nor admirable, now living out its afterlife through a long unnatural evening. The whole shadowy, locked, unvisited villa seemed almost cut loose from time and Europe, drifting far out on the airless dark and the overpowering breaths of the jasmine and *dama de noche*. A place becalmed where nothing could change – devouring heat and the flawless manners that were never courtesies. The strain born of decorum and the gunshots from the hills and the August thunderstorm gathering and thickening and mounting but never breaking.

CONTEMPLATING MICHIEL SWEERTS'S PICTURE, I hear again finely tuned English sentences on sweet, heavy air – smartly clipped English, learned in the first decades of the twentieth century. Vicious civilities that compose themselves into one elegant sneer at my father, and at all candour and virtue and honour. The powerless children in picture and in memory overlay each other – the one who looks out of the scented shadows of the garden at the mother in 1650 on the terrace under the arbour, or at the father in 1965 on the terrace within earshot of the fountain.

John Atkinson Grimshaw, *In the Gloaming*, 1878, oil on canvas.

2

ENGLISH MELANCHOLY

Mist from the river, fog drifting in from the wet ploughed land. Early dark, broken by sparse lamps in stone courtyards. Bitter east wind and damp cold rising at evening. Sodden twilight and the shouting from the sports grounds. Most of us had first visited the town for a winter interview and then arrived as students when autumn had already taken hold, so that the lasting impression was of a place grown almost otherworldly in short-lived, failing light.

The book that I read and reread, as though it would help me to find a way through this unfamiliar land, was Christopher Isherwood's *Lions and Shadows*, the lightly fictionalized autobiography of his early years:

> The train clanked through the iron-coloured fen landscape,
> with its desolate pointing spires, infinitely mournful in the fading
> December afternoon. Chalmers said: 'Arrival at the country of
> the dead'.
>
> Cambridge exceeded our most macabre expectations. It seemed
> a city of perpetual darkness . . . the shop lamps were already blurred
> in the icy fog . . the outlines of college buildings, half seen, half
> suggested, were massive and shadowy as the architecture of the
> night itself.[1]

This was the Cambridge experienced in the 1920s by Isherwood and his schoolfriend Edward Upward ('Chalmers' in the memoir); it was the Cambridge in which T. C. Lethbridge developed his spiralling wartime fantasies about traces of espionage and infiltration.[2] I can remember winter dusks, even in the 1970s, in what was still a citadel

of young men, when Isherwood's myths of a shadowy enemy, and
even Lethbridge's paranoid decodings, their fantasies that the misty
town was full of infiltrators and spies, seemed almost plausible.

As late as the 1970s, the unnatural demographic of a vast
university that was only just beginning to admit women on equal
terms gave a disquieting feeling of the world of thrillers and the
past: a John Buchan world, a garrison town full of the officers of an
army on constant alert. In those years Auden's earliest verse, set in
a masculine dusk between the old Norse saga and the 1920s thriller,
menaced by agents and infiltrators, was the other thing I read
constantly, again in an oblique attempt to understand the society
in which I intermittently found myself.

It was still one that Isherwood and Auden would have recognized.
Footballers mudded like trench soldiers filled the wintry streets at
the end of the afternoon, boots slung round their necks by the laces.
The shops themselves seemed to be catering for a last generation of
patrician athletes: sports equipment, college blazers, scarves and
colours. (There were also numerous fine antique shops, as though to
serve an equally patrician cadre of tutors and regimental chaplains.)
Only three colleges (one of them mine) then admitted both women
and men and our lodgings were all on the far side of the river from
the town. For me to cross the baroque stone bridge, through the
light-scattering mists moving on the surface of the water, was to
enter what felt like a secondary world, almost like making a journey
into the past, where the streets seemed full of short-haired, broad-
shouldered young men in tweed jackets.

But who was the enemy of this garrison of sporting officers?
Was it the Cold? The Dark? The Winter? The hostile states of
Eastern Europe? Was it that recognizably modern world which was
at that time coming tentatively into being elsewhere, in London, and
on the raw verges of the new motorways? What were they shouting
from the sports fields on the misted levels at the edge of the town as
their games ended and the diffused light started to fail? I cannot forget
the jolt, the exultant menace, of that unfamiliar virile shouting in the
half-dark: at nightfall all distant shouts of triumph have an undersong

of lamentation. (Where there is triumph there is defeat as its inevitable companion.) It was utterly unlike the chanting on two falling notes of a Scottish football crowd, heard on damp wind on the coal-smoke Saturdays of a Lowland town, as the floodlights lit up at half time above the rooftops.

But who was the enemy who waited in the shadows of England, in the mists and the early dark? Isherwood had fantasized an inimical organization of bizarre complexity.

> Everywhere, we encountered enemy agents, we recognised them instantly by the discreetly threatening tone of their voices . . . There was a college waiter who murmured into one's ear as he took the order 'Most certainly sir'. This man seemed positively fiend-like: he must surely be an important spy . . . For the present, they contented themselves with warning us, through the mouths of their myriad underlings, that we had better be careful, we were observed, we were only here on sufferance.[3]

A constant thread of conversation in the all-male colleges in those days was besiegedness and decline, the decline of institutions, of manners, education, traditions. Much of this was little more than the ill-informed praise of past times, neither experienced nor understood, but under it all, and real enough, was a sense of the 'wreckness', the wretchedness, that attends the ends of even lesser things. Paradoxically, these young men constantly used the word 'greyness' to describe what they saw as a conformist and monochrome new world coming into being outside the locked courts of golden stone where they drank their beer or claret at nightfall.

I lived on the edge of all this because of being a student at one of the first mixed colleges (as were many of my friends), so that our experience of university was very much an anticipation of the changed future, exceptional then, but in retrospect simply ordinary. But to go to dinner in one of the men's colleges (which always involved, of course, crossing the water at evening) was in some degree an expedition into the past, into the world that had nourished

Isherwood's and Lethbridge's paranoid imaginations. I saw, as
an outsider, the last years of an exclusive masculine pastoral: snug
studies, gas fires, ghost stories, fog at the windows. Cold staircases
with bare light bulbs; fine rooms, sometimes astonishingly fine
rooms, opening off them. Many conversations still turned on a
rich repertory of urban myths of espionage and cryptography. These
lamplit interiors, those conversations seem themselves in retrospect
like the first chapter of a fiction of espionage and infiltration, the last
moment of repose before the call to action sends the protagonists
hammering out into the freezing dark.

The more that I walked the town, the more that a key to the
nature of the whole place seemed to lie in the stone-paved slypes and
passages between courtyards – in the dimmed, anti-geography of dead-
ends, hidden lanes and closed back gates. A secretive complexity that
disclosed itself very slowly, gradually unfolding, arriving at neither
revelation nor resolution. But, as in many mythologies, the gates of
the otherworld seemed most likely to become visible as twilight gave
way to darkness. Isherwood and Upward certainly half-believed this
and in this way, in their evening explorations, they found their locked
portal:

> One evening . . . we happened to turn off into an unfamiliar alley,
> where there was a strange-looking, rusty-hinged old door in a high
> blank wall. Chalmers said: 'it's the doorway into the Other Town.'
> The Other Town could best be visited by night. So every evening after
> supper, we wandered the cold foggy streets, away from the lights and
> the shops, down back alleys to the water's edge . . .[4]

During the war, the controversial archaeologist T. C. Lethbridge (he
was a fantasist of the past as well as of the present) found terrifying
patterns in random detritus,[5] or what we can only assume in retrospect from the documents in his dossier to be random detritus. He
had been schooled in anthropology and archaeology, in the interpretation of fragments, and he was of the generation that found
their solace in crossword puzzles, and in the reading and writing of

fictions of deduction. From torn scraps of papers and scratches on telegraph poles, he deduced a whole, twilight army of enemy agents, gone to ground around Cambridge, invisible until they were ready to strike.

Deduction and narratives of action and disclosure were two of the mid-twentieth century's antidotes to the concentrated sadness of the bells, the spires in the fog, the lonely scatter of lamplit windows. Sunday evenings were the times of the greatest peril, when melancholia, the overwhelming English disease, invaded the studies with their trophies of oars over the fireplaces. Deciphering, the hermetic exercise of intellect, is the only specific to hold at a distance all that comes with the night mists rising from the river. However trivial and random the code, however shadowy and improbable the enemy.

But even the consolations of English genre fiction can falter in the long sequence of perceived personal and historical losses. One haunting example is the edgy framing of a narrative of murder in a country house in meditations on twilight and decline that dislocate, indeed render pointless, the shapely ingenuities of the story. In *The Bloody Wood* by Michael Innes[6] (whose literate and literary fictions of action and disclosure often contain episodes, imaginations and descriptions disproportionately powerful and evocative) the hostess is dying, the host is in despair, and their Georgian house, Charne, with its formal gardens, follies and nightingale-haunted groves is at the very end of its life.

The opening scene is set at dusk in late summer, in a pavilion within earshot of the nightingales, as a quarrel flickers and the detective reflects on time and decay: 'The town was creeping around Charne. Still just held invisible, it was nevertheless biding its time to strangle the place. Appleby thought of Grace Martineau, a sick woman swathed in shawls, waiting too.' When the plot has worked itself out and the family tragedy with it, the narrative draws back as Appleby drives away:

They had been climbing steadily, and were now looking back over wooded and gently undulating country in the direction of Charne.

> The house was clearly visible . . . and behind that, a fine haze of
> smoke marked the town; and out from this obscurity there seemed
> to thrust, like reddish tentacles, the roofs of its advancing suburbs.
> 'I doubt whether it has long to go,' Appleby said.[7]

With these words he accelerates away from a dying estate of England,
from a narrative that ended with his own involuntary surrender to
the (unfathomable, anachronistic, nostalgic) temptation to allow a
gentleman murderer to kill himself.

The curious name of the doomed house inevitably recalls
C. S. Lewis's allegorical fables of otherworlds, and the travels of the
children in the earliest (chronologically considered) of his fictions
of Narnia, in which they stumble into the last decline of Charn,
a civilization brought to destruction by foul magic. It is a region of
malign twilight (it is also an inversion of the English legend of the
good king sleeping under the hill until he wakes to save his people)
where the last evil Queen wakes only to work further harm. It is a
landscape of the very end, of the moment before dissolution and
endless night:

> Low down and near the horizon hung a great, red sun, far bigger
> than our sun. Digory also felt at once that it was also older than
> ours: a sun near the end of its life, weary of looking down upon
> that world. To the left of the sun, and higher up, there was one single
> star, big and bright. Those were the only two things to be seen in
> the dark sky . . . and on the earth, in every direction, as far as the
> eye could reach, there spread a vast city in which there was no
> living thing to be seen.[8]

It is a memorable, terrible episode, in which genre fiction has again
deepened into a poetic reflection of the post-war preoccupations
with abused power, universal loss and the decline of empires.

In real and fictional English twilights, there is a whole new
repertory of unfamiliar lights to be discovered. Fading sunlight
diffused in vapour, protracted frozen sunsets, and the lingering of

damp twilight are my strongest memories of what was new in my
first student years in England. Perhaps the shape of the university day
was such that we walked out most often in the later afternoon, when
the shouting faded on the sports fields, and the shops and market
stalls were beginning to light up one by one. Frances Cornford, in
Cambridge in the very early twentieth century, found the precise
words for these dimming afternoons, 'the snow in the field and . . .
the blue-grey afternoon before tea time'.[9] And then as we walked
back, the things that were most novel of all to me, after the square
stone terraces and villas of Scotland, were the lighted Gothic or
pseudo-Gothic windows sending their lights over the damp levels,
across the darkened gardens.

Victorian windows, cusped arches of yellow light, blurring in fog
or rain, bright in the frosty dusk. A haunting, carrying a whole cargo
of emotion, from that day to this. These lights sent forth no notion of
comfort within, but suggested rather dislocation and unease, as if the
century within the lamplit room might not be the century in the dusk
outside, as if all the drenched sorriness of nineteenth-century England
was shining out from those Gothic lights, and their reflections trailing
over the streaming cobbles.

The density of vapour in the English air produced a diffusing,
softening, metamorphic light as day faded, sumptuous bleeding
colours unknown from the wind-scraped skies of Scotland (or,
indeed, from the curt, dry evenings of southern Spain). This

> . . . water-shafted air
> Of amethyst and moonstone . . .[10]

as Louis MacNeice called it, was unfamiliar and beguiling, the more
so as the first autumn turned to a bitter winter, and once more new
aspects of the evening sky declared themselves:

> winter mist riddled with bird-whistles
> sunset a red scarf or a yellow scarf.[11]

I recognized those watery qualities of the winter dusk, years later, in these lines of Peter Levi's about his own student days. On the darkest days of winter, with the chapel windows lit only at the bottom by the lights thrown up from the lamps on the music desks – it was more like the stark unconsoledness of Emily Dickinson's dusk in New England:

> There's a certain Slant of light,
> Winter Afternoons –
> That oppresses, like the Heft
> Of Cathedral Tunes –
>
> . . .
>
> When it comes, the Landscape listens –
> Shadows – hold their breath –
> When it goes, 'tis like the Distance
> On the look of Death –[12]

Quality and texture of air, and all that it influences and creates, is one of the most subtle (but absolute) differences between Scotland and England. The nature of nightfall in the north is concisely expressed by Robert Louis Stevenson's *A Child's Garden of Verses*: not just in the summer verse about the child going to bed while the light lingers in the long evenings, but in his celebrated poem of Edinburgh winter afternoons, the poem about the lamplighter. This captures almost exactly the experience of dusk that I took south with me into the region of lamplit Gothic windows and mists on water meadows. Indeed the house in Heriot Row where Stevenson had lived as a child lay often on my own childhood itineraries:

> My tea is nearly ready and the sun has left the sky;
> It's time to take the window to see Leerie going by;
> For every night at teatime and before you take your seat,
> With lantern and with ladder he comes posting up the street.[13]

The poem is a curious hybrid – partly an attempt to explain the nature of a Scottish childhood to an English reader, a powerfully felt memory expressed in indifferent verse. But it has been accepted in Scotland as a record of shared experience. There is nothing here about the early darkening of the sky (the next Edinburgh street to the south up the steep slope of the hill would, in any case, have cut off much of the skyline from Stevenson's view across the lamplit street) but there is close attention to the texture of the urban day. Perhaps this poem, and the regard in which it was held by generations who had known it as children, itself contributed to the preservation of the original lamp standards in the New Town, lit by cold white light in imitation of the old gaslight. They gave that quarter of the city a clear, hard texture at nightfall: milky globes in frosty air. Light gleaming off granite cobbles, light striking upwards, deepening the rustications on the Craigleith stone, casting elongated shadows of cast-iron honeysuckle from the first-floor balconies.

In England, the visual impact of lighted Gothic windows seen at nightfall across wet fields, or looking down from a snowy hill, remained powerful throughout the nineteenth century, and remains powerful still:

> And thou hast climb'd the hill,
> And gain'd the white brow of the Cumnor range;
> Turn'd once to watch, while thick the snowflakes fall,
> The line of festal light in Christ-Church hall –
> Then sought thy straw in some sequestered grange.[14]

So Matthew Arnold's Scholar Gypsy, ageless shadow amidst the shadows that surround winter Oxford, turns away from the gaslit festivities below and presses on, away into the snow. Damp, mist, dusk: there is a thread in the English arts beginning, to some degree, as early as the 'melancholy' portraits of the Elizabethans, and growing rapidly from the later eighteenth century, that responds particularly to the fall of evening, especially in the darkling seasons of autumn and winter.

The familiar, aching images of lamplight and the early dark by the northern English painter John Atkinson Grimshaw (1836–1893) are a haunting not yet exorcized. The colours of their skies still provoke a recognition, in Eliot's words, of

Afternoon grey and smoky, evening yellow and rose;
. . .
With the smoke coming down above the housetops[15]

The west ends of the northern cities, the big villas on the gritstone roads, dimmed light behind branches, distant lamplight – all these have their visual record in Grimshaw's paintings, with their long afterlife in English poetry and imagination:

The northern master Grimshaw understood
Belatedness: the passing of an age
That does not pass.[16]

Grimshaw was a painter of light, especially of fading and absent light: twilight paintings, whether urban, suburban or of isolated houses, are part of the Victorian rediscovery of silhouette and obliquity: buildings shown not head-on but from an angle, often composing themselves into a rough pyramid. Dusk accentuates this, but the emotional effect of the paintings often comes more from the sparse artificial lights represented in them – a single lit window expresses loneliness, isolation, even desolation, if the scene is set (as it usually is) in late autumn or winter.

Yet Grimshaw goes beyond the general to the specific. Technically his suburban scenes are *capricci* – the fanciful combination of familiar buildings in imagined settings to produce a decorative or expressive effect. For most of his adult life, Grimshaw lived at Knostrop Old Hall on the edge of Leeds, a house that was the subject of many of his interior and garden paintings, which house (recast in a variety of settings) was an element in many of his architectural compositions.[17]

If the substantial houses behind Grimshaw's moonlit walls are examined, they are not often the expected gritstone mansions of West Yorkshire mill owners, but are mostly brick and Portland stone villas, early eighteenth-century in date, either with lamps lit behind the tall, small-paned windows of their drawing rooms, or seen by the falling light of an autumn afternoon. Sometimes they are older manor houses of soot-darkened stone, of markedly northern English character, lost amidst the newer streets, as was Grimshaw's own house. This represents one of the most haunting features of the great cities of the north: older houses that were once in the country, with the tide of mid-nineteenth-century building lapping around them – the old geography glimpsed under the new, the past lurking in the present.

Grimshaw's nocturnes have drawn a response, an imaginative recreation in another medium, from one of the most distinguished contemporary poets of the north: Sean O'Brien's fine imagination of the melancholy, *belated* lives lived in the great villas behind Grimshaw's moonlit walls, an analysis of the emotions evoked by the paintings and how emotion might be located *within* the paintings. In his poem simply titled 'Grimshaw' O'Brien begins by offering an evocation, an equivalent in a sequence of images for the cold twilights of the paintings:[18]

> November – copper beeches bare – the gates
> Shut fast against the poor – Disconsolate
> Illumination shed by gasoliers –
> Damp garden walls and hidden escritoires.

and moves on to a rapid summary of the emotions – with the word 'disconsolate' echoing through the poem – which so many viewers have recognized in Grimshaw's half-lit streets. But then his verse moves into what Grimshaw rarely showed – the evening interior behind the lonely, lighted windows: games of cards, boredom and loneliness, the unendurable length and tedium of the winter. The poem ends by conjecturing the thoughts of the daughter of such a silent house, the woman alone in the one lamplit room:

> The night has barely started on the clock.
> *We see noone. No letters come but yours.*

Isolated and sorrowing, she is the suffering individual who witnesses the failing light, bare trees and stone walls that repeat and repeat in Grimshaw's inventions and re-inventions of the Victorian north, and it is her loneliness that haunts them and gives them their sad power.

Grimshaw's atmosphere of isolation, the power of the image of the lonely light in the substantial dark house (and its conjectured or implied inhabitant) is a visual equivalent for the stalled, horrible slowness of the passage of time, the verbal accumulation of loneliness and squandered hours in Tennyson's 'Mariana':[19]

> . . . but most she loathed the hour
> When the thick-moted sunbeam lay
> Athwart the chambers, and the day
> Was sloping toward his western bower.[20]

Perhaps the most haunting and most Tennysonian of Grimshaw's pictures, *In the Gloaming*, gives a deserted Knostrop Hall (or a much aggrandized version of it): a moat, a bridge strewn deep with fallen leaves (thus implying unvisitedness, lostness, abandonment), and a water gate with steps leading down to a dim, limitless mere that stretches away into bare-branched, freezing woodland.[21] The water glimmers in the fading light; the composition is framed by stark black trees. It is his most poetic invention and, for many reasons, the one that is most intensely of its time. It seems probable that 'Mariana in the Moated Grange' was indeed in Grimshaw's mind when he painted it: certainly it has the same atmosphere of regret and decay, troubled by the inevitable question of 'who, if anybody, lives in this house?'

Behind the trees and reflected in the mere is a band of cold rose and crimson, smudged by drifts of grey cloud, fading into the broken, whitened yellow of the empty sky. Intense sunsets are common to Grimshaw and many of his contemporaries, increasingly so in the 1880s, but the pallid upper reaches of the sky in this picture are a specific and eloquent record of the blanking effects of industrial pollution. *In the Gloaming* is thus even more a quintessence of the later nineteenth century perhaps than its painter knew: Tennysonian isolation and mourning, an ancient house apparently in deep country, lost in time in a deserted backwater, but under skies that are those of an industrial city of the 1870s.

All his long life, John Ruskin (1819–1900) was a peerless observer of the evening sky. He had studied the sunsets of the earlier century in the company of Turner, whose paintings he praised in measured and lyrical words for their mastery of twilight:

> Take the evening effect with the Téméraire . . . under the blazing veil of vaulted fire which lights the vessel on her last path, there is a blue, deep, desolate hollow of darkness, out of which you can hear the voice of the night wind, and the dull boom of the disturbed sea; because the cold, deadly shadows of the twilight are gathering through every sunbeam, and moment by moment as you look, you will fancy some new film and fastness of the night has arisen over the vastness of the departing form.[22]

And he remembered Turner's skies as going beyond those of Claude and Poussin: 'They give the warmth of the sinking sun overwhelming all things in its gold, but they did not give those grey passages about the horizon where seen through its dying light, the cool and gloom of night gather themselves for their victory.'[23] But they belonged to an era whose domestic chimneys sent up only a low haze at evening: 'the smoke on the horizon, though at last it hides the sun, yet hides it through gold and vermilion.'[24]

Thereafter, he went on, year after year, setting down descriptions of evening skies with great and admirable precision, 'taking up the traditions of air from the year before Scott's death'.[25] He describes these evenings with greater intensity, once he feels that they are mostly lost and gone with the unnatural alteration of the English weather, the loss of 'the beauty and blessing of nature, all spring and summer long':[26]

an entirely glorious sunset, unmatched in beauty . . . deep scarlet, and purest rose, on purple grey, in bars; and stationary, plumy, sweeping filaments above in upper sky . . . remaining in glory, every moment best, changing from one good into another for half an hour full, and the clouds afterwards fading into the grey against amber twilight.[27]

On the evening of the following day, Ruskin noted: 'Divine beauty of western colour on thyme and rose, – then twilight of clearest *warm* amber far into night, of *pale* amber all night long; hills dark-clear against it.'[28]

His perceptions of alteration and loss concentrated on his memories of the twilights that he had experienced before the 1870s, corroborated by the translucent western skies of the 1850s, faithfully recorded by Millais in his *Autumn Leaves*. Ruskin had expressed his appreciation and recognition of this fidelity in his *Academy Notes* for 1856:

> By much the most poetical work the painter has yet conceived; and also, as far as I know, the first instance existing of a perfectly painted twilight. It is as easy, as it is common, to give obscurity to twilight, but to give the glow within its darkness is another matter; and though Giorgione might have come near the glow, he never gave the valley mist. Note also the subtle difference between the purple of the long nearer range of hills, and the blue of the distant peak emerging beyond.[29]

Ruskin's own accuracy of observation is attested here by his realization that counter-glows, reflected light, and the capacity of the human eye to adjust to falling levels of illumination can still show a clearly defined foreground against a dimming sky. Steven Connor has found memorable words for the phenomenon:

> For a short period, this creates a strange, faint flaring of the air, an oblique blaze in things. The glow of the gloaming, after the sun has

gone but something of its light still lingers, seems dispersed or sourceless, as though aching evenly from every surface, as though brightness were falling from the air itself.[30]

This, indeed, is a phenomenon for which Caspar David Friedrich had found inspired painted equivalents at the beginning of the nineteenth century. But most of all Ruskin observed, as the 1870s progressed, that the clarity which Millais had seen in that sky of the 1850s was being lost by unnatural drifts borne on a wind that itself heralded the disturbance and change of the weather:

> This wind is the plague-wind of the eighth decade of years in the nine-teenth century; a period which will assuredly be recognized in future meteorological history as one of phenomena hitherto unrecorded in the courses of nature, and characterized pre-eminently by the almost ceaseless action of this calamitous wind . . . It is a wind of darkness . . . whenever, and wherever the plague-wind blows, be it but for ten minutes, the sky is darkened instantly.[31]

This sombre perception found expression in his two lectures titled 'The Storm Cloud of the Nineteenth Century', almost his last public utterance before increasing adversity and mental disturbance drove him into reclusion and near-silence.[32] It is an extraordinary text, in itself a moment of the greatest lucidity produced by a mind darken-ing in bereavement and despair. The spoiled sky that he describes on 22 June 1876 dates from the summer when his mental illness had first become apparent: 'Thunderstorm; pitch dark, with no *blackness*, – but deep, high, *filthiness* of lurid, yet not sublimely lurid, smoke-cloud; dense manufacturing mist'.[33] And, by an accurate intuition, he guessed the cause of the changing weather as carbon in the atmosphere from the factories of southern Lancashire, describing the cloud as 'Manchester devil's darkness'.[34] He perceived further symp-toms beyond the sickly wind and the charcoal clouds, especially one that has a direct bearing on Victorian representations of the evening sky: 'And now I come to the most important sign of the plague-wind and the plague-cloud: that in bringing on their peculiar darkness, they *blanch* the sun instead of reddening it.'[35] From this he drew his conclusion that all of nature as he apprehended it, an interconnected whole encompassing his withered garden as much as the thickened air over Coniston, was all offering connected evidence of the same failure: 'Blanched Sun, – blighted grass, – blinded man.'[36] The blight extended wherever the storm cloud could travel on the wind – 'harmony is now broken and broken the world round'.[37]

Thus Ruskin offers a sad and true explanation for the strangely blank, yellowish-white sky of Grimshaw's *In the Gloaming*. No upward reflection from the setting sun brings any colour to the upper atmosphere: the smoke-drift of Leeds has blanched the fading sunlight, even in this haunting *capriccio* of an older England abandoned.

As the 1870s give way to the 1880s, a new phenomenon can be seen that accounts for the intensity of the sanguine horizon line, for the blooded or yellow-drenched west in many contemporary paintings of evening. The authoritative account of the science of the evening sky attributes a 'brilliantly coloured glowing background', as opposed to coloured clouds, to the presence of volcanic debris in the air.[38] It further identifies lilac colour at twilight as a frequent indicator of this volcanic debris, and recalls that the skies of the nineteenth century were coloured with saturated colour by a continual sequence of volcanic eruptions, the subject of Ruskin's despairing complaint that 'Month by month the darkness gains upon the day, and the ashes of the Antipodes glare through the night.'[39] In 1883 the drifting volcanic cloud from Krakatoa produced phenomena in the twilight skies so striking as to merit a Royal Society Report, a volume that contains much perceptive and elegant writing about the further alterations to be observed in evening skies worldwide: 'Then came records of a peculiar haze; in November the extraordinary twilight glows in the British Isles commanded general attention, and their probable connection with Krakatoa was pointed out by various writers.'[40]

The phenomenon of a saturated yellow sky can also be volcanic, and Grimshaw offered records of several such skies of burning yellow in paintings of the 1880s, especially in *Evening Glow* (1884) in the

Yale Center for British Art. It is to be noted in this picture that the atmospheric colour is so remarkable as to cause Grimshaw's usual staffage figure of a maidservant to change her position and to be looking up and directly into the west. Such a deep-yellow sky was observed precisely, in the wake of a subsequent volcanic eruption, by Edward Wilson in September 1901, when he was a member of Shackleton's Antarctic expedition:

> The sunset was even more glorious than the sunrise, for the sky was almost cloudless and we got the intense yellow ochreous glare after sunset uninterrupted by any clouds. It was almost uncanny. One felt as though something terrible was about to happen – the same sort of feeling that one gets in a dense yellow London fog, only this was beautiful, and magnificent, as well as terrifying.[41]

In the Royal Society volume of 1888, a colour lithograph frontispiece made by a Mr Ashcroft at Chelsea documents the evening sky of 26 November 1883, a fascinating series of meticulously drawn records, taken at ten-minute intervals, from sunset at three minutes to four, through a prolonged and fiery series of afterglows, to the last fading of the afterglow at quarter past five. The first of the afterglows, which appeared at four thirty, has a brilliance of saturated yellow suggesting that the glow of Grimshaw's painting is indeed likely to be volcanic in origin.

Apart from the beguiling visual record of the transient progress of one twilight sky on an evening long before the invention of colour photography, a moving instance of a transient thing snatched fortuitously out of time, the Royal Society volume gives the same sense as Ruskin does that awareness is growing that weather phenomena worldwide form parts of a single system, one which can be affected by both natural disaster and human activity. Thus the volume charts the progress of the volcanic ash cloud after the August eruption of the volcano, affecting the twilight sky in Asia and Australia in September; Mauritius and south Australia in October; central Europe in early November and Britain from late November through

TWILIGHT AND AFTERGLOW EFFECTS AT CHELSEA, LONDON.
NOV. 26TH 1883.

Nº1. ABOUT 4·10 P.M.

Nº2. ABOUT 4·20 P.M.

Nº3. ABOUT 4·30 P.M.

W. ASCROFT. DEL.

LITH. & IMP. CAMB. SCI. INST. CO.

Frontispiece to The Royal Society's report *The Eruption of Krakatoa, and Subsequent Phenomena* (1888); chromolithographs after crayon sketches made by William Ascroft in November 1883.

December and January, by which time some presence of volcanic ash was observed in the atmosphere worldwide.[42] The phenomena were everywhere consistent: 'The peculiar lurid glow, as of distant conflagration, totally unlike our common sunsets . . . the very late hour to which the light was observable – long past the usual hour of the cessation of twilight'.[43]

The most haunting aspect of the volcanic evenings was the persistence and otherworldly quality of the afterglows: the last of the light unnaturally reflected in the 'aerosols' the water drops formed around the fragments of volcanic dust, glassy ash, diffused through the atmosphere. Some of the strangeness was caught in a report from the Midwest of the United States: 'On December 28th an arc was formed in the east, the colours red and yellowish-green, very soft, and much blended. The crimson glow on the sky flooded the western side of buildings with an unearthly light, and cast faint shadows across the snow',[44] and in one from Berlin:

> At 4.30 the streets were lighted with a peculiarly pale glare, as
> if seen through a yellow glass. Then darkness followed and the
> stars became visible. But half an hour afterwards, at 5 o'clock,
> the western sky was again coloured by a pink or crimson glow.
> Persons who were not sure about its direction mistook it for
> an aurora; others spoke of a great fire in the neighbourhood.[45]

In contrast to the international scientific cooperation that charted the progress of the volcanic ash cloud worldwide, Ruskin's perception that the whole system of climate was being affected by human action, by the irresponsibility (he would have said 'impiety') of a single section of society, went largely unheard. Obsession with the weather seemed but one of the obsessions that had undermined his reason and he died in reclusion. His biography is one of the great and paradoxical sorrows of the nineteenth century.

TENNYSON WAS CALLED by his sincere admirer Auden 'the saddest of the English poets', understandably so given the recurring themes and atmospheres of his poetry, themes and atmospheres that seem intensely of his time and are shared by many of his contemporaries, painters as well as poets: remote houses and their isolated inhabitants, empty seashores, ruined gardens, woodsmoke and autumn mists. These combine most famously in his 'Mariana' but are strongly present in the early 'Song', which begins 'A spirit haunts the year's last hours' with its description of a raw, oppressive autumn evening in a garden of blackening, long-dead flowers:

> The air is damp, and hush'd and close,
> As a sick man's room . . .
> My very heart faints and my whole soul grieves
> At the moist rich smell of the rotting leaves . . .[46]

The summer poem 'Audley Court' inhabits characteristically Tennysonian regions of a great-house garden close by the seashore, approached through a secluded park and 'The pillar'd dusk of sounding sycamores'[47] – even in this serene poem the desertedness of the garden in which the characters talk provides a countercurrent to the calm of the summer day, one that intensifies as the poem ends at evening as the rising moon,

> . . . dimly rain'd about the leaf
> Twilights of airy silver . . .[48]

which move this pastoral towards the later setting of the narrative 'Maud', a melodrama of the love and failure of a dispossessed young man, again with the setting of a manor house deep in unvisited grounds near a seashore.

Tennyson's most intense autumnal evocation of the smell of damp air and rot comes in the monologue of a character who, to his anguish, can decay himself but never die. The atmosphere is entirely that of November England, despite the narrative's origin in classical mythology:

> The woods decay, the woods decay and fall,
> The vapours weep their burthen to the ground,
> Man comes and tills the field and lies beneath,
> And after many a summer dies the swan.[49]

And Tennyson's starkest twilight comes at the low point of his cycle of elegies for his dead friend Arthur Henry Hallam: total emotional stasis however the year or day may move, stasis long before the first faint movement of consolation, expressed in the image of the evening star defeated in a blooded sky:

> Sad Hesper o'er the buried sun
>   And ready, thou, to die with him,
>   Thou watchest all thing ever dim
> And dimmer, and a glory done.[50]

Mourning in a world where his loss is so obliterating that no external thing seems any more solid than the fog that rises at evening:

> They melt like mist, the solid lands,
> Like clouds they shape themselves and go.[51]

And it is only at the very end of his life that Tennyson can use the same image that has marked the depth of grief in *In Memoriam* – the evening star in the sunset sky – in a tranquil and accepting anticipation of his own death.[52]

Lighted windows in an autumn evening recur in Matthew Arnold's memorial poem for his headmaster father – intensely Victorian not only in its autumnal melancholy, but in its Gothic-revival setting – the school buildings at Rugby whose windows shine across the field are all of the nineteenth century:[53]

Coldly, sadly descends
The autumn-evening. The field
Strewn with its dank yellow drifts .
Of withered leaves, and the elms,
Fade into dimness apace,
Silent – hardly a shout
From a few boys late at their play!
The lights come on in the street,
In the school-room windows: – but cold
Solemn, unlighted, austere
Through the gathering darkness arise,
The chapel-walls . . .[54]

These verses circle around the one trope common to many twilight
paintings and poems: that sense of *belatedness*, not only of late
arrival at a place, with the light already going, but of coming to
a place after a lapse of time when circumstances have changed.
It is an atmosphere and feeling already encountered with Tennyson's
'Mariana', with Sean O'Brien's imagined inhabitant of a Grimshaw
painting: time is wasted, often by the actions of others, and then the
overwhelming feeling as the light begins to go is that it is too late
for anything to be changed, achieved or salvaged. In 'Rugby Chapel'
Arnold arrives when it is already too late to accomplish the purpose
of his journey – in this case a visit to his father's grave in the Chapel.
With the sense of belatedness goes a sense of devouring failure,
formless grief, unfinished and unfinishable business. So many feeling
citizens of the nineteenth century – an age that was in architecture
and the arts often an age of revivals and imitations of the past –
regretted that they had somehow been born too late in time. It is
unsurprising that the arrival at twilight, the watching of lit windows
as a stranger in the darkening cold, is a repeated motif of the nineteenth century in all the arts.

The contemporary poet John Ash's haunted twilight journey
in the poem 'Bespalko's Devotions' is a conscious homage to the
nineteenth century in setting and imagery, which is also a tracing

of an old itinerary though an unnamed Eastern European territory that is now in the hands of a hostile and suspicious government. So it is uncertain if the shadow at dusk is a ghost from the ancient, watery landscape or an agent of an equally shadowy contemporary regime:

> The river mist deepens. The fields are cold.
> It is not your shadow alone that follows you
> darkening the reeds at the edge of the pond . . .
> Herons rise like ghosts
> above the flooded fields.[55]

These verses intensify the belated loneliness that is the mood of so much of nineteenth-century writing about evening. It has the sadness of the journey undertaken too late, indeed it has the sense of lateness that is common to depictions of twilight in many of the arts of Europe.

A longing for such haunted evening landscapes possesses the heroine of Sylvia Townsend Warner's fantastical and beautiful novel *Lolly Willowes; or, the Loving Huntsman*:

> she was subject to a peculiar kind of day-dreaming, so vivid as to be almost a hallucination: that she was in the country at dusk, and alone, and strangely at peace . . . her mind walked by lonely sea-bords, in marshes and fens, or came at nightfall to the edge of a wood . . .[56]

These dreams are the first intimation in the novel of the quietly successful resolution of the heroine's unhappiness as a spinster on the margin of a family who take her for granted: her move to an out of the way village in the country and her cheerful compact with the devil. These fireside dreams are also the first manifestation of the otherworldly force who seeks her out, the 'loving huntsman' of the title:

Her mind was groping after something that eluded her experience, a something that was shadowy and menacing, and yet in some way congenial; a something that lurked in waste places and that was hinted at by the sound of water gurgling in deep channels and by the voices of birds of ill-omen.[57]

Her affinities are wild and twilit, her longings are prompted by the darkening evenings of autumn. In intention and imagination she has already moved far away from artificial light and bright rooms: 'Loneliness, dreariness, aptness for arousing a sense of fear, a kind of ungodly hallowedness – these were the things that called her thoughts away from the comfortable fireside.' And as the narrative unfolds she finds peace and fulfilment not only in becoming a witch but in remoteness and stillness, in the unregarded passage of a winter afternoon to evening: 'Looking into the well, she watched the reflected sky grow dimmer; and when she raised her eyes the gathering darkness of the landscape surprised her. The time had come.'[58]

THE EXPLORATION OF the winter afternoons was the object of the excursions undertaken in a crowded car later in my student years. We wanted to see everything that we could reach in the shortening autumn or winter days: country houses in their cold parks, monuments in flint parish churches and the fall of the light on the fields. Our excursions started in late morning, almost always late in the year, so the race against the falling light shaped them and gave them their character.

We were connoisseurs of the everyday, of the old fashioned, of the washed up, the washed out: gradations of grey in watery, receding East Anglian landscape, remote yellow-brick villages, willows stirring far out on the levels. Those afternoons of mists and rainy distance when *a common greyness silvers everything*. In guidebooks from the mid-twentieth century, as well as in the landscape, we looked for Victorian churches at nightfall, out past the edges of villages into the reedy fields and the black ditches, or sunken in the great, leafless trees beyond the estate gates.

Unconsciously, we were in search of that moment of other-worldliness that comes upon the East Anglian landscape at nightfall, much later recorded by Mark Cocker as a part of his lyric observations of the homing crows, what he calls his 'discovery of dusk': 'Dusk has become a purpose in its own right . . . Things become less fixed. Commonplace items are blurred.'[59] And the omnipresent winter mist isolates the solitary walker further,

> This mist first congeals over the water-filled dykes and then spills in linear shoals out across the fields, gradually back-filling the landscape, winding through the trees, submerging the fixed properties of day in a soft white nebula . . . I love most the times when it leaves the river banks just standing proud and isolated above the tide. The bank crown then marks my eerily silent route home to the village, like a dream causeway back to the land of the living.[60]

Dusk also restores a sense of the past to what the author calls 'abandoned Norfolk':

> I'm under no illusion that this is a place long beaten down
> by decades of agricultural usage and modification, but the mist
> and the dusk at least give the sense of the landscape reclaiming
> its powers of mystery. Here the ghosts emerge with the shadows.[61]

Perhaps we too hoped, or feared, that centuries would blur at nightfall, as in John Meade Falkner's strange poem 'The Last Church', where the poet-antiquarian and his friend come to a lonely English church as the sunset fades, in which a funeral is taking place by the Latin rite and where time has no meaning any more: 'The present is as the past'.[62] The knotting together of darkening evenings and ancient things is again evoked by Falkner in his poem on the discovery of a Roman villa in the Cotswolds:

Dark weeds the autumn sunset wore,
Wild winds were in the wood; . . .

It seemed as though the Earth were sad,
That she must show again
Those ancient mysteries she had
Concealed from common men.[63]

In old, grainy photographs, or in earlier wood and steel engravings, autumn and winter England opened to our memory, or rather
to our chaotic nostalgias: remote landscapes of lonely rectories and
their ghosts, manors folded in their groves, seashores at low tide –
England's territories of evening and regret.[64]

Sean O'Brien, 30-odd years later, was to describe our aesthetic
better than we could ever possibly have described it ourselves:

Those who . . .
. . . gather in galleries, mourning themselves
In the work of Ravilious . . .[65]

Indeed the silvery light of Eric Ravilious's finely composed, bone-
dry watercolours from the 1930s was already one of our daylight
pleasures (his dry silver seemed almost numinous, as though the
light of the past had been different from our own, and one painter
at least had fixed the difference) and one of our number went on to
become an authority on this painter of everyday rural landscapes
with their rusting machinery, chalk hill figures, plain brick
streets.[66] Ravilious was to some degree the topographer of what
we desired to find, the shabby but authentic England lost just back
beyond our parents' time. Again our feelings are caught precisely,
as our afternoons are described, by Sean O'Brien's retrospective
prescience:

To summon a grey English beauty
From short afternoons, to be sure

> How to live and believe
> In the dark, near a railway.[67]

We ranged through the eastern counties of England and the eastern part of the Midlands. We seemed always to come upon the best things at nightfall, come upon them too late. Second-hand bookshops, topaz-coloured cellophane in their windows, just closing in small towns in Suffolk and Lincolnshire; cathedral evensong at Ely or Peterborough with the colour fading out of the windows during the psalms, as the daylight died behind them. These were, in retrospect, the twilight years of a post-war England – shabby, not yet rebuilt, not expensive, with paint peeling on windows not yet replaced – a region that can now be glimpsed only in those mist-dimmed photographs in out-of-print guidebooks.

Even within this group of travelling friends, I felt still a little foreign: while they were revisiting I was seeing everything for the first time. What they knew well was known to me only from books, and this new country was a continuous revelation. I saw places then in much the way described by Peter Levi in his memoir of his lonely, odd Oxford education, when he was already a Jesuit novice, part of it all and yet not part of it all:

> We trotted or ambled together across the countryside, and stood to gaze as the yellow or pink stains of winter sunset drained out of the sky. The falling sun flamed in a hundred reflections from the windows of lonely houses, or it gleamed in the dark pools under our feet . . . Downs took on a pale, ghostly colour that was hardly green; the sky was hardly blue.[68]

Levi's world was to a great extent the imaginative world of myself and my student friends, especially in winter: 'our life is early rain and the dusk rain . . .'.[69] He also describes his own apprehension of how certain lights and weathers lead the observer to identify misted, backwater England almost as an otherworldly place, a secondary world perceptible only in glimpses:

In civilised Byzantium . . . the most sophisticated historian knew of
Britain the fact that the souls of the dead when they left their bodies
sailed away in boats from Gaul into Britain. Into the west he must
have meant, into the sunset. Buzzing about the lanes on my motor-
cycle in that long green twilight which you get sometimes in a wet
summer, I could see what he meant.[70]

In such lights, in blue and green landscapes drained of their
nature by winter dusk, remote abandoned dwellings, shuttered
against the season, feel as if they are summoning shadow inhabitants
to people them. In those days, there were still empty and partly
ruinous houses far into the foggy fields, open to our rash exploration.
Almost everywhere still there was the post-war sense of places abandoned, remote even then in what seemed a deserted landscape, one
that now seems intensely crowded.

There were houses then as lonely and faded as the manor house
that is the setting of a quiet interlude in the quest-narrative of *The
Hundred and One Dalmatians*, a twilight place inhabited by a benign,
very aged squire with his kindly old spaniel. The place is worn but
good, the tangled garden and red-brick house are still beautiful after
four hundred years. When the dalmatians rest by the hall fire, the
dozing squire calmly takes them for the ghosts of the carriage dogs
of his youth, in a house and a place where the divisions of past and
present are dissolving: 'I dare say I'm only seeing you because I'm
pretty close to the edge now – and quite time, too.'[71]

A doubly haunted recollection, also set in quiet country, and
on the misty borderlines of past and present, is recorded by Sylvia
Townsend Warner – a childhood visit to a Regency doll's house, still
in the possession of the very old women for whom it had been made
when they were children. Doll's houses inevitably have the uneasy
half-light presence of all simulacra, all unchanging memorials of
past life, of the past in a life. The doll's house that she remembers is
rendered stranger, more haunting, by the name its owners had given
it: Moth Hall. Moths in time destroy the fabric of things, are insubstantial creatures, inhabiting only dim lights – all of these aspects

shade the doll's house and its custodians, rendering them the more apparitional. The recollection must date from the last years of the nineteenth century 'before the time of cars', and it is impressed on the child that the old ladies are very old indeed, so it is reasonable to assume that they are in their eighties and were born, just, in the lifetime of Jane Austen. The whole episode is shaped by twilight:

> It was autumn . . . and even before we arrived haze was gathering and the perspective of the lanes led to dusk. The Victoria turned in by a white gate and we drove under the shadow of conifers . . . Inside the house it seemed to be almost dark. I could scarcely see the old ladies, and the tea table with its white cloth . . . was like a pool in a wood reflecting the evening sky. After tea we went to look at the doll's house. In order that I should see it properly, one of the old ladies lit a small taper and held it inside the doll's house rooms. They looked very real thus waveringly illuminated and I seemed to be exploring a real house by candlelight. I suppose there were inhabitants but I cannot remember them. I can only remember the shadows following the taper from room to room. Then the door was closed and the doll's house left in darkness. And then I suppose we said goodbye and drove home again.[72]

The nature of the experience is one of having witnessed a haunting, or at least a suspension of time, to have passed through the autumn twilight to a place where a house of the era of Jane Austen has been shown by candlelight, and then to have returned to the present by the paths of sleep and darkness.

IN OUR OWN INVASIONS of the past, my friends and I explored in a spirit of quiet recklessness. Haunting and haunted-seeming places drew us most powerfully of all: overgrown landscape gardens drew us in ever deeper to search for ruined follies amidst rhododendrons spread and grown vast beyond control, or in impenetrable spinneys of tightly packed saplings and tree suckers, when the pleasure grounds that had once surrounded them were overgrown and deserted. Abandoned temples by ornamental lakes, which had gone to silt and rushes years ago. Fallen, delicate stucco on their dusty floors, the stumps of an artificial ruin in an overgrown coppice. These were the most prized trophies of our chases because they took us straight into the already retrospective visual world of interwar artists – the praeterite evocations of Rex Whistler, the antiquarian topographies of John Piper – and the aesthetics of place expressed in Piper and his circle's series of guidebooks to England and Wales, the *Shell Guides* – first published between the wars and revived from the 1950s – which were in those years fading towards the end of their time, still under his guidance. The post-war series was abandoned in the early 1980s, with many counties still undescribed.

These, as well as their rivals, the scrupulous and encyclopaedic *Buildings of England*, were witnesses to a post-war Britain not yet reconstructed, far less gentrified, a country of provinces linked by 'serviceable motoring roads' and railways, whose admirers would still use phrases such as 'pleasing decay' to express appreciation of worn-out, beautiful, well-used things. In the unvisited provincial places that we sought out, a great term of approval was 'unimproved' – perhaps all this was a conscious swimming against the tide of the modern world (against redevelopment, against the swirling colours of the newspaper supplements, an imaginative harking back to the revived half-modernist 'picturesque' of the world between the wars). In some degree ours were a sequence of afternoon and evening travels in search of a world itself far gone into its evening.

In retrospect, it is easy to simplify the object of our travels as the exploration of what was left of the pre-war world. Our pleasure in old-fashioned shops was paralleled by an old-fashioned innocence in our recreations – willingness to spend hours on end combing through any stock of second-hand books and prints. We also seem, in retrospect, to have been axiomatically inclined to attend any Anglican or Catholic religious services that we came across, so that many of our winter afternoons ended with Evensong or Benediction, and our evenings began with coming out of a lit church into the frosty dark.

It is one of the loveliest things in Europe, the patterned singing of the Anglican psalms as the light goes behind the great cathedral windows. Boys' voices in the empty stone forests, light draining away. (The stark contrast between this and Charpentier's *Leçons de ténèbres* in their cool, virtuosic, fabulous baroque, place them in different worlds of feeling altogether.) Ely, Lincoln, Peterborough and then out into the worn, frosty streets. A kind of solemnity and reflection on the past attended this scrupulous musicianship in near-empty churches. Retrospection, *smokefall*, a thing right in its place.

English sadness could be felt particularly in the less-used churches of the nineteenth-century Gothic Revival: crimson and golden stencilling on plaster half-gone with the damp. Pugin's great church at Cheadle in Staffordshire, for all that it is in fine condition and complete in every detail, has the intrinsic instability of his fierce attempt to remake a medieval England – his attempt to force a twilight to be a noontide. The very act of recovery has to acknowledge the violence of the break in the tradition, however much the result may have convinced one generation that it offered a perfect facsimile of a longed-for age of faith.

We ate winter picnics out on the windy levels, or in the scant shelter of bridges over fenland canals. We bought sandwiches in what were then uniformly shabby village pubs. The smell of beer and misty, Saturday-afternoon sunlight changing to grey and blue, while I played Schubert and ragtime and 'Tom Bowling' on out-of-tune pianos in empty public bars. And once a hunt, scarlet and hound music, desolate-echoing cries, passed, revenants, down what had a moment before been a deserted village street.

In that decade we began to form a transitional, crepuscular aesthetic of our own – backward-looking, apprehensive of the more brutal aspects of change and redevelopment. Always in search of the overlooked, the true, what Myfanwy Piper had called 'Deserted Places . . . beauty neglected by others'.[73] We were aware of inhabiting the twilight years of the Britain into which we had been born – almost harking back at times to what Rex Whistler – a talismanic figure for us, whose reputation is only beginning to be reassessed in the twenty-first century after decades of modernist obloquy – called the 'de la Mareish'. As Whistler's brother recalled it, even between the wars, the painter already felt that de la Mare's writings had defined an England of dusks and longings and apprehension:

> How often he would apply the epithet 'de la Mareish' to some scene in his mind or actually before us – an old house at twilight, withdrawn into the premature night of great elms; the last lamppost of a town shining down on a creepered wall; numberless moods and moments in which there might be an element of stillness that seemed to hover indecisively between the innocent and the uncanny.[74]

The dusk of evening in forgotten places is crucial to de la Mare – a writer whose emphasis on nightfall as a time of *visitation* often stops short of an explicit haunting. The poet Peter Scupham catches precisely this sense that time and place in de la Mare are often themselves almost the protagonists of his narratives:

> The daylight shutters down, the white moths climb,
> The house aches into whisper and desire . . .
> Mist curls where willows clarify, or dim.
> As murmurs thicken in the Servant's Hall,
> The callers gather; you are not at home.[75]

(The splendid ambiguity of Peter Scupham's last phrase, 'you are not at home', succeeds wholly in evoking de la Mare by his own means of suggestion, evasion and uncertainty.)

As late as the 1970s de la Mare seemed far more central to twentieth-century British poetry than he does now: established critics who had studied literature between the wars would sometimes esteem his 'Mad Prince's Song' (however mannered it may seem to us now) on the same level as the poems of Owen or Eliot as a response to the First World War and its aftermath. Eliot himself accorded de la Mare the rare honour of a 75th birthday tribute, which constitutes, so far as I know, Eliot's only published verse in

praise of a fellow poet. In it Eliot recapitulates both the themes and
the processes of de la Mare's work: hints, revenants and half-lights in
'the delicate, invisible web you wove':

> . . . ghosts return
> Gently at twilight, gently go at dawn,
> The sad intangible who grieve and yearn[76]

The identification of what is characteristic of de la Mare, and what was
especially valued by his contemporaries, is precise, but the intensity
of praise that Eliot bestows reads strangely today– so many of de la
Mare's poems now seem no more than adroit exercises in pastiche,
contrived echoes of the seventeenth-century lyric. But the slender
thread of real originality in his verse visits and revisits the same
territories as his understated, compelling ghost stories, circling endlessly the idea of a remote house at twilight and a child or children
in communication, sometimes in direct conversation, with revenants
who gather at dusk. De la Mare at his best distils his own kind of
shadowy uncertainty, as with his lyric about a family of children living
– the circumstances are wholly unexplained – in what seems an otherwise abandoned country house, set amidst snowy formal gardens:

> Above them silence lours,
> Still as an arctic sea;
> Light fails; night falls; the wintry moon
> Glitters . . .[77]

The strangest of his poems about children and deserted houses,
where the twilight is implied but never described explicitly, is a
snatch of dialogue – child and mother and phantom:

> 'Child it is such a narrow house,'
> The ghost cried; and the wind sighed.
> 'A narrow and a lonely house,'
> The withering grass replied.[78]

Here the house seems barely a house but more a mausoleum or grave. Even the familiar and kindly is estranged in these poems – the robin in his 'coat of blood' is no familiar companion of the winter garden, as in Peter Levi's little elegy,

> The air was dark and misty before five
> When the robin lay dead by the house door . . .
> My friend for whom the star of twilight burned.[79]

De la Mare's bird acts rather as a summoner, calling the humans out into the 'death-still wood' at the heart of winter:

> Ghost-grey the fall of night,
> Ice-bound the lane,
> Lone in the dying light
> Flits he again;
> Lurking where shadows steal . . .[80]

De la Mare's idiosyncratic art finds its most intense expression in the short story 'Crewe', a narrative that moves through layered veils of twilight. Indeed, different kinds of dusk constitute the moving force and motif of the whole story. It begins with a railway waiting room at the end of a winter afternoon, a place so transitional as to be almost menacingly inhuman, somewhere that is as near as possible to nowhere. The wrongness of the loquacious figure who haunts it is that he is driven (presumably by sheer terror of solitude, and of the unearthly company that solitude may invite) to make a home out of this doubly darkened place with its dying fire and unlit gas lamps.

The story begins with the evocation of grimly redoubled twilight in the fading winter afternoon, light further muted by the roof of the train shed and the steam of the trains: 'When murky winter dusk begins to settle over the railway station at Crewe its first-class waiting room grows steadily more stagnant . . . The long grimed windows do little more than sift the failing light that slopes in on them from the glass roof outside.'[81]

The dweller in this dim place is a loquacious manservant in the coat of his dead master. De la Mare is always chilling on the person (or place) who has slid down society, even a little – an old family coming to an end in a haunted wastrel or an angry spinster whose vehemence survives her death. This unease attending the narrator here – the ghost story proper is the story that he tells his about last employment and how it came to a dark end – reaches out and affects the bleak totality of the story.

It is the same social revulsion that is the crux of Henry James's *The Turn of the Screw*, revulsion at the servant usurping the place of his master, the servant in his master's clothes. For a society obsessed by the gradations of class, this trespass into the twilight areas between what are meant to be absolute social divisions is one of the most unsettling contemplations – in James's story this trespass is almost as bad as the crossing of the permeable frontiers that divide the worlds of the living and the dead. *The Turn of the Screw*, on examination, is not much preoccupied with twilights – its horror does not particularly inhabit the dark, although there are some night scenes – the real terror lies in the ease with which the revenants can come by day or night into the company of the living children who they have corrupted. Indeed, the only times when the children are safe are those moments that would constitute the crisis of a conventional ghost story, those moments when the ghosts become visible to the children's governess.[82]

In de la Mare's 'Crewe', it is only at the very end that we are assured that the narrator who haunts the waiting room is not himself a ghost, but in truth (if he is telling the truth) a traumatized and hunted ghost-seer. The crisis of his narration begins with his description of the remote rectory in which he has been butler, a crepuscular house that seems in itself both animate and malevolent:

Too dark, too vaulty, too shut in . . . and in winter freezing cold, laying low maybe. Trees in front, everlastings . . . and dim and dark, according to the weather . . . anyhow the Vicarage reeked of it. A low old house, with lots of little windows and far too many doors;

and, as I say, the trees too close up on one side, almost brushing the glass. No wonder they said it was what they call haunted. You could feel that with your eyes shut, and like breeds like.[83]

He hints that something had happened at least once in the past in the house, palpable enough to cause an ineffectual exorcism by the incumbent before last, but all the time the atmosphere that builds is one which implies that the house itself is willing the suicide and the haunting and the unexplained death that eventually stem from a quarrel between servants. At the emotional height of these recollections, tellingly, the manservant in his master's coat gives away his own origins with one misplaced 'h' in his pronunciation and his listener, who tells us the story in turn, is jolted enough to interrupt the reported narrative to remark on it.

Then the vicarage goes to silences and mutterings and heat hazes and scarecrows misplaced in fields already reaped and, all the while, its master lies mortally ill in the best bedroom. Then voices inside the locked house, outside the windows at night. Then crisis and death. The story hangs in the last dimming of twilight (in absolutely every sense) before the porter comes in to light the gas, unexplained, as the present state of its teller is unexplained save for hints and implications.

De la Mare's stories rarely explore the kinds of horrors that infest the fictions of M. R. James: the random assaults of malevolent demons, of the sentient and wicked dead. The territory of de la Mare's stories is continuous, rather, with those of his stranger, more successful verses: there exist very withdrawn, very haunted places that declare something of their nature to the attentive visitor, but the reader is rarely offered more than glimpses and implications of what can happen there. Only exceptionally in these stories does the ghost-seer die of the experience. Thus, in a fictional aesthetic so heavily dependent on suggestion, atmosphere becomes crucial and twilight and remote and empty places are the insubstantial substance of his art.

Once these stories had been absorbed, the landscape of the comparatively empty rural England of the 1970s seemed changed by our knowledge of them, and nightfall on the wet fields brought with it further imaginative possibilities, not all of which were entirely comforting.

A true story (or a story recollected as true 50 years later) in a similar key to de la Mare is told in Harold Owen's memoir of his own childhood and that of his brother Wilfred, *Journey from Obscurity* (1963).[84] It is a strange account of entering a series of natural and unnatural twilights, and the events are never explained, although the place visited, it emerges eventually, is believed locally to be haunted, or in some sense malign.

His relation begins with his recollection of an afternoon walk at the end of a modest family holiday in Ireland: a narrow lane leads to the 'broken-down entrance gates of a forbidding looking avenue', which leads through dense woodland. So a dim afternoon with rain coming on is dimmed further by the twilight under the trees of an abandoned demesne: 'Inside our avenue it suddenly became very dark, a bleak feeling seized hold of us all and we became very silent.'[85] Something 'large and animal-like' moves along a branch high up in one of the trees. The darkening rain intensifies and ceases:

> My mother was now quite desperate to get out of this dark wood and return to the friendly village, but my father would have none of it. The rain had now stopped and he was absolutely determined to find out what was at the end of the drive . . . we went deeper into the narrowness of the avenue.[86]

The drive darkens, takes two bends and then they come out into the open in a place that is like nothing natural at all:

> open bare-looking ground with what appeared to be a sheet of water. It was separated from us by about thirty yards of stony fore-shore. It did not somehow quite look like real water . . . a strange high wall of mist cut across the water in a perfectly straight line. In

this way every bit of background was obliterated and it seemed that behind this mist there was just nothing at all.[87]

By now they are all terrified but their father insists on walking on, even though they realize that

> The water and the wall of mist were receding from us at exactly the same pace that we ourselves were moving . . . it was darkening now and there was a chill in the air. My father advanced once more and the same thing happened – the water and the mist again went back, only this time the normal background of trees and sedgy grass seemed in a horrid way to be coming through as if they were real and solid and the water and the mist were nebulous. This was too much for my mother and, swinging round she turned to get away from it. It was as she turned that for the first and only time in my life I heard her give a stifled scream . . . standing ten yards away from us was the shadowy figure of a tall man. This figure seemed to radiate the same cold incandescent quality that even now was permeating the hallucinatory lake . . . the whole attitude of this illusionary being diffused a mute declaration of his intention to do harm to us.[88]

Owen's father tries to talk to this figure, which appears to be possessed by malign rage, but it retreats as he advances towards it, advances if he retreats. The apparition remains absolutely silent and Harold Owen cannot apparently recall any details of its appearance except that it was carrying a heavy stick. Finally his father has the courage to pursue it right to the edge of the dark wood and it vanishes. At this moment, fear leaves them all, although the darkness seems to be falling with unnatural swiftness, and the illusory water behind them vanishes. The family flees, forcing their way through all obstacles until they come to a road and make their way back to the village.

The narrative is not explained in any way. Although it became part of family folklore, and thus remained lively in Harold Owen's memory even until he wrote his memoir in the 1960s, he seems never to have tried to investigate the episode, or the place where it

occurred, in later life. Indeed, his memoir is evasive as to where in
Ireland the episode took place. The whole experience is bounded
by the twilight – unlike most stories of the supernatural, nightfall
comes as a relief and brings release from the malign lure into which
the family have stumbled, not a worsening of their circumstances.
The apparition vanishes rather than becoming more powerful as
the twilight ends. It is as though twilight has played the part here
that it plays in many traditional narratives: a way has been opened
into an otherworld – in this case only what seem the outer reaches of
an exceptionally unpleasant otherworld – and nightfall paradoxically
comes as a release. Day and night are clear, ambiguous twilight opens
the frontiers. All that seems certain is that the Owen family found
their way into what had been the demesne of an Ascendancy big
house without ever coming to the house itself, if it still existed, and
that their Irish hosts regarded the place with some of the fear and
revulsion that first-millennium Britons felt for deserted Roman sites.

SOME OF THE MOST remarkable things we found in the churches
that we visited on our winter journeys were monuments dating from
the first half of the seventeenth century. By this time, I was becoming
fascinated by inscribed words, beginning to realize that seventeenth-
century tombs often preserved in stone verse of high quality
unrecorded elsewhere. And, most importantly, this verse was
sometimes by women, otherwise unknown as poets, often by widows
lamenting their husbands. In a parish church in Bedfordshire,
St Denys at Colmworth, is the tomb of Sir William and Lady
Katherine Dyer, erected in 1641, long after his death in 1621 and
some time before hers in 1654. Husband and wife are shown as they
must have been in their youth, he in tournament armour, she in
elegant clothes of the time of James I. They lie on their sides, facing
out into the church. The long verse epitaph that she made for
her husband is painted on the tall black slabs behind them in the
dimness under the tomb's canopy, shadowed enough on a winter
afternoon that, to be sure of reading the verses accurately, it was

necessary to climb on a chair and lean into the tomb, very conscious of the nearness of the life-size marble figures.[89] The verse repays any effort made to decipher it: it is one of the most passionate poems of the earlier seventeenth century. Katherine Dyer imagines the tomb and the marriage bed as shadowing each other so closely that her years of widowhood are to her only the long twilight of a day when her husband has retired early:

> My dearest dust could not thy hasty day
> Afford thy drowzy patience leave to stay
> One hower longer . . .

But the twilight deepens, under the heavy dewfall of winter in a low-lying, watery county, and she prepares, in brave imagery that is all her own, to join him:

> Mine eyes wax heavy and the day growes old,
> The dew falls thick, my bloud growes cold;
> Draw, draw the closed curtaynes: and make roome:
> My deare, my dearest dust; I come, I come.[90]

Another monument of the same era remains powerfully in memory: the recumbent effigy of Lady Bruce on her table-tomb among other fine monuments in the parish church at Exton in Rutland. It is not memorable for its inscription but for the exceptional beauty and accomplishment of the sculpture itself. Dating from shortly after her death in 1627, the sculptor of the sophisticated recumbent effigy with its finely handled drapery is not documented. The face is as beautifully made as the rest: calm and withdrawn, but a likeness of an individual. The pillow on which the head rests is the single element that lifts the whole to a high degree of poetic invention: it is carved with two cherubs' heads and wings in shallow relief. It is immaterial whether these are meant to represent a decorated textile – the effect is of an audacious metaphor from Caroline poetry enacted in marble – the dead lady reposes sustained by the angels. The whole monument is achieved, confident baroque – southern fluency in northern Europe.[91] It is a fine expression of that brief Caroline flowering of free discourse with Europe in all the arts, of complex and refined cultural achievement in the Britain of the 1630s. It is a shadowy period, an exceptional decade for which the vexed descriptor 'English baroque' seems the only sensible or honest designation.

In retrospect, given the violent end of this brief cultural flowering during the interrupted reign of an unstable king, the works of this period are difficult to fit into the histories, so that this period of remarkable attainment is, strangely, often marginalized as a period of decadence – a mannered aberrant moment, a silver age, which had no positive influence or posterity. There is no room for the cultural champions of the 1630s, except an appropriated Inigo Jones, in the Whig Temple of the British Worthies. There is still considerable confusion attending the description of the cultural production of the late 1620s and the 1630s: despite much excellent writing about it, it remains somehow unaccepted and not fully assimilated.

This finds its reflection in cross-cutting, ambiguous metaphors of shadow and autumn used to describe the period. The Interregnum after the Wars of the Three Kingdoms, a decade of theocratic hostility to the arts, used sometimes to be described as 'the Cavalier winter', a metaphor influenced perhaps by Richard Lovelace's poised consolatory poem 'The Grasshopper', with its assertion that a seasoned mind and heart can weather out any adverse climate with friendship at the fireside.[92]

The catastrophe of Caroline England in confrontation and war, the court under siege at Oxford, is never described as an autumn – it was too sudden and violent in its onset. Yet clearly, among the besieged loyalists at the shadowy court in Oxford, twilight was current as a metaphor,[93] although seldom if ever used in writing – no Stuart loyalist acknowledged defeat or the possibility of defeat in words. However the sequence of portraits painted during the siege by William Dobson,[94] portraits which seldom disguise the fatigue and desperation of his sitters, almost all have landscape backgrounds and their skies are winter evening schematic skies, skies showing stormy red streaks in after-sunset clouds. Desperation is seen particularly in Dobson's remarkable portrait of James Compton, 3rd Earl of Northampton, thin and distracted, for all his black armour and the transient swagger of the martial bas-relief behind him, his defeat by Cromwell only months in the future.[95] The head and shoulders portrait of Dobson's friend and patron Charles Cottrell also contrasts gilded armour and crimson sash with a countenance of exhaustion and near-despair.[96]

In the most expressive of all these portraits, the dignified and sombre full-length of the slight, controlled figure of Sir William Compton, the whole composition has been overtaken by twilight and evening.[97] Although the sitter and parts of the bas-relief and columns behind him to his right are lit by a high, fictive light source, even the foreground tonality is comparatively dim, muting the brightness of buff coat and scarlet sash. The background to his left is entirely composed of a very dark evening landscape, with a boiling angry sky, a bleeding sunset still flashing up into gashes in the clouds. This dusk and turbulence dominate the whole atmosphere of the painting to the degree that it is difficult to read them as anything other than a metaphor for the broken hopes and desperate condition of the royalists.

The court composer William Lawes was killed in the same war: he died at the siege of Chester in September 1645. 'Will. Lawes was slain by such whose wills were laws', as the grim contemporary epigram expressed it.[98] His music is at the centre of the achievements of this exceptional epoch, both in its complex Elysian beauty and in elements whose unfamiliarity and strangeness clamours to be interpreted in retrospect as fears and anticipations of how this bright world will end.

Lawes's consort music for viols, sometimes with harp or organ, has a sophistication that seems almost precociously mature, given the rapid development of English music in the previous two decades. It is an expression of the true baroque, at once dishevelled and worldly, carnal and transcendent, expressing its complexities in its 'lascivious grace'.[99]

William Dobson, *Sir William Compton*, *c.* 1643, oil on canvas.

It can give a disconcerting impression of something at the end of its time, weary in all its virtuosity. Its decorum, its intricate protocols, can on occasion simply break down altogether. Sometimes the texture of the music strips itself to a bare bass, to the skeletal progressions of an implied bass, over which angular improvisatory lines move in patterns that are only comparable to the most sombre manoeuvres of jazz. Once the ear has attuned to the complexity of Lawes's musical language, it is inevitable that it receives contradictory messages of beauty and complexity and disconcerting simplicity and hard-won maturity. It is music that has found a language for disaster: in the fourth movement of the viol consort set a6 in F, 'Fantazy a6 No. 2', the strain of contending voices moves into unresolved discord and impending breakdown, until the sound simply stops (music taken beyond endurance), silence (the end of music) and then restarts in a barely imaginable atonal grinding (anti-music, the sound that comes after the end of music).[100]

This is intensely twilight music – in the sense of being the music of the end of a day – a distracted day, a day in which the arts have flowered in a forced maturity and collapse has followed. The elegiac beauty of the viol repertory is about the end of things, but Lawes, one of the most audacious artists of England in any era, can imagine a sound-world for the time after the collapse, after the end of the light. Sound that is, in a most profound and troubling sense, 'night-music'.

The literary scholar Harold Love has written most persuasively about the viol music of Lawes and his contemporary John Jenkins in the context of the musical lives of gentry families who withdrew into the country as disaster overwhelmed England, as metropolitan music was silenced.[101] John Jenkins passed the dark time of the interregnum in a peripatetic life, moving between the country houses of patrons, bringing with him music characterized by a 'well-organised sociability'.[102] Love contrasts this with the sheer strangeness of the music that Lawes had composed before his untimely death in early 1640:

[It takes] the listener to strange and rarefied domains of sensibility. This was not unusual in either the music or the poetry created for the artistically self-absorbed court of Charles I. Sometimes Lawes's music seems to ring with an anticipation of coming political disaster as in the repeated, cannon-like hammerblows in the bass parts of the second strain of the air of the G minor six-part suite; yet, at other times . . . it wants to retreat from political stress into a private world of introspection . . . at moments in Lawes's fantasias one can hear 'the bottom dropping out of the world'. Wonder and amazement are the proper response to music of this kind.[103]

The most complex response that this music has drawn from another artist is the book-length, oblique elegy by Geoffrey Hill, *Clavics*, first published in 2011, the fruit of a lifetime's meditation on loss and England and the arts and landscape of England. The evasive, patterned verses are at times equivalents for Lawes's music, not a transcription of it. Their rhythms relate to some of the experimental irregular verse-forms of the mid-seventeenth century but, more directly, they match the irregular, nervous phrasing of Lawes's own music, the half-rhymes his unstable, passing consonances:

> The day cuts a chill swath,
> Dark hunkers down.
> I think we are past Epiphany now.
> Earth billows on, its everlasting
> Shadow in tow
> And we with it, fake shadows onward casting.[104]

The 'fake shadows' have considerable resonance: implications of the unknowable nature of the future and also of the way in which Lawes's music seems often almost explicitly prophetic of disaster. His breakdowns and dissonances are mirrored with remarkable ingenuity in the verse which describes his own death, especially in the unseasonal, emphatic '*broke*':

> The strings are slack
> Will Lawes is *broke* at Chest-
> er; Lycidas lies in the sand;
> Both justified. England rides rich on loss.[105]

Hill has used the dusk of winter, the insistent mid-afternoon twilight, to evoke the Interregnum before, in the second sonnet of his meditation on English history, 'An Apology for the Revival of Christian Architecture in England', an extraordinary sequence about faith and loss of faith, destruction and revival, indirect expressions of passionate longing for a past that needs to be recovered in imagination to heal the England of the present.[106] Later in that sequence, in the eighth sonnet, 'Vocations', when his contemplations have reached the nineteenth century, evening England appears again. This time the sonnet is a consideration of one of the elderly clerics who has survived the religious conflicts of the 1840s, who 'stayed and was sure' as if a Tractarian who didn't defect to Rome, but is living in what sounds like dignified internal exile, his room 'lit with the flowers and moths from your own shire' and with watercolours of late-summer landscapes, 'silvery . . . with convolvulus'. Then the poem cuts away sadly to the gardens and shrubberies outside the windows in damp twilight, with the distant voices of children.

> The twittering pipistrelle, so strange and close,
>
> plucks its curt flight through the moist eventide;
> the children thread among old avenues
> of snowberries, clear-calling as they fade.[107]

There is a sense of loss created simply by the juxtaposition of inside and outside – by the faltering half-rhyme of 'tide' and 'fade' – and by the approaching darkness and silence. Once more this remarkable sequence of sonnets comes to rest on a moment of dusk and empty quiet, inhabited by what are at one point articulated as 'the phantoms of untold mistakes'. This is quietly echoed by the twilight room of mourning and loneliness in 'The Eve of St Mark', the second from last sonnet in the sequence:

> Stroke the small silk with your whispering hands,
>   godmother; nod and nod from the half-gloom;[108]

A woman alone with her testimonials and souvenirs, with photograph albums of the dead, fading images of missed chances and 'untold mistakes' in the likenesses of 'the lost, delicate suitors who could sing.'

In Hill's later sequence *The Orchards of Syon* there is another meditated glimpse of crepuscular England, the light shifting through a day of snow in Lancashire, coming at evening towards something near to revelation:

> Closer to nightfall the surface light is low-toned.
> This is England; ah, love, you must *see* that;
> her nature sensing its continuum
> with the Beatific Vision . . .[109]

And in his *Scenes from Comus*, again a meditation on Milton and on eschatology, there is a momentary sight of England at nightfall as a place of transformation:

> The sun is drawn away, darkness advances
> bleeding our scene, mysterious dry ice
> tinctured with earth-smoke, Orphic harbinger.[110]

The transformation is partly of the masque-stage, but potentially actual.

Hill is, in this aspect of his work, aligned with aspects of the long tradition in the English arts that finds a common theme of a past, still living under the texture of the present, lamented or desired, recalled or half-recalled at evening. At the beginning of the twentieth century, A. E. Housman made a reputation for the crepuscular melancholy of his verses. A major scholar and a very

accomplished minor poet, Housman displaced his irrecoverable
unrequited love for a fellow-undergraduate into an elaborated fantasy of a lost past – an imaginary boy from a Shropshire farm gone to
London and remembering fights and comradeship and fairs and
carefully undefined youthful freedoms – imaginary loss, imaginary
happiness in westerly countryside. The subtext of the poems is
infinitely darker: Housman's imaginary comrades go for soldiers,
end on the gallows. It is hardly original to observe that in his
strange imaginary shire death is a faithful substitute for mutual
love. The frequency of evening in his poems is remarkable – partly
because he sets them in the Shropshire countryside around the
hills of Bredon and Wenlock Edge, so that the poems are repeatedly
aware of the light retreating westwards across the broad plain
towards the Welsh hills:

> The vanquished eve, as night prevails,
> Bleeds upon the road to Wales[111]

or

> . . . I would climb the beacon
>   That looked to Wales away
>   And saw the last of day.

While the plain below darkens in the adroit image of floodwater,
'Night welled through lane and hollow'.[112] Longing is piled on
longing in the westward gaze, sometimes so intensely that
Housman warns his imagined, desired comrade of the power
of the western sky:

> The long cloud and the single pine
>   Sentinel the ending line,
>   And out beyond it, clear and wan,
>   Reach the gulfs of evening on.[113]

The territories of the west which

> . . . take your thoughts and sink them far,
> Leagues beyond the sunset bar[,]

sinking thought in fantasies of suicide in the western sea, thoughts of arrival at the westerly land of the dead. In the end Housman equates gazing on the twilight sky with gazing on anticipated death. Indeed, sometimes the whole of the remembered countryside, rising to the mind at twilight, is a territory given over to the dead:

> The farms of home lie lost in even . . .

> There if I go no girl will greet me,
>   No comrade hollo from the hill[114]

And in the most complete of his twilight fantasies, he imagines climbing the beacon with a group of his friends, all longing for an escape from their native shire – 'plains we longed to leave' – and its constraints. This ends in one of his saddest verses, one of his most intense statements of the felt, constrained compass of his poetry:

> I see the air benighted
>   And all the dusking dales,

> And lamps in England lighted,
>   And evening wrecked on Wales;

> The starry darkness paces
>   The road from sea to sea,

> And blots the foolish faces
>   Of my poor friends and me.[115]

It is finely observed; in every sense the phrasing and cadence are classic, but it is the sense of a reservoir of feeling pressing behind the relatively conventional surface of the verse that has perhaps kept these restricted poems of evening and loss in circulation. What is most surprising about Housman and his work is simply how very popular it was. His verses were often set to music and in the first half of the twentieth century his reputation was secure, even in those progressive circles that were building links between Britain and Continental modernism.[116] Leaving aside the whole question of Housman's sexuality, the neatly articulated longing and despair in the poems makes them unlikely candidates before the First World War for such wide popularity. And yet they seemed to speak to the very generation in the 1890s that saw Britain at its unthreatened, shadowless meridian. Housman, even in a confessed act of impersonation, speaks as messenger, outsider, writing only of evening and loss and impossible love – casting cries of sexual and personal despair into conventionally elegant lyrics.

Even in the confident 1870s there are moments of exceptional melancholy at evening: in Charles Dickens's last, unfinished novel, *The Mystery of Edwin Drood*, part of their purpose is to cast a shadow around the sinister Cathedral Choirmaster, opium addict and potential murderer John Jasper, whose rooms above the gatehouse to the Close are described as a region of shadows, and rooms in Dickens seldom lie about their inhabitants: 'Mr Jasper['s] voice is deep and good, his face and figure are good, his manner is a little sombre. His room is a little sombre, and may have had its influence in forming his manner. It is mostly in shadow.'[117] But what is stranger is the sadness that attends the first description of the cathedral itself. It is an intense, late manifestation of Dickens's recurring trope that the past and its institutions can weigh all too heavily on the slender shoulders of the living – as perverse testaments and coercive legal trusts can try to force the living to act in accordance with the whims of the dead. Here there is no consolation nor serenity to be found in quietness nor antiquity, everything is as grim as Isherwood's apprehension of the stony courts of Cambridge:

Not only is the day waning, but the year. The low sun is fiery and yet cold behind the monastery ruin, and the Virginia creeper on the Cathedral wall has showered half its deep-red leaves down on the pavement. There has been rain this afternoon, and a wintry shudder goes among the little pools on the cracked, uneven flag-stones, and through the giant elm-trees as they shed a gust of tears . . .[118]

One of the most sombre evocations of English winter dusk, Thomas Hardy's 'The Darkling Thrush', is apparently unconsoled and unconsolable:

> I leant upon a coppice gate
>   When Frost was spectre-grey,
> And Winter's dregs made desolate
>   The weakening eye of day.
> The tangled bine-stems scored the sky
>   Like strings of broken lyres,
> And all mankind that haunted nigh
>   Had sought their household fires.[119]

For all that, the poem finds an uncertain balance in its close between the beauty of the thrush's song as the light fades and Hardy's own intrinsic conviction that neither the winter evening nor the future offer real causes for rejoicing:

> Some blessed Hope, whereof he knew
>   And I was unaware.[120]

But the poem finds its meaning in its timing: the winter twilight is that of the last day of the nineteenth century, the Hope, however conditional, in the thrush's song is a tentative hope for the future.

The nineteenth century in Britain returns unceasingly in painting, as in literature, to the close of the day, the last of the light. This awareness of evening is inevitably a characteristic of those northern territories whose geographical position gives them protracted spring and autumn twilights, white nights in summer, midwinter dark. The mid-Victorian Scottish painter William Dyce transformed the planted woodlands of a Scottish castle in the afterlight of an early summer

William Dyce, *Pegwell Bay, Kent – a Recollection of October 5th 1858*, c. 1858–60, oil on canvas.

evening into the Garden of Gethsemane by the addition of one
bowed figure. Dyce's painting *Pegwell Bay* in Tate Britain is a wholly
familiar image of the end of a holiday day, donkeys being led away,
the figures rather detached from each other, the light beginning to
go, happiness suddenly seen as fugitive and circumscribed with the
chill falling on the seashore. The focus of the picture is on the foreground child, looking out of the picture away from the gentlewomen
gathering shells, whose stance is balanced by the somehow enigmatic
figure in white, possibly another child, wading a little way into the
water in the middle distance. The spade hangs loosely in the hand of
the child in the foreground and the emotional focus of the picture
seems to be on her and how she feels about that moment: while all
the other figures are in some way occupied as evening falls, she alone
is responding fully to the feeling of loss, not only of the end of a
day by the sea, but the ends of all holidays, all summers. In fact
the picture is dated precisely by its full title, *Pegwell Bay, Kent – a
Recollection of October 5th 1858*, so it places itself at the very end

of the warm days of the year even in a sheltered southern place: the shawls and hats of the foreground women will be needed on the walk home. As with so many English evening pictures and poems dealing with evening, the feeling of belatedness, of time running out, is very strong in this picture.[121]

Seashores are often sad places in the Victorian arts: reflections in wet sands, ebbing tides, the irrecoverable lapse of time. The seaside episodes in Lewis Carroll's *Alice* books – 'The Walrus and the Carpenter' and the Gryphon and the Mock Turtle – both have rather melancholy undercurrents, far beyond the demise of the innocent oysters who get eaten. Of course these episodes are set at the seaside only in second-hand narrative or by implication – it is actually Tenniel's illustrations that place the Gryphon and Mock Turtle on a rock by the shore. The atmosphere of these episodes is certainly oddly unsettled: the sun shining in the night, the very sight of the expanse of sands being the occasion for uncontrollable tears. Memory of evenings on the coast of northern England haunt Tennyson's poems of departure and farewell, and the proximity of the sea plays a considerable part in conjuring the menaced stillness of the opening chapter of Wilkie Collins's *The Moonstone*.

The other locus of the sadness of cold England, strong in memory, is the landlocked melancholy of the northern cities. Autumn, raw stillness at twilight: 'memory and regret and unalterable past mistakes'.[122] Winter skies of ivory and umber, streetlamps and bare trees, city sunsets of smoke in stained, freezing air. Football, floodlights, the movements of thinning crowds through brick or gritstone streets. Response to these images is a kind of recognition, even resignation, even today, as has already been suggested of reactions to the paintings of Grimshaw (the same would be true of the Manchester artist Adolphe Valette).

But some writers have responded with something more like detached aesthetic appreciation to these industrial twilights. In the mid-twentieth century Louis MacNeice observed precisely the polluted elegance of the evening sky over Birmingham:

On shining lines, the trams like vast sarcophagi move
Into the sky, plum after sunset, merging to duck's egg, barred with
mauve Zeppelin clouds, and Pentecost-like the car's headlights
bud . . .[123]

MacNeice's friend Auden produced one of the most memorable and
haunting expressions of the fall of an autumn evening on an industrial
landscape:

Watching through windows the wastes of evening,
The flare of foundries at fall of the year.[124]

And Sean O'Brien, our contemporary, sketches a whole lost industrial
north in one couplet:

A sketch of smoke and ash at dusk,
An England hoisted to the light again[125]

seeing in quotidian places a region of potential where, at twilight,
the supernatural (or genius of this particular place) might be
summoned:

How to appease or even wake the deity
From brick and iron and this evening-afternoon?[126]

There is a whole sequence of night walks in his poetry in the twilights
between the streetlamps on foggy evenings and nights – those who
would want to walk in such places at such times he calls 'Novembrists',
as if adherents of an esoteric artistic or political movement, those
who have:

futile knowledge of the spirit's appetite
For somewhere in between this world
And its discarded shadows . . .[127]

Simon Armitage also walks through the regions of evening above northern industrial towns, but his vision is that of a realist pastoral, like the painter John Sell Cotman's, and he loves what does not change in place. Field boundaries, field names on the edge of a Pennine mill village. His poem 'Evening' is an elegant consideration of the phenomenon of belatedness in a day and a life: the evening walk, the habits of days and years in one particular place:

> You're twelve, thirteen at most
> You're leaving the house by the back door . . .

But however slowly we walk, all of us are rushing through our lives, falling through time, and nightfall always comes sooner than we expect:

>   . . . But
> evening. Evening overtakes you up the slope.
> Dusk walks its fingers up the knuckles of your spine.[128]

And he returns to the house that he has left as a child, a grown man, a father of a family, astonished at the way in which belatedness can overwhelm an evening walk, can overtake a life – 'How did it get so late?'

The idea of a room painted so that it would appear to be surrounded by a landscape of perpetual twilight might only occur in a life suspended, temporarily brought to a standstill by exceptional circumstances. One such room survives, coarsely executed, but haunting in idea and intensity, a work with the power of outsider art, made in the early nineteenth century. It is an upstairs room in an eighteenth-century building called the Council House, on the main street of Llanfyllin in Powys, where Lieutenant Jacques-Pierre Augeraud, a French officer in the armies of Napoleon, was held as a prisoner of war on parole around the year 1812.

This handsome small town, sheltered in a deep valley under steep slopes, was perhaps chosen to receive officer prisoners, allowed one servant each, and some freedom of movement within a restricted compass, because it is deep in the country, removed from main coach roads, and so far from the sea. Perhaps the painted room was begun for diversion in his enforced rustication, but as completed it inevitably becomes a reflection on place, on enforced idleness while years are passing, indeed on belatedness. The whole room has been made into a twilight world of rocky outcrops, waterfalls and mountains and ruins and lakes and inlets of the unreachable sea.

The most immediate impression that Lieutenant Augeraud's painted room makes on the visitor is the impact of the restricted tonality of its painted walls, presumably dictated by the small number of available pigments. The simply painted feigned arcading is black with stylized sprigs of yellow flowers. The landscapes placed within these arcades, making an implied continuous landscape on all four walls, are confined to two tones of blue, greys, black and white and a pinkish-brown, with some small touches of red on the minute foreground figures. This restriction in itself produces the most extraordinary effect of the room, that of an imagined world at dusk: shadowy arcades with a watery, mountainous, very blue landscape beyond.

It could be conjectured that it would make its best effect by candlelight and (in so far as, in their naivety, they work at all) the recession of the perspectives would read best from a seated position by the fire, from which the dado or balustrade would appear at about eye level. Probably this in itself tells us a little about how the artist (who was also its inhabitant) intended to use his painted room as a place of retreat and candlelit escape in the evenings.

The dreamlike quality of the naive landscapes is partly conveyed by the mistiness that its tonality implies. Coincidence of available pigment produces a generalized impression of diffused and rain-shadowed light clearing towards evening (whether this is intended or not, the effect is still powerful). What is bizarre and engaging, and the single factor that gives the room its undeniable strangeness and power, is that no attempt is made to follow the fall of the real light from the window overlooking the street, so that every wall is equally painted with the representation of a prospect looking westwards at evening.

Interior view of the Council House in Llanfyllin, Powys, Wales, showing a wall painting of *c.* 1812–13 by a French POW, Lieut. Jacques-Pierre Augeraud, taken prisoner during the Peninsular War.

There are mountains and sea, but it is all a view out to evening waters, to a hidden place round the corner of the mountain lake or the inlet.

The landscape is schematically represented: mountainous and almost treeless. Foreground staffage (cottage, ruin, temple, bridge, a few very small figures that exaggerate the implied towering height of the mountains) is minimal. The starkness of the landscape is notable, as is the steepness of the slopes, and the omnipresence of water. (A distant visual analogy would be with the imaginary, highly stylized Scandinavian mountain landscapes of the twentieth-century Finnish writer and illustrator Tove Jansson.)

The painter would appear to be a man of his time – but without any of the formal training in drawing that a contemporary British military officer might have received – naive as a painter but personally highly sensitive to place. The landscapes in the room are to some

degree a transformed version of the landscape of Wales itself in
steep slopes and waterfalls, partly a reflection of the experience of
confinement to one deep, well-watered valley, but partly too an
imagined region of escape – the generalized, otherworldly, blue
landscape of the pan-European Romantic imagination. None of the
waterways or roads appear to lead anywhere, neither to mountain
pass nor open sea, although they continually hint that escape and
open water might lie just out of sight. Significantly, in an era when
the horizon line is essential to the composition and expressiveness
of landscape painting, it is hardly visible here at all. Part of the
strangeness of the imagined world derives from this fact, the other
part from the curious way in which it is evening and the west all
around the room – an effect derived from the restricted palette but
also the most powerful element contributing to the dislocated, twilight atmosphere of these unskilled but haunting paintings.

Another amateur artist of the turn of the nineteenth century,
but one who achieved a standard of draughtsmanship bordering on
the professional, showed an exceptional awareness of light as it is
affected by season and time of day. Thomas Kerrich (1748–1828)
was a clergyman and University Librarian at Cambridge whose
life was shaped by the acute visual sensitivity that he developed on
an extended Grand Tour in the 1770s.[129] He was a precociously
scholarly medievalist, art historian and collector. But he was also
a connoisseur of night and evening skies, a member of that generation who saw the light and landscape of northern Europe with
a fresh intensity, new accuracy and depth of feeling. He made a
spectacular *Moon Sketchbook* late in his career, from 1811 to 1818,
with scientific, memorable, poetic sketches of the moon in different
conditions of weather and cloud, riding in the vast skies of East
Anglia. These sketches have been compared, in the depths of feeling
that they convey, to the work of Dahl and even Friedrich.[130]

During the 1790s he made a set of slight but impressive sketches
in chalk on coloured paper showing coastlines and skies in Norfolk.
The point of these is their immediacy, the rapidity of their execution,
their attempt to fix a passing moment in the fleeting and changing

light and weather of northern Europe. A pair of evening seascapes was made at Burnham in Norfolk in 1794, an attempt to record the minute shifts of light in the evening sky as the sun sets.

With such sketches, the depiction of northern European landscape has moved away decisively from the imitation of Mediterranean painting. The imitation of the long-admired Claudian afternoon light, or of the curt, purple twilights of the south have ended, to be replaced by a depiction of northern landscape based on observation rather than idealization. The wars of the late eighteenth century have ended the era when Rome was the art academy and art market of Europe; it has become very much more difficult for northern painters to travel to the south. For British painters it became intensely problematic, indeed, to travel on the Continent at all, which forced a generation of artists in upon themselves and upon their northern native places.

This coincides with a revolution in domestic lighting, which made it possible for the first time to appreciate painted depictions of the subtle, cold, watery skies of the north by artificial light. Indeed the extraordinary degree of change in domestic lighting towards the end of the eighteenth century demands investigation for the profound alteration that it must have worked to all ideas of place, season and home: 'The first revolutionary developments in lamp design since prehistoric times may be claimed, if lighting power is to be the criterion, by Ami Argand of Geneva . . . suddenly in 1782–4, there came a tenfold increase in the light available from a single wick.'[131]

With this on the one hand, and with the closing of southern Europe to northern artists, came the cultural development of the picturesque tour of the Lakes or of Wales, and of the solitary walk to observe season, time and nature. It was the era of the Claude Glass, shading and composing the reflected view, and the era of guidebooks that systematized the viewing of landscapes under carefully considered conditions as though they were works of art.[132] As soon as the landscape of northern Europe is viewed as itself, without the coloured filter of the landscape conventions of Claude and Poussin, long twilights and refractions in frost and mist become a defining characteristic of the visual experience of northern nature, and thus of northern art, which becomes increasingly focused on depicting the fugitive effects of changing light and season.

It might be observed in passing that, where western Europe only developed a rounded aesthetic of twilight, obscurity and longing in the early nineteenth century, the fullest aesthetic potential of this complex of experience and feeling had long formed part of the aesthetic awareness of Japan, another telling instance of the Japanese ability to articulate fully the aesthetics unique to a northerly light and climate:

> *Yūgen* as a concept refers to 'mystery and depth'. *Yū* means 'dimness, shadow filled', and *gen* means 'darkness'. It comes from a Chinese term, *you xuan*, which means something too deep either to comprehend or even to see. In Japan the concept became (in Brower's words) 'the ideal of an artistic effect both mysterious and ineffable, of a subtle, complex tone achieved by emphasising the unspoken connotations of words and the implications of a poetic situation.' . . . It is also the term for a style of poetry . . . it was also early linked with *sabi* by Fujiwara no Shunzei to describe beauty accompanied by sadness. The interpretation was approved by Kamo-no-Chōmei (1155–1216) who wrote . . . that for him *yūgen* was to be found 'on an autumn evening when there is no color in the sky nor any sound, yet although we cannot give any definite reason for it, we are somehow moved to tears.'[133]

In Europe, evening had been coming into focus slowly through the length of the eighteenth century. 'Ode to Evening' by William Collins (1721–1759), written as early as 1747, is very much a transitional poem devoted mostly to a classicizing allegorical personification of Evening, but giving way occasionally to real memory and observation, as with 'Hamlets brown and dim-discovered spires' vanishing into 'the gradual dusky veil'.[134] The twilight landscape moves apprehensively into cultural focus in this poem. Gray's 'Elegy' is really a poem of night, although it begins with the very end of the day's toil, and the rapid onset of the dark – twilight is only present for a moment in this reflection on mortality and long perspectives of time, in the finely accurate lines,

> Now fades the glimm'ring landscape on the sight,
> And all the air a solemn stillness holds.[135]

One poem of Coleridge's, 'Dejection, an ode', subtly explores the association of the twilight of evening with melancholy, anticipating that whole nineteenth-century nexus of feeling that became wholly characteristic of the arts of England:

> All this long eve, so balmy and serene,
> Have I been gazing on the western sky,
> And its peculiar tint of yellow green:
> And still I gaze – and with how blank an eye . . .
> I see, not feel, how beautiful they are![136]

and bringing forward what will become the familiar trope of belatedness, of an emotion that cannot be realized as evening overtakes the poet:

> It were a vain endeavour,
> Though I should gaze for ever
> On that green light that lingers in the west.[137]

The observation of the northern landscape and season is nowhere more acute than in the journals of Dorothy Wordsworth: there is a real sense of seeing things unfiltered, times and circumstances having thrown the observing eye and feeling mind back on that which lies immediately about them. This is exemplified in this entry in her Alfoxden journal for 23 January 1798, in her beautiful, scrupulous observation of distinctness fading from the landscape:

> 23rd. Bright sunshine, went out at 3 o'clock. The sea perfectly calm blue, streaked with deeper colour by the clouds, and tongues or points of sand;

on our return of a gloomy red. The sun gone down. The crescent moon, Jupiter, and Venus. The sound of the sea distinctly heard on the tops of the hills, which we could never hear in summer. We attribute this partly to the bareness of the trees, but chiefly to the absence of the singing of birds, the hum of insects, that noiseless noise which lives in the summer air. The villages marked out by beautiful beds of smoke. The turf fading into the mountain road. The scarlet flowers of the moss.[138]

Or, later in her life, a January day in the Lake District, a walk to Ambleside at nightfall, and the precise observation of the colours and feelings of evening as counterpoint to their sadness at receiving 'a heart-rending letter from Coleridge':

There was an unusual softness in the prospects as we went, a rich yellow upon the fields, and a soft grave purple on the waters. When we returned many stars were out, the clouds were moveless, in the sky soft purple, the lake of Rydale calm, Jupiter behind.[139]

This sense of the importance and aesthetic claims of the landscape at hand is fully achieved in these writings, a reminder that a quiet life in Cumberland was both a retreat to a remote province and a life in a region whose natural beauty had made it but recently the focus of aesthetically motivated travellers.

This reopening of vision and sensibility at the turn of the nineteenth century is everywhere present in the works of John Sell Cotman, whose attention to the world around him is exceptional, as is his originality in making scrupulous records of overlooked, ragged places: tree-brash washed against the bank of a river, brambles under deep tree cover long after the footpath has faded into wilderness.[140] The weight of emotion, the sheer gravity of Cotman's monochrome *Horses Drinking* is at once apprehensible, but it is inexplicable in its profundity and affect. It is one of the great images of daytime twilight, of the places in the shadows. The emotional impact of the darkness under the boughs is immediate, a real and flawlessly represented twilight under overshadowing trees, as is that of the depth of recession to the distant landscape and the mysterious rhythm set up between the dark horse and the light horse in the foreground. It is the perfect example of Cotman's capacity to invest the quotidian with weight and emotion, to instil feeling through his skill, apparently out of all proportion to a subject no more romantic in 1806 than the fuelling of a car today.

Cotman lived until 1842, living just into the era of the beginnings of photography, as if the will and desire to capture the passing moment, the fall of light, the shift of the tide, had been willing photography into being through the first half of the nineteenth century.[141]

As time passes, my student years in the 1970s begin to look like the last, fading decade of a sensibility of twilight that had persisted in one form or another since the 1790s, a sensibility very much formed by a whole sequence of perceived losses and falls and endings,

John Sell Cotman, *Horses Drinking*, 1806, wash drawing.

by awareness of passing time and the attrition of time, of the slow nuances of the misted winter afternoons passing into evening in remote and unregarded places. A movement that appreciated loss and cold afternoons, and the measured sadness of English music. This aesthetic was prophetically defined by Ruskin in his contemplation of Venice, his meditation on 'the city and the shadow': 'Perfection of beauty is still left for our beholding, a ghost upon the sands of the sea, so weak – so quiet – so bereft of all but her loveliness.'[142]

These feelings for belatedness and the past, which are visible in Britain in the Kerrich circle in East Anglia in the later eighteenth century and find their first great exponent in John Sell Cotman, continue through the nineteenth century and have a memorable last manifestation in the conscious 'picturesque revival' of Regency sensibility in the mid-twentieth-century *Shell Guides*, with their monochrome plates of misted towpaths and coverts.

Gone and lost those cold twilights, lost as the England through which we moved, lost as the selves who travelled there. The decade of our explorations was itself a dusk, the last glimmering of a way of seeing – the darkening afternoon of post-war, provincial England before the wholesale demolitions and reconstructions of the 1980s. It is lost and built over and gone now: and the only way to go back there is to stare into the black and white photographs in the out-of-print guidebooks – gazing alone by the light of the reading lamp, as if longing to be absorbed into their substance – to inhabit once more their fogged streets and ploughlands, their soot-skied provinces. Always to be damp-haired, never to be in a hurry. Always to have a cold coming on, the chill striking in from the wet tweed of your jacket. To see your breath in the air of winter rooms, half-thawed by gas or anthracite fires, and there to be 'unhappy and at home'.

3

CITIES OF EVENING

On my last few visits to my tutor, before I left university, I would lose myself in the umbered, haunted little painting by James Pryde that hung on the panelling of his outer room. Shadow and disquiet reached out from the canvas to overwhelm the light striking up from the sunlit courtyard below. A formal garden, gone to irrecoverable ruin, seen from a high viewpoint under gathering clouds, with tattered hangings to either side, the foreground a placeless region of twilight. Possessed by devouring shadow and disquiet – a painting by Pryde is seen as an apparition is seen. If Caspar David Friedrich positions the viewer of his pictures as the belated, melancholy traveller pausing on the Dresden Heath as the winter day goes over into evening (see below), then James Pryde (1866–1941) positions the viewer of his few, intensely individual pictures as a reluctant witness to a crime at nightfall, a witness lost past hope in a maze of derelict slums that had once been palaces, a witness who could become by force an accomplice. Or they find themselves under a great, tattered arch; in the shadows at the edge of a desolate formal garden; at the foot of a broken shrine in a dark street. Pryde's viewer becomes the haunted observer, the reluctant ghost-seer, in a world populated by phantoms.

All Pryde's canvases show what happens after the worst has happened: the mob after a revolution prepare 'a masque or a lynching' on a scaffold amidst the wreckage; soaring baroque rooms in the last stages of abandonment and decay are populated by revenants who repeat past acts of violence with every nightfall. Twilight is of the essence of these pictures: the dim light filtering from above into the alleyways between tattered palaces, shuttered rooms amidst the ruins. Pryde, to borrow a term from sixteenth-century Italian art, is a master in 'the dark manner'. The brief description that attaches to him most frequently is 'the Edgar Allan Poe of Painting',[1] but the extraordinary feeling of hinted disquiet that attends his work goes beyond Poe's melodramatic inventions. Pryde was a lover of the most extravagant manifestations of the late Victorian popular theatre, but his paintings transmute their violence into a disturbing reality. His presentation of himself, in the latter part of the life of what might be called an 'extreme bohemian', was of a grand, sinister old actor, beautifully dressed in worn good clothes, dusted with a touch of make-up. Or as a failed prizefighter, a ruffian living in London apartments furnished with grand plunder, baroque detritus:

> The room had that indefinable air of eighteenth-century mystery which Pryde imparted to many of his canvases. A fine Jacobean sideboard was flanked by two wooden pillars – Pryde declared that they were made for Sir James Thornhill – and between them hung a large Dutch picture of some military scene, in a black and gold frame. On the sideboard were pistols and two curious old Italian carved wooden figures . . . he placed a dog grate in the chimney recess, showing rough masonry or brickwork. He slept in a four poster bed in the studio gallery.[2]

His dreams grew ever more disturbing, more despairing, and his output slowed and dwindled to almost nothing as *Death of the Great Bed* remained unfinished on his easel.[3] It seems unremarkable that this vision of crepuscular grandeurs destroyed by vengeful revenants should remain unfinished: it is as if receiving and transcribing dispatches from the region of his imagination had become so painful, so destructive, that alcohol and procrastination were his only recourses to keep them at bay. The unfinishable pictures are at the centre of Augustus John's description of the environment in which Pryde spent the latter part of his life:

This studio had the lofty, dignified and slightly sinister distinction of
his own compositions. Upon the easel stood the carefully unfinished
and perennial masterpiece, displaying under an ominous green
sky the dilapidated architectural grandeur of a building, haunted
rather than tenanted by the unclassified tatterdemalions of
Jimmy's dreams.[4]

Pryde's output is an extraordinary one: after the posters and
portraits of his youth, he turned to the sombre bravado of his litho-
graphs of eighteenth-century criminals, made just after the turn of
the century.[5] The coarse, unapologetic swagger of the figure of John
Price, executioner, actor and murderer, is diametrically opposed
in feeling to the bright, roguish stylizations of Claud Lovat Fraser's
posthumously published *Pirates* (1922), or his genial sets and
costumes for *The Beggar's Opera* in 1920:[6] Pryde softens nothing,
indeed seems beguiled by real violence as he was beguiled by the
roughness of barnstorming penny theatres and boxing matches.
Thereafter he painted almost nothing except his haunted ruins:
wrecked, magnificent rooms; mysteries enacted in the palaces

James Pryde, *The Red Bed*,
c. 1916, oil on canvas.

of the slums. His rooms and places lie in darkness, lit only by a small spillage of illumination – thus the moment of depiction is always a twilight moment. It is as if he shows the instant when an observer casts a glance or a torch-beam into the habitual darkness of obscure places. His imagination inhabits rotten grandeurs and the dark, and something of the taint of slumming and seances hang around his work.

Throughout his series of pictures *The Human Comedy*, the baroque room with its towering bed is lit only by chance lights, from the opened door and shutter that half-illuminate the birth in *The Doctor*, to the brutal incursion of blank, white brightness into the posthumous scene of the dismantling of the bed in *Lumber*. In *Death of the Great Bed* the clustering phantoms and memories are lit by an impossibly high light from the left, as though the vast, dim room in which the grim comedy has been enacted lay, at this last crisis, in a deep vault, a Piranesian ruin or prison.

Piranesi's extraordinary capacity to haunt the shadows of the British imagination goes some way to explaining Pryde's imaginative world, as does a recollection of some of the stranger aspects of Venetian genre painting of the eighteenth century. Many of his effects are deliberately coarsened versions of baroque effects: his claim that the columns in his studio had been made for Sir James Thornhill is indicative of his debt to one of the few English grand manner painters, especially a debt to the technical mastery of Thornhill's oil sketches.[7] Although Pryde's fascination with *The Newgate Calendar*, with the worlds of prizefights and executions, has suggested comparisons with Hogarth, the influence would seem to be generic and confined to figure-pieces. In a technique making extensive use of highlight and shadow sketched in with glazes (as well as in fascination with lumber, ladders, scaffolding, stacked timber), Pryde owes a considerable debt to Velázquez's *View from the Villa Medici* (c. 1649–50, Museo del Prado, Madrid), of which he owned a reproduction. Velázquez's free, almost improvisatory, handling of the garden statues reappears in Pryde's *The Shrine* (c. 1915)[8] and the dislocated, weary and melancholy mood of

Velázquez's sketch, with its central *Rückenfigur*, haunts all of Pryde's garden paintings.

Affinities in Pryde's work haunted me after I had left university and embarked on migratory postdoctoral years, spent in London and Scotland. In essence, Pryde's visual imagination is grounded in Edinburgh and Venice with curiously little reference to the city in which he lived most of his adult life. He wrote of his memories of the verticality of the buildings in the Old Town of Edinburgh, which in his youth still contained extraordinarily fine eighteenth-century rooms in what had become tenements in multiple occupancy – gilded bolection mouldings, overdoor and overmantel paintings – castle rooms in decay. He wrote also of the numinous lumber at Holyrood, and the dim narrows of the wynds through which he passed on his way to school. He did not specifically mention the late Georgian Edinburgh in which his family lived, their house deep in the winter shadows at the bottom of the slope of the New Town. There, the extraordinary scale of the porch of St Stephen's Church, designed to be seen down a plunging street vista, would have overwhelmed him from close at hand as he turned the corner on his way to school, and the high stone avenues would have loomed over him as he toiled southwards up the hill. That monumental porch set the scale for the rooms, palaces and beds of his mature imagination, as did the great rough stone arch that carries Waterloo Place over Calton Road. The great volutes around the dome of S Maria della Salute in Venice would only have confirmed lessons of scale learned in childhood.

It is hard to identify the precise quality of the darkness in Pryde's work: for all that he painted murders, music halls and back streets, the works of Pryde's near-contemporary Walter Sickert are always tempered by some suggestion of regret or compunction. Or else Sickert finds a kind of weary elegance in cabarets and lodging houses, as in *O Nuit d'amour* (1922, Manchester Art Gallery), where the glimpse of a restaurant violinist playing the hackneyed Barcarolle from Offenbach's *Les Contes d'Hoffmann* is transfigured by the beautifully precise observation of the fall of the streetlight on the restaurant shutters and of the chandeliers' light within. Again the quality of

alienated darkness that attends Pryde is absent in the younger
painter of low-life to whom he might be compared, also a painter
much preoccupied with the baroque, Edward Burra (1905–1976).
Burra's dance halls and harbour bars have a sympathetic quality of
vernacular energy. Burra's fascination with the sinister, the soldiers
in carnival masks, the darkly peopled landscapes, is tempered with
humanity, with an element of humane lamentation for the wars
of the mid-century. Burra's baroque affinities are with Hispanic or
Mexican art, and his own paintings of religious subjects are, in their
unfathomable degree, serious in the way that late baroque art is
serious. Perhaps the only point where the two painters overlap is in
intensity of allusion to the Iberian seventeenth century, as manifested
in Burra's Mexican church interiors, in the bleeding statue facing
down the iconoclasts in Pryde's *The Monument*.[9] In this, one of
the strangest of Pryde's imaginations, an iconoclast with a long pole
pauses at the foot of a partially destroyed baroque figure of Christ in
a once-magnificent aedicule. The buildings around are in absolute
ruin, most levelled to the ground with saplings rooted amongst their
stones. The wounded statue is bleeding from the heart, heart's blood
welling and running onto the broken draperies. There are some
ambiguities of depiction, but tears appear to have dried on the
statue's cheeks.

It was difficult not to find memories and traces of Pryde in
those migatory years between London and the Lowlands of Scotland.
Blue-misted air, blue mist in a glass of gin; greyed evening skies of
overlapping flat brushstrokes – winter air thickened with coal
smoke and cloud; high, wrecked Georgian rooms in Spitalfields or
Bloomsbury. Supper parties in houses whose walls and ceilings still
showed cracked plaster, scraped panelling, lit by firelight and candlelight before the electricity was reconnected. Those half-repaired
dwellings – coal fires, shutters, frozen air in the stairwells – could
offer hints of Pryde's paintings, and his visual world was evoked
often in the course of long evening walks into what remained of
eighteenth-century London. The hunt for dim splendours hidden
behind decaying facades – gilded panelling, ceilings painted with

fictive architecture and Italian skies – gave an ostensible object to endless evening wanderings through the city. Summer evenings with the tattered theatre of a thundery sky at the end of a stock-brick street, Baudelaire's colours of evening, *hyacinth and gold;*[10] winter evenings with lights coming on in the long windows. Once, unforgettably, a lit window in Bloomsbury showed a ceiling painted with the apotheosis of Bacchus and Ariadne, at odds with the narrow street that had grown up since it was made.

The sense that twilight London might disclose any mystery or wonder was one shared by Pryde's contemporary G. K. Chesterton (1874–1936). Although they had interests in common, in popular art and narrative, street life and sport, Chesterton's view of the evening city is essentially optimistic: there is crime, there is much evil (especially in destructive thought and belief), but there is nothing that will not yield to the Thomist deductive logic, the benign clarity, of his detective. For all their apparent affinities, Pryde seems isolated from his contemporaries by his bleak perception of the city, by the authenticity of the darkness and menace, the despair and revenance, which are the freight of his paintings.

Chesterton saw the twilight metropolis as a site for adventure, a gaslit Forest of Logres, and thought of the detective story as the modern successor of the epic or the romance:

> The first essential value of the detective story lies in this, that it is the earliest and only form of popular literature in which is expressed some sense of the poetry of modern life . . . Of this realization of a great city itself as something wild and obvious the detective story is certainly the 'Iliad.' No one can have failed to notice that in these stories the hero or the investigator crosses London with something of the loneliness and liberty of a prince in a tale of elfland . . . The lights of the city begin to glow like innumerable goblin eyes, since they are the guardians of some secret, however crude, which the writer knows and the reader does not.[11]

The secretive potential of Chesterton's London becomes most palpable at nightfall, when the lamps are lit – more than once he uses the images of eyes shining in the dark but concealing the thoughts behind them:

> But since our great authors . . . decline to write of that thrilling mood and moment when the eyes of the great city, like the eyes of a cat, begin to flame in the dark, we must give fair credit to the popular literature which, amid a babble of pedantry and preciosity, declines to regard the present as prosaic or the common as commonplace.[12]

Early twentieth-century narratives of crime and detection, the works of Chesterton and Louis Feuillade (1873–1925),[13] drew heavily on the unknowability of the darkening metropolis, its qualities as a fluid place of adventure where double lives and private worlds alike could be hidden behind uniform facades and brick garden walls. In an era that often saw its cities as places of exile and alienation, as well as of hidden wonders, twilight acts as the moment that opens out the city's potential for splendour or crime:

> Let us go then, you and I,
> When the evening is spread out against the sky
> Like a patient etherised upon a table.[14]

And it is in that twilight landscape of fog, cheap restaurants and 'half-deserted streets' that Chesterton's philosophical but ultimately consolatory fictions of crime and disclosure unfold: again and again in his fictions, it is the fall of evening which discloses the marvellous or terrible secret hiding in the vastness of London. Nightfall opens the door to Chesterton's 'other town', whether it is in a suburban garden ('The winter evening was reddening towards evening, and already a ruby light was rolled over the bloomless beds, filling them, as it were, with the ghosts of dead roses') or in the city itself ('in the cool blue twilight of two steep streets in Camden Town, the shop at the corner, a confectioner's, glowed like the butt of a cigar'). Or a lonely winter nightfall which brings its own cold illumination:

> The pale green sky of twilight with one star like the star of Bethlehem, seemed by some strange contradiction to be a cavern of clarity . . . the priest hardly understood his own mood as he advanced deeper and deeper into the green gloaming, drinking deeper and deeper draughts of that virginal vivacity of the air.[15]

All of Chesterton's evening stories have an element of benign fairy tale and share that paradoxical function of the detective story, which is actually one of reassurance. They are, in the end, a series of instances of the dark illumined, danger contained, in a theatre of mysteries that is essentially optimistic.

Dickens's evening London can be ambivalent, a place of apprehension of the future and incursion from the destroying past, anticipating the loneliness and sadness of Eliot's city as evoked in the lines:

> The winter evening settles down
> With smell of steaks in passageways,
> Six o'clock.
> The burnt-out ends of smoky days.
> . . .
> And then the lighting of the lamps.[16]

Bleak House is perhaps his gravest novel of the Victorian twilight: from its fogbound opening, with the shops 'lighted two hours before their time',[17] its short days are shadowed by darkness and polluted air (as well as by the dead weights of lawsuits and buried lives). The country is as dimmed and shadowed as the town: the rain and floods in Lincolnshire under a lightless sky imprison Lady Dedlock:

> The view from My Lady Dedlock's own windows is alternately a lead-coloured view, and a view in Indian ink. The vases on the stone terrace in the foreground catch the rain all day; and the heavy drips

fall, drip, drip, drip upon the broad flagged pavement called, from the old time, the Ghost's Walk, all night ... My Lady Dedlock (who is childless), looking out in the early twilight at a keeper's lodge, and seeing the light of the fire on the latticed panes, and smoke rising from the chimney, and a child, chased by a woman, running out into the rain to meet the wrapped-up figure of a man coming through the gate, has been quite put out of temper.[18]

When, in the novel's crisis, she runs away from her husband's London house, away into the dark and cold on a journey of expiation of her own past mistakes that will end in her death, those who watch around the bedside of her ailing husband become devastatingly conscious of nightfall. It is one of Dickens's most beautiful extended parallels between characters, their ebbing fortunes, their dwellings, and the great, overshadowing, metaphoric things – the sluggish Thames in *Our Mutual Friend*, the walls and prisons in *Little Dorrit*, the bad law and smothered daylight here in *Bleak House*. Control has gone, the household is shattered, time and light have become the enemies of the stricken Sir Leicester, who begins to learn the limits of his own power as if for the first time. Every detail of the scene maintains the parallels, deepens the expression of the internal by external things:

> The day is now beginning to decline. The mist, and the sleet into which the snow has all resolved itself, are darker, and the blaze begins to tell more vividly upon the room walls and furniture. The gloom augments; the bright gas springs up in the streets; and the pertinacious oil lamps which yet hold their ground there, with their source of life half frozen and half thawed, twinkle gaspingly, like fiery fish out of water – as indeed they are ...
>
> Now does Sir Leicester become worse; restless, uneasy, and in great pain. Volumnia lighting a candle (with a predestined aptitude for doing something objectionable) is bidden to put it out again, for it is not yet dark enough. Yet it is very dark too; as dark as it will be all night. By and by she tries again. No! Put it out. It is not dark enough yet.

His old housekeeper is the first to understand that he is striving
to uphold the fiction with himself that it is not growing late.

'Dear Sir Leicester, my honoured master,' she softly whispers,
'I must, for your own good, and my duty, take the freedom of
begging and praying that you will not lie here in the lone darkness,
watching and waiting, and dragging through the time.
Let me draw the curtains and light the candles, and make things
more comfortable about you. The church clocks will strike the
hour just the same, Sir Leicester, and the night will pass away
just the same.'[19]

But Lady Dedlock has passed beyond recovery into the night and
the foggy streets, into territories where few women in nineteenth-
century fiction or life would have wished to go alone. It is clear,
even in Chesterton's benign fictions, that respectable women
who have a job are always depicted as 'hurrying' home from
their work after nightfall, as though the streets of the evening
city, through which the affluent pass in their carriages, are doubtful,
even compromising, territory.

In George Eliot's *Daniel Deronda* (1876) the woman abroad in the
darkening metropolis is in the last extremity of personal crisis, failed
and betrayed by her father, unable to find her mother in a city that is
much changed since her childhood. The scene of her attempted suicide
by drowning and her rescue by Daniel offers an extreme contrast of
how different urban twilight is for a woman and a man, even on a July
evening. For her, homeless and friendless, the approach of night is an
absolute that tips her over into despair. For him, the river upstream
of London is a place of private recreation away from the benign
grandeurs of his guardian's house: 'It was his chief holiday to row till
past sunset and come in with the stars.'[20] For Daniel, the evening river
at Richmond is simply a place of delight where he can row and sing
and think:

It was his habit to indulge himself in that solemn passivity which
easily comes with the lengthening shadows and the mellowing light,

when thinking and desiring melt together imperceptibly, and what in other hours may have seemed argument takes on the quality of passionate vision. By the time he had come back again with the tide past Richmond Bridge the sun was near setting; and the approach of his favourite hour – with its deepening stillness, and darkening masses of tree and building between the double glow of the sky and the river – disposed him to linger as if they had been an unfinished strain of music.[21]

Then he sees the woman on the riverbank, 'the small face with the strange dying sunlight upon it', and his infinitely gentle rescue of Mirah from attempted suicide leads him in the end to find himself, his history and his future.

By the end of the war of 1914–18 much had changed in the nature of the city and the self-perception of an intelligent woman at liberty in it. After she had left her mother's house, Sylvia Townsend Warner lived with pleasure and ingenuity in London:

> With £150 a year from the UK Trust and no acquaintances, I led an ideal life, with all of London to walk in . . . For some one with a fair amount of ingenuity and no ambition, it was a paradise. Oh, those long stuffy summer evenings, full of melancholy and the sound of washing-up in the basements of cheap hotels![22]

And by 1930 Virginia Woolf, in her celebrated essay 'Street Haunting', can survey the streets of twilight London as axiomatically a place of pleasure, a rich diversion for an educated woman walking alone:

> The evening hour, too, gives us the irresponsibility which darkness and lamplight bestow. We are no longer quite ourselves. As we step out of the house on a fine evening between four and six, we shed the self our friends know us by and become part of that vast republican army of anonymous trampers, whose society is so agreeable after the solitude of one's own room.[23]

Indeed, feeling so safe and anonymous in the crowd that she can play with ideas of the London square as wild and empty country, all the time enfolded in the safety of company and the beauty of the patterns of branches across the lighted windows:

> How beautiful a London street is then, with its islands of light, and
> its long groves of darkness, and on one side of it perhaps some tree-
> sprinkled, grass-grown space where night is folding herself to sleep
> naturally and, as one passes the iron railing, one hears those little
> cracklings and stirrings of leaf and twig which seem to suppose
> the silence of fields all round them, an owl hooting, and far away
> the rattle of a train in the valley.[24]

Certainly the American painter and aesthete James McNeill Whistler (1834–1903) anticipated this perception of the twilight beauty of the city, the benign tranformation of clear definition to suggestion, the dissolution of perspective to massing blocks of shadow, with the highlights of falling fireworks or streetlights over or across the water. His 'Ten o'Clock Lecture' seems to speak for a whole era in painting and writing, for a way of seeing and apprehending the city as the late nineteenth century turned to the twentieth:

> The desire to see, for the sake of seeing, is, with the mass, alone
> the one to be gratified – hence the delight in detail – and when
> the evening mist clothes the riverside with poetry, as with a veil –
> and the poor buildings lose themselves in the dim sky – and the
> tall chimneys become campanile – and the warehouses are palaces
> in the night – and the whole city hangs in the heavens, and fairey-
> land is before us – then the wayfarer hastens home – the working
> man and the cultured one – the wise man and the one of pleasure –
> cease to understand, as they have ceased to see – and Nature,
> who for once, has sung in tune, sings her exquisite song to the
> Artist alone, her son and her master – her son in that he loves
> her, her master in that he knows her – To him her secrets are
> unfolded – to him her lessons have become gradually clear.[25]

Whistler puts this perception into practice in his own riverside *Nocturnes*, bold studies of late summer twilight passing into night. His first paintings of water and darkness were made on his sudden journey to Chile in the 1860s – studies of boats at anchor, points of illumination from the shore reflected under a lucid sky still pale with reflected light. He continued to develop this idea on his return to London, the idea for the *Nocturnes* coming to focus during an August excursion by steamer in 1871, being stirred by an echo of the tonality that he had found in Valparaíso bay of 'the river in a glow of rare transparency an hour before sunset'.[26] The borrowing of the musical designation from John Field and Chopin, and Whistler's explanation of it, are well known: 'By using the word "nocturne" I wished to indicate an artistic interest alone, divesting the picture of any outside anecdotal interest which might have been otherwise attached to it. A nocturne is an arrangement of line, form and colour first.'[27]

Whistler painted his first London *Nocturne*, which echoes his night-piece of Valparaíso harbour in tone and colour, as one of two paintings completed in the course of the same night.[28] The *Nocturne* is bold, improvisatory, very free in technique, with layers of pigment applied over a grey ground, layers of pigment so thin that almost every brushstroke can be traced. The view is of Chelsea, from the Battersea bank of the river, flattened and schematized, but highly recognizable.

The allusion to the blocks of flat colour of the Japanese wood-block print is unequivocal and has often been observed: although Whistler's illusion holds, the means by which it is achieved are perilously visible on the surface: the barge painted with a serpentine flourish of thin paint and one dot of yellow, the mist dragged in one pale brushstroke across the dark buildings. The restricted tonality of the painting is wholly successful in conveying reflected light in river and sky, the reflections fixed in place by the small points of light from windows on the opposite bank and their trails of light in the water. The whole evanescent composition is held in balance by one small point of red – a fire on the distant foreshore and its watery reflection.

James McNeill Whistler, *Nocturne: Blue and Silver – Chelsea*, 1871, oil on wood.

These images are counterparts to the twilit poetry of T. S. Eliot, which itself shadows and counterpoints the urban poetry of Charles Baudelaire: the city defined by river mist and the 'violet hour' of evening, 'the smoke coming down above the housetops' over winter London, calls paid 'among the smoke and fog of a December after-noon'.[29] Almost all these lines have their doubles in Baudelaire: '*nous plongerons dans les froides ténèbres*' (we will sink into the frozen shadows), and the fall of evening that stalks into Paris as the animate fog in Eliot pads around the house, '*Voici le soir charmant, ami du criminel; / Il vient comme un complice, à pas de loup . . .*' (Observe the charming evening, the criminal's friend, who comes like an accomplice with a wolf's tread . . .), the end of autumn and winter haunted by the pale shadows as the air-frost comes down.[30] Some of Eliot's most celebrated lines evoke the cold evening, the sad flow of the crowds through the 'unreal city' (Baudelaire's 'swarming city full of dreams') from office to station, with a joyless allusion to Sappho's homeward star:

> . . . when the eyes and back
> Turn upward from the desk, when the human engine waits
> Like a taxi throbbing waiting,
>
> . . .
>
> At the violet hour, the evening hour that strives
> Homeward, and brings the sailor home from sea,
> The typist home at teatime . . .[31]

Leading in the end to a sorrowing vision of evening London as but one of a succession of brilliant capitals, all overtaken by darkness and time:

> What is the city over the mountains
> Cracks and reforms and bursts in the violet air
> Falling towers
> Jerusalem Athens Alexandria
> Vienna London
> Unreal[32]

The French pioneer of photography Camille Silvy (1834–1910) spent eight years of his short career in London, from 1859 to 1867, living and working in the house in Porchester Terrace that John Linnell (painter and father-in-law of Samuel Palmer) had built for himself. As well as immensely successful *carte de visite* portrait photographs, Silvy undertook an ambitious series of studies of light, which were published in the *London Photographic Review* in 1860, having been shown to the Royal Family in the closing months of the previous year.[33] The coal smoke and fog that lent atmosphere to his photographs in London, however, had affected his lungs and, exacerbated by service in the Franco-Prussian War, his physical and mental health broke down entirely for the rest of his life.[34]

Camille Silvy, *Studies on Light: Twilight*, 1859, composite photograph.

Of the studies dating from 1859 to 1860, it was the picture of *Twilight* that was particularly admired, by Queen Victoria among others. *Twilight* (or *The Evening Star*) shows a wide residential street on a dank winter evening – water in the gutter, damp pavements shining, the roadway muddy. The evening sky is still lit by low reflected light around the horizon, but a darkening cloud ceiling is dim enough to constrast distinctly with the streetlamp in the fore-ground, under which a man buys a paper from a newsboy. Other streetlamps shine with diffused light through mist, which blurs bare trees and substantial houses in the distance. On the left, amongst the branches of the closest tree, is a faint point of light, which may just be the 'evening star' of the alternative title.[35] Some hundred yards away on the near pavement, is a bulky figure, cloaked and hooded, blurred by motion into, or away from, the foggy distance.[36]

This figure, and the region of blurred streetlamps and fog in which it moves, is crucial to the atmposphere of a composed photograph that Mark Haworth-Booth contexts not only with Baudelaire's definition of 'fugitive, fleeting' modernity, but also with reference to the disquieting twilight world of Wilkie Collins's novels of crime and clairvoyance. He also quotes a precise analysis of the degree of artifice that went into the making of this work. It is a composite image formed of four negatives – streetlamp, figures, foggy background, wall and railings. Joins are visible – the boy's back and the lamp, the pavement to the right of the group of figures; there are discrepancies of illumination and shadow especially in the reflections in the wet pavement. The light of the foreground lamp may have been drawn onto the negative as it is surrounded by no diffusion of its light in the foggy air.[37] Indeed, it is almost impossible to tell whether part of the blurred, cloaked figure may have been drawn across the join between two negatives.

The degree of manipulation of photographic technology required in the mid-nineteenth century in order to produce even a convincing appearance of twilight is notable in Silvy's image, as is his skill in overcoming these technical difficulties.[38] Much the same difficulties attended cinematic representation of twilight for a surprisingly long time, and twilight scenes tended to be avoided accordingly, with the exception of supernatural narratives where a race against the sunset to a place of safety was essential to the plot.[39] The many difficulties that attend a time of day when the quality of light changes minute by minute – the 'magic hour' after sunset is called the 'magic moment' by realistic American directors – are compounded by the considerable difficulties that attend any attempt to counterfeit dusk. Urban dusk – fading blue daylight and intensified tones of yellow in artificial light, the colours of Whistler's London *Nocturnes* – presented particular problems.

Stanley Kubrick's *Barry Lyndon* (1975), a film that minimized the use of electric light using the fastest lenses then available to film indoor scenes by candlelight, had to make lavish use of its budget to film numerous external scenes at twilight by natural illumination, regardless of the need to assemble each scene from a mosaic of moments captured in the course of a long sequence of evenings. This accumulation of dim lights patiently captured plays a considerable part in the creation of the film's atmosphere of removedness and apartness, consistently remote from the brightness of the present.

Until comparatively recently cinema cameras have been far less flexible than stills cameras. It was only in the 1950s that cameras small enough to go on location became commonplace. Before then, cinema cameras used relatively slow film that required the strong illumination of harsh studio lights. This in turn made lighting crucial: the role now usually known as 'cinematographer' was often described as 'lighting cameraman'. The person in charge of the camera department was responsible for the lighting of the scene: they would spend all of their time on this, the most difficult and critical job, leaving the operation of the cameras to others.

Filming in low light was impossible for many years, and so external night scenes presented a significant problem. These were achieved by filming 'day for night' (or *nuit américaine*, as it was called in France, due to its prevalence in Hollywood films), filming under natural daylight of answerable strength, but manipulating the film to create the illusion of evening or night. The film acts as the shadowing Claude glass worked for the eighteenth-century painter. The simplest means of counterfeiting darkness is to shoot in the natural twilight of a wood. Alternatively, the use of a blue filter darkens the image and gives it a blue tint. In practice, it hardly produces a simulacrum of twilight, far less night, and the greatest care has to be taken to keep the sun and cast shadows out of the frame. It is also possible to 'stop down', to adjust the camera exposure a few stops downwards to reduce the light and produce a darker image.

Alternatively, the fall of evening could be simulated entirely in the studio, as Hitchcock did for his two claustrophobic thrillers *Rope* (1948) and *Rear Window* (1954). The former counterfeits the sky and skyline seen from a Manhattan penthouse progressing in near-real time from about 7.30 until 9.15, using devices that resemble those of baroque opera: a Kircherian 'light organ' and clouds made of spun glass, for all that the progress of the fictive light was based on the real findings of photographers sent out by the director to document the New York sunset at five minute intervals.

The most effective uses of *nuit américane* show clear sky and silhouette figures against it: anything much more than this will begin to show the flaws in the illusion. As film stock became faster, it became possible to shoot later in the day, and so a finer effect could be achieved by shooting around sunset, although the available time in 'golden hour' and, even more, in 'blue hour' is of necessity severely limited, especially if a number of camera angles have to be set up to cover a scene.

In filming at evening, there are two consecutive but quite different stages of twilight: golden hour (or magic hour) and blue hour. Golden hour is the time around sunset (or sunrise) when shadows are soft and the light is diffuse and shaded gold or red from the low sun. Photographers and cinematographers love this time of day for the light it gives, and a disproportionate amount of filming gets done, inevitably in a rush, at this last hour of the day. The actual length of 'golden hour' depends on latitude and time of year: very far north, golden hour conditions may extend through much of the day. In the extreme north, golden hour can last all night. A considerable number of scenes in Aleksandr Rogozhkin's anti-war comedy *The Cuckoo* (2002), set in the Sami territory of northern Finland, are lit by the infinitely extended golden hour of the northern white nights. Many of Ingmar Bergman's most celebrated films depend for their atmosphere on the lingering, undiminished light of the Scandinavian summer evenings, used to create atmospheres of otherness and transformation.

'Blue hour' is the period of twilight in which filming remains possible without additional light. The colour balance changes noticeably from the reds of golden hour to a domination of blue. Blue hour is relatively brief, little more than twenty minutes in average conditions, and however much it is used in still photography it is too short for most cinematic purposes, unless expense is a minor consideration.

For both golden hour and blue hour, the languorous colour tones of the evening and the elegant photographic results belie the frenzied activity usually required to obtain them, with the film crew rushing to beat the dying light. With a small film crew, and given the favouring length of northern twilight, much more is possible, and constraints of budget can be turned to advantage. Thus, the Scottish director Bill Forsyth in his gentle, proudly regional *Gregory's Girl* (1981) can make relaxed use of a sustained period of evening towards the end of the film, as the hero is led eventually to a meeting with the heroine, creating a long summer's evening of youth, an evening long in memory. In capturing and showing an actual twilight, the director is in fact helped, not hindered, by the fact this is low-budget film-making. By necessity this means a small, fast and agile crew, able to set up and shoot scenes quickly – quickly enough to respond to the changing light conditions and film scenes set before, during and after twilight. Much the same is true of his more ambitious, more international *Local Hero* (1983), which centres on the resolution of potential conflict between a remote Scottish community and the international oil industry. Again, the long, the endless, summer evening brings the fable to resolution – a time outside time when truths are told and the supernatural is oddly, credibly close. All the lessons learned from ingenuity on a low budget are carried over into this film's response to the slowly moving summer light.

All this, of course, changed for ever with the introduction of the digital camera with its capacity to shoot in much lower light than ever before. As a consequence, since it is far easier to manipulate digital footage, brightening, darkening or tinting the image to simulate different times of day, a gradual change in aesthetic has taken place in current cinema and television, both of which are able to film into evening or even night.

The limited time for twilight shooting remains a serious constraint, however, and twilight scenes are still relatively few. Aesthetically, and in terms of audience perception, it is possible that ambiguities of representation remain from the earlier cinema, from the 'day for night' shooting of *nuit américaine*. Conventions of cinematic representation may be so strongly established that scenes shot digitally in genuine twilight remain confusing: is the low light 'really' twilight or is it to be understood to be night?

It is a paradox relating to the ability of painting, as opposed to the most scrupulous photography, to convince the human brain that it is seeing a close approximation of what it believes that it sees in actual conditions of low light. The infinite adaptability of the eye casts doubt on the most scrupulous photography or cinema, and the inventions and approximations of painting carry their perverse conviction.

There are many painted evocations of low light in the winter cities of the nineteenth century and the early twentieth – of the urban melancholy that is one constant of the era: 'toute la misère des grands centres'.[40] Few paintings capture this more absolutely than those of Vilhelm Hammershøi (1864–1916), the connoisseur of muted light, light gone to green, to grey, to nothing. He painted a few evocative renderings of wintry London, of afternoon gone early into evening and fine rain. One is a frozen, fogbound view out from a high, cold room into Brunswick Square (*The Jewish School in Guilford Street*, 1912). The other, *Street in London*, is one of the most persuasive images of the monochrome of winter England, painted during Hammershøi's third visit in 1905–6. The absolute restraint of his palette here represents the absence of light, that northern light which is a negative, a lack, the day which is never truly light. It invokes too the wonderful sculptural quality of the great iron railings by the British Museum, the damp chill in the air. It is one of the deepest likenesses of London in the early twentieth century, the visual rhyme to Eliot's misted, dusk-besieged city.

Hammershøi was the most precise of all the *fin de siècle* masters of the twilight (that precision encompasses the indeterminate, hour-less afternoon blankness that lights his London street) and one who

Vilhelm Hammershøi, *Street in London*, 1905–6, oil on canvas.

explored lower levels of light than almost any other painter. This
is especially true of many of his interior paintings, likenesses of
the rooms and enfilades in his family home at Strandgade 30 in
Copenhagen, some of them in the deepest shadow furthest from the
already fading window light.[41] Indeed some of his domestic interiors
are almost as dark as Pryde's shuttered palaces, dusk lurking in
rooms being a constant element that shapes both of their paintings,
although Hammershøi is habitually calm and meditative where
Pryde is sinister and despairing. Although, Hammershøi did paint
one or two emotionally ambiguous pictures of empty, windowless
palace halls, and one disquieting work shows a room in his familiar
Copenhagen apartment, shabby and emptied, almost decayed, as

though it were in a long-deserted house.[42] It is a strange picture, exceptional in his oeuvre, and one in which it is extremely difficult to discern the implied position of the artist, or indeed the viewer. It is often asserted, not absolutely accurately, that Hammershøi's paintings are 'without narrative',[43] but this particular painting is problematic precisely in that it seems to render narrative inescapable.

Hammershøi is most celebrated as a master of the fading light in his depictions of the interiors of the Copenhagen flats in which he and his family lived. Occasionally these show a bright morning throwing sunlight across Biedermeier furniture and grey-painted panelling. But usually these are evening or night pictures, some of the most haunting depictions of the northern twilight and its fall. They are often extraordinary experiments with the very last of the light, the ebbing of definition from grey things, the catching of a sliver of belated reflection on the moulding of a panel, in the polish of a table or piano, or along the bevel of a mirror.

Often in Hammershoi's evening paintings the figure of his wife has her back to us, a conscious homage to the *Rückenfigur* of Caspar David Friedrich's wife at the window, to the figures who turn away from the viewer in Friedrich's metaphysical landscapes. Sometimes the sombre greys and greens of Hammershøi's works evoke melancholy and silence in the dusk. The last of the autumn light falters over the quay and the inlets of the Baltic, with the Greenland icebreakers lying at anchor almost under the windows. Perhaps it is easy to place too much emphasis on this aspect of his work: there are other inhabitants of Hammershøi's rooms, they have other moods and tones. Sometimes his son leans in a doorway on a spring morning, or examines a coin by candlelight. His wife sews or plays the piano; a table is set with fine white plates; a group of friends gather around the dinner table. In all this there is much of the Scandinavian interest in the depiction of family life and the domestic interior: the paintings show the quiet recreations of a small and sophisticated family, living in elegant rooms deliberately arranged to evoke the sparseness of rooms in paintings of the Danish 'golden age'.

The most consistent feature of Hammershøi's work, however, is his use of the tonality of northern twilight, his palette of greens and greys. This is as true of his landscapes and his still, formal views of Copenhagen as it is of the interiors for which he is famous. It is the defining feature of his portraits. The exploration of the last of the light, of the lowest light, lies at the centre of his practice as a painter.

There is an extraordinary anticipation of Hammershøi's tonality in a portrait of an anonymous young man by Gerard ter Borch (1617–1681), dating from the late 1630s or 1640s.[44] The whole work is sombre, distinguished by a precocious fascination with the meticulous depiction of a very low level of light. The young man stands in his black clothes, in a room whose walls are shadowed in grey and green. On them hangs one map, but no paintings. There is a table, like a scholar's table, but it has only his black hat on it, no papers and no books. The table is covered with a finely painted, almost shimmering, grey silk-velvet cloth. There is an open door in the shadows behind the young man. His clothes are plain but costly. His room, too, is rich but empty – the colour of the walls is almost impossible to guess – if they are whitewashed, the room is very dimly lit indeed. The whole ensemble of rich austerity is hard to read, it seems to be trying to communicate something about the subject of the portrait, about privilege and self-imposed austerities, but the message is elusive. It is the dimness, the studied representation of a very low level of light in which the young man stands, that is haunting and exceptional.

The painter has his back to the window, which is implied as a light source, but almost no light comes filtering over his shoulder, only enough to cast a faint illumination on the floor in the foreground. It is an anticipation of Hammershøi's Strandgade paintings in tonality, in sparseness, in its implication of silence, silence tempered perhaps only by the faint sound of rain. Indeed, the light in the picture only makes complete sense if late afternoon rain is running down the window behind the painter's shoulders, diffusing and obscuring such light as is fading out of the clouded sky. Brown brick houses and pollarded trees on the other side of the green canal, its waters pitted and

Vilhelm Hammershøi, *Interior, Strandgade 30*, 1908, oil on canvas.

starred by the intensifying rainstorm. Greys and greens from those shadowy ripples in the waters stretch up to possess the room. It is hard to attribute precise meanings or intentions to this exceptional painting: in an age and a country where the 'art of describing' reached an unparalleled sophistication, it may constitute simply an intense act of observation of a particular figure in a particular room on one overcast autumn or winter day in the seventeenth century, however much the context and colouration appear to a later eye to suggest a narrative about the figure depicted, a reflection on melancholia and riches that is of its time, but expressed in a visual language that looks to the future.

In the writings of W. G. Sebald an abandoned Europe and a failing England enact and re-enact their conflicts and recollections under a darkened sky. Especially in his novel of lost identity, lost hopes, memorial and admonishment, *Austerlitz* (2001), again and again the most important episodes are enacted in the urban twilight of European cities or in the shadowed, nostalgic spaces of the great railway stations – Antwerpen-Centraal or Liverpool Street. It is in the latter that the eponymous hero is meditating on the generations of the dead whose lives lie under the platforms and train sheds, in a place which is itself a kind of node in the journey between Europe and Britain, the journey to and from the complex condition of exile:

> As for me, said Austerlitz, I felt at this time as if the dead were returning from their exile and filling the twilight around me with their strangely slow but incessant to-ing and fro-ing. I remember, for instance, that one quiet Sunday morning I was sitting on a bench on the particularly gloomy platform where the boat trains from Harwich came in . . .[45]

A dark epiphany is the consequence of his meditations: he follows the porter through a door in the builder's hoardings and finds himself in the disused waiting rooms, where he has a vision of a Piranesian prison, of infinite ruinous vaults, 'Viaducts and footbridges crossing deep chasms thronged with tiny figures . . . like prisoners in search of some way of escape from their dungeon'.[46] He relates this to scraps of retrieved memory of mists rising over the flat lands of East Anglia, of his own first arrival in Britain,

> Memories like this came back to me in the disused Ladies' Waiting-Room of Liverpool Street Station, memories behind and within which many things much further back in the past seemed to lie, all interlocking like the labyrinthine vaults I saw in the dusty grey light, and which seemed to go on and on for ever.[47]

When he goes searching for his own past in Europe the courtyard of the archives building in Prague presents itself to him as another dusk-haunted place of departure, an entrance to the fugitive past:

> it also suggested a monastery, a riding school, an opera house and a lunatic asylum, and all these ideas mingled in my mind as I looked at the twilight coming in from above, and thought that on the rows of galleries I saw a dense crowd of people, some of them waving hats or handkerchiefs, as passengers aboard a steamer used to do when it put out to sea.[48]

And when he finally discovers the apartment of his childhood friend and nurse, twilight again offers the hour, and almost the element, through which a measure of the past can be regained:

> Věra had risen and opened both the inner and outer windows to let me look down into the garden next door, where the lilac happened to be in flower, its blossoms so thick and white that in the gathering dusk it looked as if there had been a snowstorm in the middle of spring.[49]

And the whole complex past that Austerlitz recovers is inevitably involved in the twilight, nostalgia and longing, which attends all the places and moments of transition in this narrative:

I saw Věra as she had been then, sitting beside me on the divan
telling me stories from the Riesengebirge and the Bohemian Forest,
I saw her uncommonly beautiful eyes misting over in the twilight,
so to speak, when after reaching the end of the story she took off
her glasses and bent down to me.[50]

At the very end of the novel, the narrator makes a sort of secular
pilgrimage of memory to Antwerp and to Willebroek fortress. At
the very end when he has meditated upon Austerlitz himself, on
the unknowable past, that past recovered only in dim glimpses, and
on those lost (and those innocents who lost their selfhoods) in the
twentieth century's wars and disasters, he sets forth so that he
enters an ancient city at dusk: 'And then set out on my way back
to Mechelen, reaching the town as evening began to fall.'[51]

The unconsoled twilight in which *Austerlitz* ends is paralleled in
Angela Carter's justly celebrated evocation of Baudelaire's autumnal
Paris:

> Sad; so sad, those smoky-rose, smoky-mauve evenings of late
> autumn, sad enough to pierce the heart. The sun departs the sky
> in winding sheets of gaudy cloud; anguish enters the city, a sense
> of the bitterest regret, a nostalgia for things we never knew, anguish
> of the turn of the year, the time of impotent yearning, the incon-
> solable season . . .
>
> Soft twists of mist invade the alleys, rise up from the slow river
> like exhalations of an exhausted spirit, seep in through the cracks
> in the window frames so that the contours of their high, lonely
> apartment waver and melt. On these evenings, you see everything
> as though your eyes are going to lapse into tears.[52]

This passage captures the essence of an infinity of mournful urban
evenings of the nineteenth century and their literary expression – the
cities of Baudelaire and Laforgue, and of Victor Hugo's *Les Chants du
crépuscule*. Hugo's evening effects are in the grand manner of the century,
the poet giving formal voice to a society troubled and in trouble:

De quel nom te nommer, heure trouble où nous sommes?
Tous les fronts sont baignés de livides sueurs.
Dans les hauteurs du ciel et dans le cœur des hommes
Les ténèbres partout se mêlent aux lueurs.[53]

What name should be given to you, troubled hour which we inhabit?
All foreheads are wet with livid sweats. In the heights of the sky and
in human hearts, everywhere the shadows mingle themselves with
the feeble lights.

Jules Laforgue's poems of the last light in the city form a nervous
and colloquial counterpoint to Hugo's measured verses, deliberately
quotidian, pathetic and engaging:

Blocus sentimental! Messageries du Levant!...
Oh, tombée de la pluie! Oh! tombée de la nuit,
Oh! le vent!...

La Toussaint, La Noël et la Nouvelle Année,
Oh, dans les bruines, toutes mes cheminées!...
D'usines...[54]

Sentimental blockade! Levantine frieght lines! Oh rainfall, oh, nightfall,
oh the wind, All Saints', Christmas, New Year, Oh all my factory
chimneys in the drizzle...

Laforgue is much concerned with the ignoble horrors of Sunday evenings
in bachelor lodgings, with the serial dullness of autumn afternoons:

Adieu! les files d'ifs dans les grisailles,
Ont l'air de pleureuses de funérailles
Sous l'autan noir qui veut que tout s'en aille.[55]

Farewell, the rows of yews in the greyness have the air of mourners
at a funeral, under a black wind that would blow everything away.

The plural Sundays are endless as the winter with the aimless, pitiless
rain outside, '*le ciel pleut sans but*' – rain falls, night falls, lights come
on and the downpour never lets up all the winter through:

Le crépuscule vient; le petit port
Allume ses feux. (Ah! connu l'décor!)[56]

Twilight comes, the little quay lights its lamps. (Ah! familiar scene.)

Lights reflected in darkening water appear repeatedly in the
works of Georges Rodenbach (1855–1898), whose subject is almost
exclusively the towns of the old Spanish Netherlands, seen in their
nineteenth-century decline. Where Laforgue is elegantly bathetic,
Rodenbach and his characters are overwhelmed by the melancholy
solemnity of places that then seemed far gone into their twilight:
'recurrent imagery of empty provincial Sundays, solitude, autumn
and winter nightfall'.[57] The protagonist of *Bruges-la-Morte* is
defined by bereavement, by the intensity of the mourning that leads
him into an affair with an actress who resembles his dead wife and,
eventually, to disaster. But the city, with its waters and shadows,
is the other character in the work – so strongly present and so
powerful as to shape the whole contour of the text, from the
opening,

> *Le jour déclinait, assombrissant les corridors de la grande demeure*
> *silencieuse, mettant des écrans de crêpe aux vitres.*
>
> *Hugues Viane se disposa à sortir, comme il en avait l'habitude*
> *quotidienne à la fin des après-midi. Inoccupé, solitaire, il passait*
> *toute la journée dans sa chambre . . . dont les fenêtres donnaient*
> *sur le quai du Rosaire, au long duquel s'alignait sa maison, mirée*
> *dans l'eau.*

The daylight was failing, darkening the corridors of the
large, silent house, putting screens of crepe over the windows.
Hugues Viane was preparing to go out, as was his daily habit
at the end of the afternoon. Solitary, with nothing to occupy
his time, he would spend the whole day in his room . . .
whose windows looked out onto the Quai du Rosaire,
along which the facade of his house stretched, mirrored
in the canal.[58]

He identifies himself inevitably with the city in its decline,

> *Et comme Bruges aussi était triste en ces fins d'après-midi! Il l'aimait*
> *ainsi! . . . Une équation mystérieuse s'établissait. À l'épouse morte devait*
> *correspondre une ville morte . . . Il avait besoin de silence infini et d'une*
> *existence si monotone qu'elle ne lui donnerait presque plus la sensation*
> *de vivre.*

> And how melancholy Bruges was, too, during those late after-
> noons! That was how he liked the town . . . A mysterious equation
> gradually established itself, he needed a dead town to correspond
> to his dead wife . . . He needed infinite silence and an existence
> that was so monotonous it almost failed to give him the sense of
> being alive.[59]

After his attempt to rejoin the living has ended in catastrophe, the city
itself seems animate still, almost articulate at the end of the novella,

> *«Morte . . . morte . . . Bruges-la-Morte . . .» avec la cadence des dernières*
> *cloches, lasses, lentes, petites vieilles exténuées qui avaient l'air – est-ce*
> *sur la ville, est-ce sur une tombe? – d'effeuiller languissamment des fleurs*
> *de fer!*

> 'Dead town, Bruges-la-Morte' – the cadences of the last bells, weary
> and slow, little, worn-out bells which seemed to be shedding petals
> – was it on the town? Was it on a grave? – from flowers of iron.[60]

Rodenbach's novel, as Frances Fowle has traced in detail,[61] drew painters
to Bruges at the turn of the twentieth century – Henri Le Sidaner,
Fernand Khnopff – to produce sombre variations on the themes of
sparse lighted windows along empty quays and the light going over cold,
charcoal-dark canals.

ALTHOUGH THE ATMOSPHERE of the cities of the Low Countries has
changed absolutely from this silted melancholy of the *fin de siècle*, the
light from uncurtained windows still trails reflected in canal water with

the fall of the autumn evening. Lighted houses on the Rapenburg, near
the University in Leiden, display rooms of some splendour: one is hung
with verdure tapestries, themselves representations of twilight, of the
shadowy recesses of medieval hunting forests. Eighteenth-century
rooms are painted with continuous sequences of panels, forming a
panorama, whole rooms show summer evening coming down over
the trim country houses, the slender islanded towers that stretch
along the river Vecht.

My most intense memory of such an October twilight is of crossing misted lakes in south Holland in late afternoon, my expert friend
guiding our little powered boat through the leaf-strewn waterways of
Leiden as evening came on, seeing a whole city of lighted rooms from
the water, seeing the houses on the quays from the canal, as their
architects had intended them to be seen.

The most memorable twilight painter of nineteenth-century
Holland is Anton Mauve (1838–1888). While many of his works are
engaging, freely painted representations of farmwork and husbandry,
there is a distinct and haunting sub-group of his works that are concerned with riders and distance: even in his *Morning Ride along the
Beach at Scheveningen* (1876), all the figures in its elegant group of
horsewomen and men on a bright morning turn away. As in many
works of Hammershøi, Friedrich or Giandomenico Tiepolo, these
figures place the viewer in a complex but disconcerted relation to
them and to the landscape in the painting. It is remarkable how
often the painters of twilight are also the painters of *Rückenfiguren*.[62]
There is a cold seriousness to Mauve's picture of the Haagse Bos,
the old hunting forest, which still touches on the centre of the city.
In his *Riders in the Snow* (1880) the *Rückenfiguren* are moving far
away along the trampled snow of the ride, being placed surprisingly
deep into the picture plane, hauntingly distant from the viewer.
Evening is coming in mist that already thickens the air between
the trees, and much of the effect of the picture depends on the
transience of the depicted moment, the evocation of damp cold.
Very soon indeed, the riders will have passed out of sight and fog
and darkness will close the scene.

Caspar David Friedrich (1774–1840) explored more territories of the twilight than almost any other painter. Failing light and the slow movement of the northern European evening preoccupied him throughout his career. The feeling of belatedness that his works convey has been described with great precision by Joseph Leo Koerner – his example here is focused on the two *Rückenfiguren* in Friedrich's *Der Abend*:

> What we saw becomes what they had already been seeing in a past long before our arrival. Their anteriority, expressed as our view of their backs, deepened our sense of 'evening'. It enabled the canvas not only to depict a late time of day, but also to elicit within us an experience of our own lateness as subjects of landscape.[63]

Or in the solitary place in which the viewer is positioned by Friedrich's screen of alder bushes in *From the Dresden Heath*:

> You are afterwards . . . you arrive in the dead of winter, after all signs of life have vanished save the one. Your belatedness deepens as you revert to the initial traveller on the heath only then to discover that he, the artist Friedrich, has already viewed the scene in retrospect.[64]

Friedrich's intense awareness of winter colours, colours of evening studied in solitude, parallels Goethe's description of a winter twilight:

> On a winter journey through the Harz I climbed down from the Brocken towards evening . . . the sun was just setting over the pools of the Oder. While the shadows on the yellowish snow had looked slightly violet during the day, one would have to describe them now as deep blue, as a more intense yellow was reflected off the areas in sunshine. But as the sun finally moved towards setting, and as its rays, much reduced by the denser vapours, coated the world around me in the most beautiful purple, the colour of the shadows turned into green, a green as clear as the sea and as beautiful as emerald.

Anton Mauve, *Riders in the Snow in the Haagse Bos*, 1880, oil on canvas.

The display became more and more lively – it was like being in a fairy world – for everything had clothed itself in these two lively and so beautifully matching colours, until the sun finally set and the magnificent display turned to grey twilight and was gradually dissolved into a night of moon and stars.[65]

This purple and green dusk, so faithfully observed, is matched by Friedrich's autumn and winter twilights, as in his lonely depiction of a disregarded place in his *Ploughed Field* in Hamburg, a corner of cultivated land with its shadowy figure in profile expressing involvement with the landscape in isolation and regret, in contrast to Goethe's growing exhilaration in contemplation of the colours of evening. Although they would appear to have much in common, Goethe remained ambivalent about Friedrich's work.

Even Friedrich's summer sunsets are to some degree troubled or questioning. *The Evening Star* (c. 1830–35), a beautiful and yet apprehensive work, shows the golden evening sky seen from the hill above Dresden with the figures of his wife and one of his daughters passing in profile along the crest of the hill. Friedrich's son, Gustav Adolf, waves his cap with raised arms, as though reaching out to the invisible star, which may be conjectured to be hidden by the grey cloud-bar above him and to his right. Despite the child's gesture of spontaneous joy, it is a sombre portrait of a family already under the strain of the artist's insecurity and instability. They are together and yet not together – the two women pass in profile in their dark clothes almost like mourners. The artist is separated from them by the turned earth of the foreground, earth which relates the painting strongly to his earlier view from the same hill, *Hill and Ploughlands near Dresden* (1824–5) in the Kunsthalle in Hamburg. In this, the whole foreground is occupied by the furrowed soil, towards which a flock of crows is descending, birds which always carry implications of sorrow and disaster in Friedrich's work. In *The Evening Star* he is isolated on the wrong side of the turned earth as he sets down his family's likenesses moving away against the fading, complicated evening sky, with the first indication of grey mist gathering in the valley beyond the city.

A contemporary painter who has explored to the very end of evening, further into the twilight even than Friedrich or Hammershøi, is Victoria Crowe. She has long painted shadowed rooms, mirrors and windows, reflected and distant things, with scrupulous observance of the finest gradations of changing and refracted light. She has recently made a sequence of studies of deep winter dusks, all seen through windows. Snowy landscapes of the Scottish Borders are framed by a window that faces out and upwards to trees, hillside, an upland horizon.[66] Or bare trees and hills are reflected in the great mirror that hangs opposite the north-facing windows in her Edinburgh studio. Many of these paintings play with an ambiguity of the last of the light – vision in cold glass – of the very end of deep-blue evening, when any increase of the light level on the painter's side of the pane would cause the winter trees and their dusk-shadows on snow to disappear, as the window would be turned to a black mirror, reflecting only the room inside, where the painter stands, silent and invisible. The sheer transience of midwinter light is always remembered in these pictures – sparse rays from the setting sun touch the snow and the foreground trees with short-lived rust and ochre, when the distance is already rich with the darkening blue of nightfall. These twilight pictures are silent, intensely still, so much of their skill and concentration focuses on the moment when twilight passes to darkness.

Considered Silence shows black trees diminishing into latest dusk beyond the window, their smaller branches already fading into the shadowy clouds behind them, with the delicate silhouette of a lily visible inside the room, like a memory of a barely recoverable summer. A small light coming from far behind the painter and the viewer draws a scatter of golden light out of the pattern in the curtain. This only serves as a more intense reminder of the lateness of the hour – how vulnerable the whole meticulously depicted world outside would be to the introdution of any light to the foreground. This painting works at the extreme of the transition from 'nautical twilight' to 'astronomical twilight', at the last moment when the infinitely adaptable human eye can still see clearly what a camera would capture

Caspar David Friedrich, *The Evening Star*, c. 1830–35, oil on canvas.

only with difficulty. These paintings are not only beautiful in themselves with their scrupulous recording of branches seen against the profundity of the sky, they have also a specific poetry that comes from their fragility. They have captured the last colour in the fading world, before the monochrome of night vision and the fading of sight into darkness take over. Unlike many paintings of twilight, these pictures convey no regrets, no melancholy. They consider the death of the light in wisdom, in calm, almost with detachment, observing the infinity of blues in the cold nightfall outside, the wonderful patterns of the motionless trees over the snow.

The contemporary poet Helen Tookey also finds stillness at nightfall in deep winter in her perfectly poised poem 'In the dying days of the year we walked . . .'. Two people are walking along a tidal river at evening in the ambiguous endtime between Christmas and New Year. Everything is observed in terms of harmonious exchange: light giving way to dark, fresh water to salt.

Victoria Crowe, *Considered Silence*, 2014, oil on linen.

In the dying days of the year we walked
by the river and wondered at the meeting of
salt water and sweet as the tide swung like
the weighing of day against night . . .[67]

Everything external is at its furthest, at its turn: year, day and river.
It is a beautifully oblique poem of consolation and mutual love: the
understanding between the two people walking together in affection
and shared memory, untroubled by the unknowable intricacy of the
city, and the spreading estuary under the vastness of evening.

. . . We walked by the river and weighed
our small works as the year swung and
turned like the tide in its saltsweet dying days.[68]

4

Dark Corners

Misted, drowsy midsummer morning, setting out southwestward from Hereford through rich country and old trees for The Cwm, the secluded country house where a Jesuit college had been hidden in the seventeenth century. As we moved away from the city, the roads began to narrow and the valleys grew steeper. The villages grew more infrequent, farmhouses sparser, trees denser. We came to the village of Welsh Newton at the foot of its sloping fields, a road up into the trees led to the plain stone church. There, an indicator of the dissident history of this remote and beautiful country took the form of a sign by the gate stating simply that the grave of St John Kemble could be found at the foot of the Preaching Cross. This notice is a quiet reminder of the history in the Welsh Marches of one of the communities within Britain who could be thought of as overshadowed or twilight people: the post-Reformation Roman Catholics, criminalized by statute, excluded from public life, exiled or confined to such remote 'dark corners of the land' as this. The recusant Catholics were by no means the only inhabitants of the shadows of upland Britain as the divided centuries of British history progressed from the Henrician Reformation to religious and political détente at the end of the eighteenth century: after the revolution of 1688, the Jacobites inhabited much the same territory, as did the Episcopalians of northern Scotland and many of the remote, ceremonious communities of north Wales.

This grave at Welsh Newton is the one that Sarah Siddons, the great tragic actress of the late eighteenth century, visited with her ladies, so that she might honour her martyred kinsman and pray for his intercession. As a member of the Herefordshire family of Kemble, and whose brother John Philip may have gained his early acting experience in the exiled Catholic college at Douai in northern France, she was clearly aware of the unspoken topography of dissident Britain and moved at ease through its shadows.

We drove on into soft wooded country and made a right turn into a sunken lane, wide enough for only one car, the branches meeting in layer upon layer of green twilight overhead. Deeper into the dim recesses of the summer and the shadows. And then, at the top of the slope, there were glimpses of sky and distance through gaps in the leaves.

As the road swung round, a hidden valley spread below us, and we arrived at The Cwm – now a handsome nineteenth-century house, with the remains of the old building that had housed the secret college in its cellars – folded in the shelter of the hill, settled deep into its trees. And so perfectly sited in a place that is itself an ambiguity: a place where every road, every path, leads to a frontier or a border. Two minutes' walk westwards into the valley takes you into Wales, a short walk to the north or south into another jurisdiction, diocese, shire. Indeed whatever local agent of central government was sent against the Jesuits of The Cwm, from whichever direction, escape into another polity could be achieved at walking pace assisted by 'a very private passage from the houses into the wood'.[1] The whole is absolutely hidden from the approach from Hereford, surrounded by slopes and woods with many places to post sentries and with the deep groves and all of Wales as territories into which to escape. If ever there was a place that is a deep, dark corner of the land, the end of every line, the dark margin of the very edge, this is it.

Sometimes a visit to a place, particularly to a place as removed and undisturbed as this one, can be almost the only point of access to its history, particularly if that history is a shadowed account more perceptible in the gaps between documents, than in the documents themselves. The Jesuit poet and scholar Peter Levi wrote of aspects of this phenomenon, from a lifetime's experience of patient walking among the obscure corners of Britain, in search of the vestiges of antiquity:

> Gazing at places is never a short cut to what happened in History,
> but a sense of place, of the small scale of the bright green ramparts,
> the dry, cracked tongues of the forest still stretching out, the
> flowering weeds, the lapwings in sunlight, the murmurations of
> starlings, an accurate sense of place is the fruit of a lifetime
> of patient scholarship.[2]

Mainstream historians write of the 'dark corners' of Britain: remote
areas that resisted metropolitan ideologies of progress and reform
through religious, social and industrial revolutions. To this day,
those territories of dissidence – Lancashire, the Herefordshire
Marches of Wales, northeastern Scotland – seem to retain a palpable
atmosphere of removedness. This is partly because they are upland
areas distant from the main transport routes and at some distance
from a major centre of population, those areas where proscribed
ideas might persist for simple reasons of remoteness from enforcing
authority. But common to all of them is a sense that the landscape
of the 'dark corners' feels deepened, by the dense trees of Lancashire
or north Wales or, in the case of northern Scotland, by the skulking
castles of the gentry sunk deep into their plantations below the
snowline, with the bare slopes rising above. The signposts are fewer,
and the sparse minor roads cut deeper into the fields. A farmhouse
with the Five Wounds carved over the door; a castle with a simple
Kaisersaal displaying portraits of the Jacobite shadow-dynasty from
James VIII to Henry IX; a whitewashed cathedral at the end of a
potholed farm track. An awareness of alternative realities comes
out of the unreconciled realities of a double education.

Sometimes the nature of a dark corner seems to communicate
itself urgently in silence and the density of the trees: the turning off
the A96 in Aberdeenshire towards the Pictish Maiden Stone, ferns
growing in the broken wall under the beeches along the minor road.
The lands of a powerful family gone abroad; the estate wall decaying,
because they have been gone so long in Salamanca, Rome or Vienna;
in the alternative Britain-in-exile of officers in the continental armies,
of the wine merchants, of the picture dealers and *virtuosi*. Or a dark

corner may manifest its nature simply in undisturbed stillness and ancientness, as with the church of St Seiriol at Penmon, on the far tip of the island of Anglesey. The stone crosses dating from the first millennium, which have never left the site, stand in the church. It is the enclosed garden of flowering hawthorns below the church, with the saint's holy well in its little well-house, that feels farthest and deepest: not only in that it guards stone foundations that may be those of the original church, but in the way in which it is walled on one side by the rough face of the cliff. And the water in the well stirs and is still with the movement of the spring, as it has done from then until now.

These are the places associated with some of the societies and communities – defeated, often exiled, or living at home under legal disability – who were considered as *shadowed* or *overshadowed* peoples. A covert poetic of symbols and allusions attends the places where they lived and the works that they have left behind. The shadowed community changed and realigned over time: during the Interregnum the defeated Royalists swelled their numbers for a decade. After the final defeats of 1746, the scattered Jacobites communicated in a series of symbols by then a century old. From the ruling metropolis, the shadowed twilight of the recusants or Jacobites was always characterized as a recidivist darkness, opposed to the brightness of their progressive rule. In the end, the term *gens lucifuga*, 'the light-shunning people', was defiantly adopted by the emancipated Catholics of nineteenth-century England as a badge of identity, an assertion of continuity with the persecuted Christians of the first millennium. However, the image retains its ambiguities, its endless poetic potential as well as its doubts.

The arts of the *overshadowed* communities inevitably offer an alternative reality to those of the mainstream canon, a society turned upside down in which the great ones of the bright world act out a meaningless pantomime, while the true king is in pensioned exile and the real bishop is in prison. For overshadowed communities, evening light may indeed act as a reminder of daily experience of defeat or adversity, but it is more often the metaphorical light in which these communities are perceived by those outside them for whom 'progress is idolized as another name for good',[3] which sees them as having reached their twilight, having a past only and no future. Can places draw twilight into their being, can a region or a community draw shadow over itself? And can shadow and twilight linger in the places of their memory?

The paradox endures of dark corners being viewed historically from outside as old and alien, whereas, once their thresholds have been crossed, they can seem cohesive, serene and welcoming: the northern Arcadia spread along the banks of the Hodder, and folded under the flank of Pendle; the profound and tranquil Scotland beyond Aberdeen. The most celebrated imagination of the lives of those who dwelled in dark corners is found in Bl. John Henry Newman's sermon on 'the second spring', on the condition of English Catholics of the penal times as opposed to their vastly improved state by the mid-nineteenth century:

> a mere handful of individuals, who might be counted, like the pebbles and detritus of the great deluge . . . perhaps an elderly person, seen walking in the streets, grave and solitary, and strange, though noble in bearing, and said to be of good family, and a 'Roman Catholic'. An old-fashioned house of gloomy appearance, closed in with high walls, with an iron gate, and yews, and the report attaching to it that 'Roman Catholics' lived there; but who they were, or what they did, or what was meant by calling them Roman Catholics, no one could tell; – though it had an unpleasant sound, and told of form and superstition.[4]

This is a memorable account, but in its very use of the imagery of twilight, it unconsciously takes its tone from the mainstream rather than from the exceptional community that Newman had joined with his conversion. But his yoking of the ideas of dissidence, the 'recesses of the country' and evening light, has persisted, to colour subsequent perceptions of places and those who live in them:

Such was about the sort of knowledge possessed of Christianity by the heathen of old time, who persecuted its adherents from the face of the earth, and then called them a *gens lucifuga*, a people who shunned the light of day. Such were Catholics in England, found in corners, and alleys, and cellars, and the housetops, or in the recesses of the country; cut off from the populous world around them, and dimly seen, as if through a mist or in twilight, as ghosts flitting to and fro, by the high Protestants, the lords of the earth.[5]

Such an atmosphere might be perceived, if only in romantic hindsight, to attend the northern recusant houses such as Samlesbury Hall, to the northwest of Preston, with its coded inscribed stones, or the secluded manor house of the Fitzherberts at Norbury in Derbyshire, with its panelled study inscribed with quotations from the Latin Bible; these are partly prudential maxims, but most are an articulation of defiance, resolution and resistance. If they are read as a whole, with a consciousness of the symbolic charge of their positioning within the room, the study becomes a place of memory, charged with depths of meaning in a way that only reveals its full pattern to the instructed reader moving mentally or physically about the space.[6]

Similarly, the celebrated grotto under the Twickenham house of the poet Alexander Pope can be perceived (and almost certainly was perceived by its creator) as a place of meditated recusant withdrawal into the shadows.[7] It is often forgotten that Pope's recusancy was a central part of his experience, and imagery of brilliant light and withdrawn shadow in his work is only intermittently read in that context. Pope suffered anxiety, financial loss and humiliation as a result of his religion, and remained dependent, for all the powerful friends made in his maturity, on the marginal circles among whom he had grown up. In Pope's own summary of his own position:

Yet like the Papist's is the Poet's state,
Poor and disarm'd and hardly worth your hate.[8]

An index of the seriousness of his suffering under legal penalty is that he was unable, because of the laws forbidding a Catholic to reside less than ten miles from central London, to go to London in his last illness for medical treatment.[9] He was also excluded from owning property or land, in a century when the neoclassical consensus endlessly emphasized the desirability (indeed the moral beauty) of the one thing that Pope could never have, an *inherited* estate. The house at Binfield, among the sequestered shades of Windsor Forest, in which Pope spent his youth was owned in fact by his father, but had to be owned as a legal fiction by complicit Protestant cousins. It was sold in panic in the year 1716, when the penal laws were rendered yet more stringent in the wake of a failed Jacobite rising the previous year.[10] After the enforced removal from Binfield, Pope gardened with passion and made his celebrated grotto, but all of it on rented land, and on rented land that he had occasionally to vacate on account of the laws against Catholics.

So Pope had to invent alternative mythologies for himself and for his community, mythologies which weave shadows and twilight – perhaps more acutely felt by him living so close to London and the court that he could never visit, rather than in the companionable remoteness of the dark corners of the land. One of these is the mock-heroic of *The Rape of the Lock*: the reiterated bathos of the poem has a completely different resonance within Pope's community, disarmed, disenfranchised and disqualified from ownership or action. Another is the praise of withdrawal from public life and the city in his *Imitations of Horace*, a poised praise of the virtue of a necessity.

But the grotto is at the centre of Pope's myth, in every sense. The place, and the range of associations with which he surrounded it, represent an alternative mythology of virtue in internal exile, an embracing of shadow and ruin as though they were choices freely made. Pope's letter to his friend Francis Atterbury, giving his reasons for continuing a Catholic after the death of his father, is well known and has been extensively discussed. The image of bright light is used by Pope for all the implications of acceptance into the governing ascendancy: 'It is certain, all the beneficial circumstances of life, and

all the shining ones, lie on the part you would invite me to.'[11]
The use of the word 'shining' here sets up a powerful contrast:
the shining world is everything that goes with public life, benefices
(and apostasy); Pope's construction of an environment for himself
is in the shadows, particularly in the shadows of his grotto, the
obscurity of the loyal subject (the loyal Papist) placed outside
the law. The grotto, enchanter's cave, fane of justice, is a substitute
for the inherited gardens that Pope can never own nor transmit.
The imagery of light and shade with which Pope attends his grotto
(and with which he expresses the retired life of the recusant as
opposed to the active life of the conformist) appears throughout
his verses in related contexts. As early as *Windsor Forest*, his pastoral
of an intermission in the application of the Penal Laws, the lines
that open the poem characterize the retreat of Pope's parents, as
well as of the nymphs of pastoral convention:

> Unlock your springs, and open all your shades.
> . . .
> Here waving groves a chequer'd scene display,
> And part admit, and part exclude the day[12]

Again eminence and brightness come together in the first of the
Ethic epistles to Henry St John, Viscount Bolingbroke:

> The few that glare, each Character must mark,
> You balance not the many in the dark.[13]

In the third Epistle, the shadowy, ancient country house of the
fasting miser Cotta (a place, 'like some lone Chartreuse', with a
strong suggestion of the retired houses of the recusants, the kind of
house that might have been ornamented with the sculptured stones
later used at the entrance to Pope's grotto) is thrown open to the day
as the woods, the overshadowed integrity and continuity of the family,
are felled by his spendthrift son,

Last, for his Country's love, he sells his lands,
To town he comes, compleats the nation's hope,
And head the bold Train-bands, and burns a Pope.[14]

In Epistle IV, the good Genius of the place floods the green garden with 'Shades from Shades', as opposed to the glaring Dutch-style gardens of Villario, where:

The strength of Shade contends with strength of light;
His bloomy Beds a waving Glow display,
Blushing in bright diversities of Day

So here, too, shadow is associated with wisdom and consideration, brilliant light with the passing fashions brought in with the Revolution.[15] The careful tracing of the imagery of shadows and shining are in themselves a key to unlock one particular and deep-seated train of thought running through Pope's work.

It would be presumptuous to write at any length of Pope's grotto, in the cellars of his riverside villa at Twickenham, as a location which embraced shadow and obscurity, which set itself forth as a place of withdrawn virtue in opposition to the prevailing brutality and veniality of Walpole's England. Maynard Mack has written superbly and at length of this aspect of the grotto,[16] on the Horatian inscription dedicating it to a life spent out of the light – '*secretum iter et fallentis semita vitae*' – an obscure journey by the unfrequented paths of life – and on Pope's verses on the status of the grotto as the 'Aegerean Grott' of virtue in opposition, in seclusion, almost in hiding.

The words associated by Pope with his grotto are all opposi-tions to the 'shining world': shadows, recesses, retreats. The only thing that shines in Pope's verses on his grotto is the sunlight on the river Thames and that is specifically mentioned in opposition to the glimmering 'drops' and 'crystals' of the 'shadowy cave'. Glimmering as opposed to shining, spangled points of light moving in twilight. The imagery of the Nymph Egeria that Pope attaches to his grotto carries the idea of supernatural wisdom instructing politicians (the legend is of the instruction of the primitive king of Rome, Numa) from a cave and grove just outside the city.[17] Pope's writings about his grotto will also bear, among their many meanings, the identification of the grotto as the location of the integrity that refuses compromise in religious as well as in political matters. There are many senses in which we can take the word shadowed – 'umbratus' – and 'removed to the margins by legal disability' cannot be discounted amongst them, any more than we can rule out a further implication in the famous couplet that concludes Pope's verses on the grotto:

> Let Such, Such only, tread this Sacred Floor,
> Who dare to love their Country and be poor.[18]

There is a special sense in which a recusant would write these lines: an implication of having chosen an English life under penalty rather than the easier life of a Continental exile.

This construction of an environment that is also a world withdrawn from the world is characteristic of many societies that have lived under shadow and penalty. The Jacobites come particularly to mind with their paper palaces and secret meetings: the defeated Earl of Mar's projected London for James VIII, his fantastically detailed Scottish paper palace for himself.[19] Baroque splendours in the imagination, hidden and disguised places of resort in the remote country – the church like a row of cottages, the Kaisersaal on an upper floor.[20]

When we try to take these speculations on Pope's grotto further, we have to proceed with considerable caution: there is no full documentation of the remodellings of the grotto even in Pope's lifetime.[21] The official description of the site as a listed monument is extremely cautious in dating any element of it.[22] This is important here, because of the presence of two carved stones of unmistakably recusant Catholic origin. Even in its present dilapidation, the roof of the grotto still bears these two carved slabs apparently dating from the seventeenth century.[23] These show respectively the crown of thorns and the Passion Shield or Arma Christi, the arrangement of the Five Wounds that constituted the badge of the last Catholic rising, the Pilgrimage of Grace of 1536. These stones seem to originate in the recusant north: the nature of the 'raised and sunk' lettering of the 'AK 1626' at the top of the Passion Shield is of a kind much more frequently encountered in the north than the south of Britain. We can conjecture that these are remnants from a recusant house, just possibly a house associated with the family of Pope's mother. The placing is highly significant: these stones are at the entrance to the grotto, echoing the use of the Passion Shield as a discreet (or sometimes deliberately indiscreet within a 'dark corner') visual signifier of a Catholic house. Modern scholarship has associated the Passion Shield with the mysterious line 'Five for the Symbols at your Door' in the British counting song 'Green Grow the Rushes', and certainly the figures '5555' are inscribed above the door of Sir Thomas Tresham's oppositionally recusant Triangular Lodge at Rushton in Northamptonshire.[24] The Passion Shield itself is found in the recusant chapel of Provost Skene's House in the Guestrow at Aberdeen and on recusant castles across the north of Scotland. So, in this respect, the grotto is associated with the Catholic tradition of secret places and secret writings, houses which declare their nature to the instructed by carved stonework at a door. With citizenship of dark corners goes the ability to read the covert and allusive elements of their inscriptions, the shadow-meanings half-concealed even in such a canonical work as *The Rape of the Lock*.

William Dobson's evening portraits of the Civil War Royalists find their culmination, forty years later, in the emotive likeness of *Lord Mungo Murray* (1668–1700), painted in 1683 by John Michael Wright.[25] This member of a highland Stuart-loyalist family was painted by the most accomplished painter of the recusant community towards the end of the reign of Charles II, when the hostilities of the century had again surfaced in Oates's Plot and the Exclusion Crisis of 1678, and the imminent succession of the Catholic James VII and II was to precipitate another sixty years of conflict and repression. So the picture of this very young aristocrat, deer-hunting in Wright's

John Michael Wright, *Lord Mungo Murray*, *c.* 1683, oil on canvas.

imagination of the upland landscape of Scotland, occupies an uneasy time of truce, a truce wearing to its end. It is difficult to interpret the contrast between the youthful sitter and Wright's stark landscape and autumnal twilight as anything but an expression of apprehension. The Murray family were to some extent ambiguous magnates, Marquesses and Dukes of Atholl, owning lands on the borders of highland and lowland Perthshire, who had held to an adroit middle course through the 'killing time' of Charles II's reign in Scotland, although they were unable later to avoid being drawn into the Jacobite conflicts that polarized upland and lowland Scotland for half a century from 1688.

The whole way that light is manipulated in Wright's portrait expresses anxiety about Lord Mungo's future, fear for the vigorous sportsman in his fine clothes (clothes which would accord exactly with the external attributes of a Celtic nobleman as they might have been itemized in a contemporary Gaelic praise poem)[26] in a society with an uncertain political future.

Wright intensifies the effects of light that had been used by William Dobson in the 1640s in his portraits of the beleaguered Royalist commanders of the Civil War: Lord Mungo is lit by a high fictive light from the right, casting his left side into strong shadow. This light is in unresolved contrast to the late-evening light on the landscape, after-sunset afterglow on a stormy autumn evening, against which the mountain peak in the distance is shown in dimming silhouette. The disquieting contrast is intensified by the care with which the foreground landscape is depicted as twilit in carefully worked browns with grey highlights, and the dim rocky shadows in the foreground, which suggest that Lord Mungo stands on a track through high moorland, despite the lowland nature of the foliage beside him. This foreground is a remarkably inventive passage of painting, rendering undergrowth shadowed by evening by means that owe a good deal to the depiction of underwoods in verdure tapestry. While there is a convention in European art of twilight portraits with a fictitious or theatrical light in the foreground, the contrast here is extreme enough to render the picture troubling; this early representation of an upland landscape seems to express only foreboding, anticipated sorrow.

Wright's career reached its high point in the brief and controversial reign of James VII and II when he acted as steward (and, presumably, iconographer) to the injudicious Royal embassy to the Papal Court in 1685–7. As well as breeding exponential mistrust of the king at home, James's diplomatic proposals to escalate sectarian conflict in Europe found no favour in Rome. The publication of Wright's magnificent (if suicidally tactless) illustrated account of the embassy on the ambassador's return to London can only have served to hasten the coup that drove his master into exile and the British Catholic community (himself included) back into obscurity.[27]

The 'Jacobite' conflict, which Wright's publication brought closer, lasted until the middle of the eighteenth century. Soon after the failed rising of 1715, James settled in Rome as a Papal pensioner and remained there throughout his long life, dying in 1766. For those 50 years his presence under the wing of the Papal Court greatly complicated the visits of those young members of the British elite who visited Rome, a city which remained the archaeological centre of a world that still looked to Greek and Roman antiquity as setting the standard for all the arts, as well as the contemporary art school and art market of Europe.

But for a young British gentleman or nobleman to visit Rome, the inevitable goal of the Grand Tour, was to enter what had to be considered in some degree as enemy territory. In one cogent sense, to make the Tour was to undertake a journey to the underworld. More than one enemy of the Whig and Hanoverian polity of Britain sat in state in Rome, and their community held the gates of the past and the gates to the world underground.

The Rome that encompassed both the last Stuarts and the Cavalier Piranesi was a place of twilight and rumours, with espionage operating on both sides, requiring the fair northern boys on the Tour to come to some kind of accommodation with the noontide shadows surrounding them: their exiled Catholic and Jacobite countrymen who were essential intermediaries through whom to obtain admission to the museums, palaces and monuments. The degree to which this was a source of anxiety can be seen in the letters that the architect Robert Adam wrote home in the 1750s: his family of builders and architects had Hanoverian contracts for military engineering in the Highlands, but the success of his Roman life depended on introductions from the Pretender's physician and the Abbé Grant. His assertions that his own position was uncompromised by such contacts, and that 'the best Whigs' did the same, are nervous and are repeated often.[28]

When Edward Gibbon made his 'cool and minute' survey of the antiquities of Rome, in the 1760s, his guide and instructor for the eighteen weeks of his course of study was James Byres (1734–1817), art dealer, antiquarian and architect.[29] Byres is almost a paradigmatic figure from the 'dark corners of the land' – an Aberdeenshire Catholic, whose Jacobite father had fled to the Continent after Culloden, with family connections in the priesthood and the wine trade. His works are scattered, dispersed and mostly forgotten. His greatest architectural work is the (unbuilt) late baroque palace at Wynnstay, which he designed for Sir Watkyn Williams-Wynne in drawings of extraordinary beauty and detail, finished down to the titles of the books in the library.[30] His chief archaeological enterprise was a study of the Etruscan painted tombs at Corneto (now Tarquinia), of which fragments were published posthumously.[31] This work holds traces of an analogical history, whereby the overshadowed Etruscans are paralleled to the Jacobite northern Scots, and their Roman adversaries to the conquering forces of Whig Britain. Byres can also be held to have exacted a quiet personal revenge on the Grand Tourists in the course of his Roman career as picture dealer and dealer in heavily restored antiquities.

It was after his studies with Byres that Gibbon had the first impulse to write of the decline of the Roman Empire (originally conceived only as a history of the City itself in its twilight years), an idea that came to him at evening at the end of summer:

> In my Journal, the place and moment of conception are recorded; the fifteenth of October, 1764, in the close of evening, as I sat

musing in the Church of the Zoccolanti or Franciscan friars, while they were singing vespers in the Temple of Jupiter in the ruins of the Capitol.[32]

It is a curious thought: the author meditating on Roman decline was a citizen of a polity that felt as never before that it had taken on the power and rising authority of the ancient empires; his guide and tutor was a displaced citizen of a defeated polity claiming a fantastical antiquity of its own, through the mythological early kings of Scots from whom the shadow-king in the Palazzo Muti derived his descent. And yet they met as equals, even friends, on the neutral (if not easy) ground of Rome, united in a common classical culture, if divided in religion.

Byres was a friend and associate of Giovanni Battista Piranesi (1720–1778).[33] Piranesi dedicated two etched plates of excavated antiquities to him,[34] and it is Piranesi's etchings that form an extraordinary record of the patched and inhabited ruins of Roman antiquity as repositories of darkness, chasms of twilight. Piranesi's Rome is gigantic, dwarfing the anguished, dwindled figures of contemporaries (which of course lend excessive scale to the monuments) beneath the crushing, accumulated weight of the past. And the past is even more insistent in the damaged and half-repaired condition of its remains, the poor dwelling built into the fallen portico, the plumy weeds and saplings rooted in the broken cornice. Hauntingly, Piranesi's grand effects of scale and shadow are anticipated to a remarkable degree in the built works of Sir John Vanbrugh (1664–1726), in the massiveness of Blenheim (1705–22), but above all in the lowering magnificence of his last work, Seaton Delaval Hall in Northumberland (1722). Here, on an exposed and remote site, Vanbrugh plays dark games with scale: massive rustication, oversized stoneworks, even an extraordinary flattened cushion moulding that implies that the lower courses of the building are being forced down into the earth by the weight of the towers and columns above. And the high masses of the interior seem to draw smoke and shadow into themselves.

Metaphorically, almost all of Piranesi's plates published as
Della magnificenza ed architettura de' Romani (1761) and *Vedute di
Roma* (1748–78) concern themselves with twilight. This is not only
expression of the belatedness felt daily by a society visibly inhabiting the damaged ruins of titanic antiquity, but also a late, almost
violent, manifestation of the baroque manipulation of the viewer's
emotions. Piranesi's etchings confront the viewer with unstable
viewpoints, grating or repellent textures, uncontrollable vastness,
stark contrasts of light and dark, endless ambiguitites of place and
scale. The depth of Piranesi's shadows is proverbial as a triumph
of the printmaker's art, but the emotional or poetic force of this
shadowy depth is prodigious.

The Vaults of the Villa of Maecenas at Tivoli are pierced by
openings that let in full daylight, but the shadows under the surviving
vaults are so profound as to enfeeble or defy the power of the light.[35]
The Interior of the Baths in Hadrian's Villa again shows depth of
shade in daylight, with webs of what seems sentient or even menacing vegetation springing from the vaults above.[36] *The Interior of the
Canopus*, at the same site, has a sense of shaded, even brooding, ruin
with particularly expressive and mysterious staffage figures. Below the
littered ground level, in which the frantic little figures are digging,
Piranesi hints and sketches black-dark lower vaults into which they
will soon break.[37] And all this is doubly true of the shadowy, repli-
cating, endless subterranean prisons of the *Carceri d'invenzione*.

So, in the Rome of Piransesi, which remains to a remarkable
degree the Rome of the European imagination,[38] twilight gathers
below the city, twilight as a constant is always lurking just out of the
sunlight. It is perhaps significant that Piranesi died just before the
radical improvement of artificial lighting in the eighteenth century:[39]
his interior twilight is not only born of the contrast of white noontide light with dim churches and shuttered palaces, but also from
accumulated, disquieting recollections of exploring antiquity, sunk
deep into the earth, by the light of flickering torches. All these contrasts and feelings are redoubled in the *Carceri*, which go on to be
crucial images for romantic writers and painters, perhaps beyond

their intentions, so far as those can ever be reconstructed, or conjectured. The same sense of ever-lurking interior twilight shaped some of the most memorable work of ter Borch in the seventeenth century (deep rooms and the dimness of overcast northern daylight) and will later shape most of the paintings of Hammershøi, in whose works the shadows are always gathered in the interior rooms of the enfilade, ready to return, clustering as day fades.

While Piranesi was content to record the Roman past in his etchings as a brooding, sunken, half-wrecked presence, the prodigiously skilled twentieth-century British printmaker F. L. Griggs (1876–1938) spent his whole career evoking the English past from fragments, or in the closely related enterprise of re-imagining a lost medieval England. Their uses of the medium are sharply contrasted: Piranesi massing depths of shadow, Griggs using every nuance of the inked plate to convey fading light, late sunlight refracted in gathering mist, the elegiac evening light that shines on the Catholic England whose loss he laments.

Griggs is an artist to some degree on the margins, partly because of his narrowly focused subject matter – antiquarian views of England's ruins, fragments of an imaginary holy city of the Middle Ages – partly because of the Catholicism that he embraced in 1912, thus identifying himself with a community not quite integrated to the English mainstream. Despite this, and despite the financial and artistic difficulties of his later years, he touches on, indeed constitutes a point of contact between, a number of central movements of his times. While he inherited much from Samuel Palmer,[40] especially in techniques of representing effects of diffused light in etched line, he was associated for much of his adult life with the later generation of the Arts and Crafts movement in the Gloucestershire Cotswolds, working as a repairing architect and building a ruinously expensive but faithfully vernacular house for himself. Towards the end of his life he was an important influence on the new generation of English Romantics coming to maturity in the 1930s.

What gives Griggs his place in this chapter is the passion with which he imagined a pre-Reformation England, and the elegaic

F. L. Griggs, *Duntisbourne Rouse*, 1927, etching.

transference of losses in his own lifetime – the slow erosion of
undisturbed rural England, the terrible personal and national losses
of the First World War – into one finely modulated lamentation
for the world destroyed by the Reformation. His subjects are almost
all distant and unfrequented places and almost always twilight is
the medium that crosses the aching disjunctions of then and now.
Evening light softens and moulds the ruins, smoothes or mellows
the losses of violence and time. In one of the visits to Ireland that
Griggs made during the First World War (visits which were crucial
to his development as an artist) he saw a ruined medieval church by
twilight, in remote country in County Wexford:

> I saw it one green-below-&-blue-above sort of evening . . . we never
> get that sort of blue light [in England] – it's very mysterious & lovely
> & haunted . . . there's the ruined church –ruined by Catholics rather
> than have it defamed . . . There are mysterious and beautiful huge
> trees in the neighbourhood.[41]

From this point begin his series of ecclesiastical ruins in their last
decay, pastoral but terminal, seen by the last of the light, either in late
evening or in the last sunlight before an obliterating storm.[42] Indeed
during his last wartime visit to Ireland, his mind channelled by his
own approaching sorrows – possible conscription and the ill-health of
his fiancée – he drew the compositions for almost all his subsequent
etchings in one sustained period of creative work. As he said later,
'One great period of inspiration and the rest of one's life spent working
it out.'[43] These were the designs for the imagined medieval cities
and buildings, intact and perfect, but always seen at some remove, a
reminder that only imagination can connect with a past so completely
gone. There is always some obstacle in the foreground, separating the
contemporary viewer from the pristine beauty of the past: fortification
or water, moat and wall, shadow, rough ground. There is a whole
series of these in Griggs's work: *The Ford* (1915–24), *Sellenger* (1917),
The Minster (1918) and the lamentingly named *Anglia Perdita*
(1921–6). Together, they make up an almost-reconstruction of a city
of faith of the past. There are some images that exist in a territory
between these imaginations and Griggs's pastorals of decay: the ruined
Fen Monastery (1923–6), sinking into the soil and the slow waters.
A tour de force of the rendering of light in etched line is *Mortmain*
(1918), the deserted manor house in fading, diffused sunlight (a
spoiled, haunted monastic grange according to Griggs[44]) absolutely
cut off from the viewer by black fortifications and a dark ditch.

Later in his life, in July 1925, Griggs wrote of transfiguring
summer twilight as the light he sought constantly to capture in his
graphic work, 'Above all, for me, those ineffable lights & gleams
when the source of light is invisible, like a July-evening after rain,
after sunset',[45] and it is with these last lights that he articulated his

elegiac views of ruins sunk into pastoral, the abandoned church turned to a barn. In *Duntisbourne Rouse* (1927) a remote and simple Gloucestershire church is seen at twilight across a stream, cut off from the viewer, seen by the last misty sunlight under a rising crescent moon. Griggs wrote on one impression 'presently the rooks will have passed and the sheep will be folded and the first star will shine'.[46] Much the same atmosphere characterizes *Stanley Pontlarge* (1939) and *Priory Farm* from the same year, both homages to the nineteenth-century masters of etching Samuel Palmer and John Sell Cotman: Palmer's deep country surrounding Cotman's ruined provincial churches. Perhaps the most expressive of these twilight pastorals is *Maur's Farm* (1913, with many subsequent reworkings), which embodies a personal chronicle of loss, conveyed by the fading of evening light.[47] The subject is an extensive monastic complex of buildings turned to a farm, the church tower still intact in the middle distance, haystacks on the right taking the place of vanished buildings. On the left a tree grows up through the ruined cloister. Maur or Maurus is a sixth-century saint, one of the disciples of St Benedict: Griggs implies that this farm was once a Benedictine monastery dedicated to St Maur, the saint who he chose as his own patron or confirmation saint. As the war of 1914–18 deepened, Griggs, devoured by a sense of personal and communal loss, twice darkened the sky above the farmyard, until he reached the after-sunset light striking up into the clouds, and finally mourning nightfall.[48]

While Grigg's imaginations are of distant ages of faith, the memory of the English Catholic community focuses rather on its years under the shadow – the underground years from the Reformation to the early nineteenth century, the years of the Penal Laws and the Jesuit mission to the remote 'dark corners' of England. In the 1870s and early 1880s Gerard Manley Hopkins (1844–1889) lived in rural Lancashire at the Jesuit College at Stonyhurst.

Earlier in his clerical career, in September 1874, he had recorded his own appreciation of the dimmed and uncertain light of the

F. L. Griggs, *Maur's Farm*, 1913 (with subsequent reworkings), etching.

underwoods of north Wales: 'Caerwys wood, a beautiful place. The day being then dark and threatening we walked some time under a grey light more charming than sunshine falling through boughs and leaves.'[49] And while he was in Lancashire, his intense observations of the natural world included a series of brilliantly precise considerations of evening skies: indeed, he became a member of the worldwide association of observers who recorded the atmospheric changes precipitated by the eruption of Krakatoa in 1883.[50] Long before that he had cultivated the ability to record natural phenomena in the idiosyncratic, precise vocabulary in which he composed his verses. On the evening of 12 March 1870, for example, he recorded the clear blue upper air traversed by 'a broad slant causeway rising from left to right of wisped or grass cloud, the wisps lying across; the sundown yellow, moist with light but ending at the top in a foam of delicate white pearling',[51] or, returning from the community's vacation in mid-August 1873 and walking three hours and more through rain-wet fields between Blackburn and Stonyhurst, he observed the western clouds, 'with strong printing glass edges, westward lamping with tipsy bufflight, the colour of yellow roses. Parlick ridge like a pale goldish skin without body.'[52] In the November of the same year, he recorded sunset profound in colour, projecting its depths of tone onto the field of the western sky, presumably reflecting in water-droplets formed around carbon particles blown loose from industrial Lancashire:

> balks of grey cloud searched with long crimsonings running along their hanging folds. A few minutes later the brightness over; one great dull rope coiling overhead sidelong from the sunset, its dewlaps and bellyings painted with a maddery campion-colour that seemed to stoop and drop like sopped cake; the further balk great gutterings and ropings, gilded above, jotted with a more bleeding red beneath and then a juicy tawny 'clear' below . . .[53]

In August 1874 Hopkins made the last of a series of speculative observations of the phenomenon of the evening sky called *rayons du crépuscule*, one that was much to preoccupy him later: 'I clearly saw then . . . beams rising from the horizon in the east due opposite to the sunset; this was some time before sunset . . . I think they are atmospheric merely.'[54] Hopkins was beguiled by these anti-crepuscular rays, the easternmost points of columns of intensified evening sunlight combed into light and dark by cloud-shadow. He was confused for some time by a fancied resemblance to a rainbow, later almost convinced that they were subjective phenomena. He returned to them in one of his most closely observed contributions to *Nature*.

Before the arrival of easily and accurately reproduced scientific illustrations, the discourse of science had to be evocative, and often crossed into what would now be called the discourse of literature. Here there is a remarkable convergence: Hopkins's endlessly inventive and neologistic language of description resonates with scientific attempts to render natural phenomena ever more accurately in words. Indeed, Hopkins's descriptions of the sky are not atypical of contributions to *Nature*. His letter of November 1882 appeared on the same page as an early observation of the changing skies of the 1880s, a description of 'unusual cloud-glow at sunset' by F.A.R. Russell, who was to go on to become a major contributor to the Royal Society volume on the eruption of Krakatoa.

Hopkins raises the subject of anti-crepuscular rays almost tentatively, although the phenomenon had already been discussed fairly extensively in *Nature*:[55]

> I have several times seen in this country . . . beams or spokes in the eastern sky about sunset, springing from a point due opposite to the sun. The appearance is not very strongly marked, and I used to think I must have been mistaken . . . There seems no reason why the phenomenon should not be common, and perhaps if looked out for it would be found to be.[56]

He goes on, though, to speculate about intensity of observation, and about true observation as opposed to the recognition of the expected:

> But who looks east at sunset? Something in the same way everybody has seen the rainbow; but the solar halo which is really commoner, few people, not readers of scientific works have ever seen at all. The appearance in question is due to cloud-shadows in an unusual perspective and in a clear sky; now shadow may not only be seen carried by misty, mealy, dusty or smoky air near the ground, but even on almost every bright day, by seemingly clear air high overhead.[57]

Hopkins has crossed quietly into the discourse of his own verses with the metrical and precise 'misty, mealy, dusty or smoky' coining and borrowing a sense for 'mealy' from the vocabulary of horticulture – the 'meal' or *farina* sprinkling the petals of a florist's flower. The two kinds of sky that can carry the rays are as present to the reader as is the gleam of turned earth in his poems.

A shorter, intensely poetic letter appeared a year later in the same journal, returning to 'shadow-beams in the east at sunset':

> The phenomenon of beams of shadow meeting in the east at sunset . . . was beautifully witnessed here today and yesterday. Both days

were unusually clear; there was, nevertheless, a 'body' in the air,
without which the propagation of the beams could not take place.
Yesterday the sky was striped with cirrus cloud like the swaths of a
hayfield; only in the east there was a bay or reach of clear blue sky,
and in this the shadow-beams appeared, slender, colourless, and
radiating every way like a fan wide open. This lasted from 3.40 to
about 4.30. Today the sky was cloudless, except for a low bank in
the west; in the east was a 'cast' of blue mist, from which sprang
alternate broad bands of rose colour and blue, slightly fringed.
I was not able to look for them until about 4.30, when the sun was
down, and they soon faded . . . it is merely an effect of perspective,
but a strange and beautiful one.[58]

Here, the intensity of observation inevitably recalls Ruskin's sky
descriptions, which he brought as evidence of climate change in
the 1884 lectures 'The Storm Cloud of the Nineteenth Century',[59]
and the reflection inevitably recurs that the two writers were
observing the skies of the 1870s and early 1880s from Coniston and
Stonyhurst, from viewpoints not far distant from each other. Ruskin
believed that the plague cloud of industrial pollution had blotted
the evening skies of England a decade before Krakatoa erupted,
and so in fact he attributed some volcanic phenomena of the 1880s
to his carbon cloud.[60]

Hopkins's most extensive contribution to *Nature* was in a letter
describing 'Krakatoa' skies, dated from Stonyhurst on 21 December
1883, which was published in the journal in January 1884,[61] where
it appeared as the greater part of a compilation of correspondence
about 'the remarkable sunsets' and how they differ from the colours
and forms of evenings observed before the eruption. It deserves
quotation at some length:

the sunrises and sunsets of other days, however bright and beautiful,
have not given any such effects as were witnessed, to take an instance,
here on Sunday night, December 16th . . . the remarkable and
specific features of the late sunsets have not been before or at sunset

proper, they have been after-glows, and have lasted long, very long, after . . . *intense and lustreless* and that both in the sky and on the earth. The glow is intense, this is what strikes everyone; it has prolonged the daylight and optically changed the season; it bathes the whole sky; it is mistaken for the reflection of a great fire; at the sundown itself and southwards from that on December 4, I took a note of it more as inflamed flesh than the lucid reds of ordinary sunsets. On the same evening the fields facing west glowed as if overlaid with yellow wax.

But it is also lustreless. A bright sunset lines the clouds so that their brims look like gold, brass, bronze, or steel. It fetches out those dazzling flecks or spangles which people call fish-scales. It gives a mackerel or dappled cloudrack the appearance of quilted crimson silk, or a ploughed field glazed with crimson ice. These effects may have been seen in the late sunsets, but they are not the specific after-glow; that is without gloss or lustre.

His intensity of observation is then turned to the illumination of things on earth. His comparison is drawn from painted representations of dimmed light, relating back to that foreground illumination, the 'self-luminous' quality, which Ruskin praised in the depiction of a moment of late twilight in Millais's *Autumn Leaves*:[62]

The two things together, that is intensity of light and want of lustre, give to objects on the earth the peculiar illumination which may be seen in studios or other well-like rooms, and which itself affects the practise of painters and may be seen in their works, notably Rembrandt's, disguising or feebly showing the outlines and distinctions of things, but fetching out white surfaces and coloured stuffs with a rich and inward and seemingly self-luminous glow.

From his own repertory of past observation of the varied colourations of dusk, he discerns comprehensively that the colouration of volcanic evening skies is distinctive especially in its regularity:

Four colours in particular have been noticeable in these after-glows, and in a fixed order of time and place – orange, lowest and nearest the sundown; above this, and broader, green; above this, broader still, a variable red, ending in being crimson; above this, a faint lilac. The lilac disappears; the green deepens, spreads, and encroaches on the orange; and the red deepens, spreads, and encroaches on the green, till at last one red, varying downwards from crimson to scarlet or orange fills the west and south.

He notes particularly the impurity of the colours, focusing on the mixed quality of the red:

The red is very impure, and not evenly laid on. On the 4th it appeared brown, like a strong light behind tortoiseshell, or Derbyshire alabaster. It has been well compared to the colour of incandescent iron. Sometimes it appears like a mixture of chalk with sand and muddy earths. The pigments for it would be ochre and Indian red . . .

and goes on to itemize the texture of the coloured surfaces – 'streamers, fine ribbing or mackerelling, and other more curious textures, the colour varying with the texture' – in his virtuoso description of the sunset of 16 December 1883:

A bright glow had been round the sun all day and became more remarkable towards sunset. It then had a silvery or steely look, with soft radiating streamers and little colour . . . there was a pale gold colour, brightening and fading by turns for ten minutes as the sun went down. After the sunset the horizon was, by 4.10, lined a long way by a glowing tawny light, not very pure in colour and distinctly textured in tawny hummocks, bodies like a shoal of dolphins, or in what are called gadroons, or as the Japanese conventionally represent waves.

Then follows further description of this particular sunset – as precisely cadenced and carefully visualized as much of Hopkins's original verse:

The glowing vapour above this was as yet colourless; then this took
a beautiful olive or celadon green, not so vivid as the previous day's,
and delicately fluted; the green belt was broader than the orange, and
pressed down on and contracted it. Above the green in turn appeared
a red glow, broader and burlier in make; it was softly brindled, and in
the ribs or bars the colour was rosier, in the channels where the blue
of the sky shone through it was a mallow colour. Above this was
a vague lilac. The red was first noticed 45° above the horizon, and
spokes or beams could be seen in it, compared by one beholder to
a man's open hand. By 4.45 the red had driven out the green, and,
fusing with the remains of the orange, reached the horizon. By
that time the east, which had a rose tinge, became of a duller red,
compared to sand . . . the ground of the sky in the east was green
or else tawny, and crimson only in the clouds. A great sheet of heavy
dark cloud, with a reefed or puckered make, drew off the west in the
course of the pageant; the edge of this and the smaller pellets of cloud
that filed across the bright field of the sundown caught a livid green.
At 5 the red in the west was fainter, at 5.20 it became notably rosier
and livelier; but it was never of a pure rose. A faint dusky blush was
left as late as 5.30 or later. While these changes were going on in the
sky, the landscape of Ribblesdale glowed with a frowning brown.[63]

These superb observations were made relatively late in Hopkins's last
stay in Lancashire, not long before his departure to Ireland, thus it
remained to his friend and colleague in the Stonyhurst observatory,
Father Stephen Perry, to make an observation and collection that
corroborates much of Ruskin's disquiet about carbon in the atmosphere in the 1880s.[64] In May 1884 *Nature* published Perry's letter on
the 'extraordinary darkness at midday' on 26 April 1884:

The extraordinary darkness that occurred here suddenly on the
morning of the 26th is deserving of record, as being the most
intense that is remembered by any of the inhabitants . . . 11 a.m. . . .
the sky became rapidly darker in the west-south-west. The wind was
blowing from the north-east with a velocity of five miles an hour . . .

At 11.30 the darkness was so great that it was found impossible to read even bold print (small pica) close by the window and at this time a dense black cloud with a slightly yellowish tinge hung over the south-west sky; the blackness being the most intense at 10 degrees above the horizon. At 11.35 it became somewhat lighter, and at 11.40 the rain began to fall, and in forty minutes 0.114 inch of rain-water was collected in our rain-gauges, the whole being almost as black as ink, and full of fine carbon in suspension. Hail that fell a mile off to the south-west by south, and both hail and snow that fell on the hills two miles to the west, were also black. At Preston, fourteen miles to the south-west, the darkness was very marked.[65]

A measure of this black Lancashire rain was preserved by the Stonyhurst observatory in a sealed bottle, which still survives in the treasure house of the museum collections at the College. Ruskin had thus described the carbon-laden air of the 1880s:

While I have written this sentence the cloud has again dissolved itself, like a nasty solution in a bottle, with miraculous and unnatural rapidity, and the hills are in sight again . . . One lurid gleam of white cumulus in upper lead-blue sky, seen for half a minute through the sulphurous chimney-pot vomit of blackguardly cloud beneath, where its rags were thinnest.[66]

Geoffrey Hill, in his poised evocation of the Hodder Valley as it is today – he is a poet who has been preoccupied through his long career with dissidents and the landscapes of dissidence – sees ragwort bright under the trees by the shadowed water that Hopkins loved, and considers the cosmopolitan and English splendours of the College and its gardens in the valley below. He sees especially the contemporary clarity of sky over the observatory amidst its shaved lawns on the terraces, as a consequence of the silenced post-industrial north having unwittingly restored the air of England to its ancient translucency:

Two nights' and three days' rain, with the Hodder
well up, over its alder roots; tumblings
of shaly late storm light; the despised
ragwort, luminous . . .

. . .

. . . Downstream . . .
Stonyhurst's ample terraces confer
with the violent, comely
nature of Loyola and the English weather;
stone, *pelouse*, untouched by carbon droppings,
now, from the spent mills. . . .[67]

Walking through the trees, up the steep slope from the river.
Turning right into the lane, pausing by the gate to look out over the
rich valley lying below the ridge of Pendle Hill. Columns of smoke
in winter sunlight, cross-hatched hedgerows, scattered manors.
Brightness from the west moulding the tower of Mytton church.
Then on, uphill and away from Hopkins's bluebell wood, past the
masters' houses. Left at the first gap, over the rough track, past the
eighteenth-century front of St Mary's House where Hopkins lived
in the 1870s, along the brothers' walk through the trees, and into the
College. The longest corridor in Lancashire, then the grand staircase
with the pale statue of the Virgin on the broad landing. Through the
top refectory – portraits of martyrs, portraits of soldiers – and on
through the far door onto the stairs to the Sodality Chapel and the
Library. The great library gallery running the depth of the building,
tall bookcases crowned with busts, and above the sequence of portraits of Inka Kings. Paintings, manuscripts, reliquaries, an archaic
cricket bat propped in a corner. Into the Square Library, galleried,
double-height, the long windows looking the length of the avenue,
the canals, the great trees. And on the table the sealed bottle of the
black rain, handwritten label fading a little, but still easily legible.

Cupping it in one hand and tilting it slowly to stir the night-black
carbon, the invasive shadow, all the sorrow of the nineteenth century,
slowly seeping up into clear water.

A bottle of polluted 'black rain' collected at Stonyhurst College Observatory, Clitheroe, Lancashire, on 26 April 1884.

..."EVENING LATE, BY THEN THE CHEWING FLOCKS
HAD TAKEN THEIR SUPPERS OF THE SAVOURY HERB
OF KNOT-GRASS DEW-BESPRENT."

Samuel Palmer, *Evening*, 1834, mezzotint by Welby Sheldon after Palmer, for a translation of the First Eclogue in *An English Version of the Eclogues of Virgil by S. Palmer, with Illustr*[*ations*] *by the Author* (1883).

5
HESPERIDES

Absolute stillness through the white nights of high summer. Absolute
quiet, absolute distance, when the sun makes its slow journey far
into the north. Time slows in these June evenings and all but halts
in the lucid twilight that lingers through into the hours of night.
It is the place and time to consider Kant's discernment of the fruits
of summer evenings:

> *Die Nacht ist erhaben, der Tag ist schön. Gemütsarten, die ein*
> *Gefühl für das Erhabene besitzen, werden durch die ruhige Stille*
> *eines Sommerabends . . . allmählich in hohe Empfindungen gezogen,*
> *von Freundschaft, von Verachtung der Welt, von Ewigkeit . . .*[1]

> Night is sublime, day beautiful. Temperaments with a feeling for
> the sublime are drawn gradually by the quiet peace of a summer
> evening towards lofty sensations of friendship, eternity, indifference
> to the world . . .

And indeed the world can seem very distant from such a secluded
northern place. Coming back to the house at the stroke of midnight
on midsummer night, with the northern sky still bright: lucent
whitish-yellow at the horizon shading into pale blue above. Small
charcoal clouds moving from right to left. Tree branches crisply
silhouetted. To the south, fences, grass and house all still show in
colour: 18-point type is still legible. From time to time there is a little
stir of wind, neither hot nor cold.

It is the stillness that Goethe evoked in his 'Wanderer's
Nightsong': late light on the ridge of the hills, birdsong hushing,
windless calm. All things stilling, quietening to the end: '*Balde, ruhest*

du auch' (Soon, you too will rest). Those eight short lines, as Schubert set them to music in the high summer of 1815, a few weeks after the Battle of Waterloo, summarize a whole epoch of feeling, in which summer twilight became a place of peace and of longing for peace. So much of the previous century had thought of itself as owning the splendour of the sun at noon. Bright empires rivalled the ancients, moving, in all the languages of Europe, towards the dubious, coercive clarity of the Enlightenment. No wonder that those defeated communities in exile and obscurity were forced to accept the metaphor of life in obscurity, so completely had the rulers of the age laid claim to the light.

A current of disquiet was the inevitable undertow of that 'great century'. Acceptance of the shades that follow the sun about the globe, acceptance of the attrition of time and of the fragility of things. This acceptance began to insinuate itself even at the meridian of eighteenth-century confidence. The shadow-king was always a distant presence in his twilight court at Rome. Disquiet found expression in verses of elegy and evening. Mourning urns and artificial ruins took their places in the great landscape gardens, which themselves became vast emblems of mortality as their leaves withered and fell every autumn. Alexander Pope's *Rape of the Lock* ends in a sudden, involuntary vision of Miss Fermor's beautiful hair laid in the dust of the grave. Lord Cobham commemorated his dead friend, the dramatist William Congreve, in a monument on an island in the lake at Stowe, with a monkey holding a mirror, unreadable and unendurable in its implications. But all this is transformed, as the century ends, in the celebration of twilight as the time of the visionary peace distilled in Schubert's song.

After the turmoil of wars and revolutions, which brought the noontide certainties of the eighteenth century to an end, all the arts in northern Europe seem to have turned together to the celebration of twilight: in Wordsworth's early work, for example, one finds the meticulously observed last rays of summer twilight in 'An Evening Walk':

> . . . small,
> Gleams that upon the lake's still bosom fall;
> Soft o'er the surface creep those lustres pale
> Tracking the motions of the fitful gale.
> With restless interchange at once the bright
> Wins on the shade, the shade upon the light.[2]

And when darkness falls on the waters, the landscape itself becomes almost sentient, and certainly the quality of the poet's awareness of it becomes something extraordinary:

> Air listens, like the sleeping water, still,
> To catch the spiritual music of the hill.[3]

I walk away from the house and down into the wood, on such a summer night, towards the sound of water from the fall of stream into pool. There is no hint of chill to make me quicken my pace, no hint of approaching darkness to hurry me on the way. A grass path stretches away to the north, into the daylight that still sends its last low rays amongst the trunks of the trees. It is as though light and summer will have no end on these evenings when the sun hardly dips below the hill, showing a streak of brilliance along the northern horizon all through the short, lucent nights. The floor of the wood is thick with ferns, self-sown foxgloves stand in ranks beside the winding path. Wild raspberries have just begun to set their fruits in the clearings between the trees. I follow the broad grass path through the trees in falling light filtering from the north through the still-young leaves and over the ferns and mossy branches on the floor of the wood.

This is the time of the summer night loved by the Romantic poets and painters of the early nineteenth century, this peaceful evening offering its glimpse of otherworlds, the physical landscape of twilight opening out into territories of the imagination whose 'spiritual music' sounds most clearly at nightfall. Samuel Palmer (1805–1881) found *his* earthly paradise in high summer, in his nineteenth year, in the twilight coming down on the fields to the south of London, 'Remember the Dulwich sentiment at very late twilight time with the rising dews (the tops of the hills quite clear) like a delicious dream',[4] and thus he began on a series of sketchbook drawings of spiritualized twilight landscapes, folded flocks and harvested corn, the crescent moon resting on the horizon and the hills. These sketches found a more lasting form in the series of paintings and pastoral etchings that he produced throughout his career. *Evening Late* (1834) expresses the senses of visitation and vision that Palmer continually drew from the twilight. The shepherd rests amongst his sheep, stooks of corn fill the field. The lower half of the western sky is faintly lit by a sun that has sunk far below the horizon, trees show black against it and a crescent moon with a nimbus about it rises into the dark upper sky. It is an image of profound calm and yet of fugacity – of one moment of captured stillness, even as evening grows cold and the summer moves to harvest and its end.

A long sequence of verses entitled 'Twilight Time', fair copied in the sketchbook, confirm that for Palmer twilight was the time when the visionary and spiritual aspects of light and landscape were most intensely manifested to him:

> . . . twilight time, doth seem more fair,
> And lights the soul up more than day,[5]

Palmer saw his darkling Kent as a foreshadowing of Paradise: life had not yet turned on him, and the new visionary influence of Blake was still powerful:

> Creation sometimes pours into the spiritual eye the radiance of
> Heaven: the green mountains that glimmer in a summer gloaming
> from the dusky yet bloomy East . . . [These things] shed a mild,
> a grateful, an unearthly lustre into the inmost spirits, and seem
> the interchanging twilight of that peaceful country, where there is
> no sorrow and no night. Every light eternally on the change: yet no
> light finally extinguished.[6]

Almost everything distinctive that Palmer achieved in his later life derives its energy from this early experience. Palmer's work resonates closely with that of his near-contemporary Caspar David Friedrich: both are landscape painters intensely focused on twilight and effects of light. Both were pietistic, contemplative, largely self-educated Protestants, mystical in affinity. Both also were sustained in their work by the attribution of intense, mostly personal and hermetic, allegorical or transcendent significance to landscape and light.

When the northern Scottish sun has set behind the trunks of the trees to the northwest, further into the north than seems possible, it casts almost exactly the light of Caspar David Friedrich's painting *Evening* (1820–21), and I might almost be standing amongst the grassy slopes and bushes in its foreground, where his two shadowy figures stand together in the underwoods. The scale of the picture is deceiving: in reproduction its depth of receding planes make it look far larger than an original that is no bigger than a large postcard, for all its force when seen across a gallery.

Or it could be in another wood with a belated glimpse of summer sky – in John Sell Cotman's *Duncombe Park* (c. 1806–8), one of the experimental wilderness paintings he made on his youthful tour of the north of England.[7] Both Friedrich and Cotman delighted in painting obscure places, retired places, even disappointing places, and transforming them by their concentration on what the westering light reveals or conceals. This shift of sensibility, the spiritual transformation of longing into feeling for light, found contemporary expression in Wordsworth's poem 'The Excursion' (1814), with its resplendent sky seen when the narrator has escaped the night and twilight of the mists on the hills:

Glory beyond all glory ever seen
By waking sense or by the dreaming soul!
. . .
By earthly nature had the effect been wrought
Upon the dark materials of the storm

Caspar David Friedrich, *The Evening*, 1820–21, oil on canvas.

Here the poet balances a feeling that the cities and chasms in the clouds amount to more than an earthly vision, with the reminder that it is 'earthly nature' that has apparently granted him a glimpse of an otherworld:

> That which I *saw* was the revealed abode
> Of Spirits in beatitude . . .

and his italicization of 'saw' is, in itself, an affirmation of the wonder and ambiguity of a moment, which shares with Palmer and Friedrich alike a sense of nature more than transformed by light.

All Romantic artists shared, to some extent, their time's intensity of feeling about light and landscape, engaging in a passionate colloquy with place as though it could answer them, respond to them, instruct them. But how different Friedrich's woodland sunset is from Cotman's. Friedrich's bears its weight of religious allegory, where Cotman's invests

personal emotion in the memory of his solitary walk amongst the
trees under the fading sky. For Friedrich, sunset is the paradise to
which the shadowed walkers are travelling. The fence of tree trunks
and the rising powder-blue mists from the valley beyond are the
barrier of years and their illusions that stand in the way of the
couple's last journey together to the bright regions of the evening sky.

For northern artists, paradise is removed to the clouds or
composed in the distant mountains by the evening light: often for
Friedrich a glimpse of paradise is implied on the far side of a river
or an inlet of the sea, in distant spires seen across darkening fields.
Palmer's paradise is hinted to be the next valley beyond his softly
wooded hills in the late summer twilight, and sometimes his still
landscapes themselves become a half-lit Eden in their fruitful stillness. This kind of allegorical landscape comes to Friedrich and
other painters of the north so naturally that it is as if their painting
is simply giving form to the shared feelings of a generation and
a region.

For the young Cotman, delight in place is bound up with the
remembered physical exultation of scrambling up outcrops of
shale and through brambles to the wild viewpoint of his picture.
The painting itself is a record of his reluctance to go back to the
lamplit house on that summer evening, one of his numbered days
of freedom before a life of responsibility and depression overcame
him.[8] His flawless paintings of obscure bends in rivers, tangled
}corners of woodland, horses drinking at a trough in the shadows,
are records of moments of inexplicable intensity of feeling about
everyday things. He rejoiced physically in the steep walk to the high
rock, the climb down the trackless riverbank in wild weather, the
storm driving through the leaves as he bent over his drawing book.
His paintings carry with them the bodily memory of toiling to a
viewpoint. Like the feeling of labouring up Tap o' Noth, to reach
the Pictish fort on the summit at evening, and to have suddenly at
my feet all the outworks of the Cairngorms in bracken and heather
and smoky pinewood and mist dimming to summer blue, summer
floating gold.

And so I watch the sunset between the boughs in the wood behind the house, and the slow evening wears on almost imperceptibly, moving unmarked towards midnight. At the end of the wood I take the path that leads on northwards up the hill. Coming out into the hilltop field, I can turn and look straight out to the north at last. Although this is on the 57th parallel, just short of the magical 60 degrees where it is truly twilight all night long, this is still very much the region of the white nights, the antechamber of the true north.

You see this, looking northwards past the stone farms and the little pinewoods as the land rolls away towards the coast. The sky is still a pale blue from horizon to zenith – the fullest expansion of the brilliant line of light that is scored along the northern horizon for a month either side of midsummer night. Tree branches and hills stand out in clear silhouette against it. And, magically and only at this height of the summer, there is a glimmer of amber above the horizon, a diffused red along the profile of the hills. The red glimmer on our horizon is the distant reflection of the true north, the same way that on clear summer nights from the north coast of Aberdeenshire the mountains around Helmsdale, far to the north, appear suddenly against the horizon like a territory risen from the sea, like dreams. In summer light, they are blue almost beyond the imagined blues of Cotman's paintings. The notch in the hills above Helmsdale, seen at midsummer across the barely moving sea, is like a gateway, leading the eye as far to the north as the imagination can follow. To move north at this season is to move into the light.

The red glimmer on the northern horizon is the distant reflection of the sun at midnight, the bright sky over Shetland, the absolute north of absolute light and dark. Turning back downhill towards the house I think of a friend's house on the mainland of Shetland, a whitewashed house on treeless slopes leading down to the sea. The light will be bright enough there to read outside at midnight. Scoured headlands, scattered houses, stone beaches, the wind never quite sleeping. And beyond that the recollection of the painted paradisal high-summer evenings of Scandinavia: the field of radiant white flowers, wooden houses by the shore with foreground pines on

a midsummer night of serene brightness, the forest lake holding
the light of the midnight sky. The true north defined by the light
in the sky above, reddened by the sun just below the horizon, 'the
simmer dim'.

How can we best think about these colours of evening, which
follow each other slowly, so slowly through the long summer nights,
those colours which blend in the western sky in Friedrich's *Evening*?
Or the lights falling from summer skies as described by Hopkins in
1869, 'The heights and groves . . . looked like dusty velvet being all
flushed into a piece by the thick-hoary golden light which slanted
towards me over them',[9] or in 1874:

> the rosy field of the sundown turned gold and the slips and
> creamings in it stood out like brands, with jots of purple. A sodden
> twilight hung over the valley and foreground all below, holding the
> corner-hung maroon-grey diamonds of ploughfields to one keeping
> but allowing a certain glare in the green of the near tufts of grass.[10]

Since the beginning of the nineteenth century, the scientists, poets
and artists of northern Europe have been intense observers of the
evening sky, and the experience of this observation has formed their
aesthetic. The colour theories of Goethe are, of course, concerned
with much more than the colours and phenomena of twilight, but
watching the setting sun and darkening sky was surely one of the
things that led Goethe to his conclusions about colour. He was one
of the most diligent scholars of the western sky, and of all colour in
nature. His consideration of colour concerns itself with much more
than twilight, but watching the setting sun and changing, darkening
sky was surely one of the chief factors that led Goethe to his conclusions about colour. His marvellous sentence in the preface to the
Farbenlehre, 'Die Farben sind Taten des Lichts, Taten und Leiden'
(Colours are the Deeds of Light, its Deeds and Sufferings), claims
his territory as both scientific observer and poet. For him, colour
is the resolution of the tension between light and darkness, which,
atmospherically expressed, is the process of twilight.[11]

Which process moves so slowly in the long evenings of summer, with the effect of the suspension of time, time turning delusive, appearing hardly to pass at all in the unchanging, unearthly twilight: the inevitable memory of a child's summer evening, playing outside, playing outside time, until finally it is too dark to see the ball. This is the slow edging and merging of lights caught in Rubens's *Landscape by Moonlight* (1635–8). The midsummer sky sewn with enormous stars, flooded with moonlight is extraordinarily bright – it carries also hints of the last of daylight washing umbers and russets along the bushes on the riverbank. It is as though the weary, magnificent painting showed the length of a whole evening with the slow transitions of daylight to moonlight to starlight, all caught in one frame, in one endless moment.

This wonderful slowness is caught in a letter of the American novelist William Maxwell, recording July 1968 in rural Ireland:

> The long twilights were even more satisfactory . . . it was like having everything you had ever lost given back to you. You are used to this phenomenon, probably, but I simply couldn't get over it. Twilight, and then the half light that comes after that, and then the quarter light, and the eighth light, and then the almost darkness that is still a kind of light, in which the shapes of things emerge in all their solidity, and people are doing very odd things – such as fishing at eleven thirty at night – and the supernatural is not at all implausible.[12]

His correspondent, Sylvia Townsend Warner, responded on the same theme, on another long summer evening, three years later: 'I am like the man wandering through the twilight meadows in Strauss's song: *ich gehe night schnell, Ich eile nicht.*'[13]

'I do not go fast, I do not hurry' – the singer of Strauss's 'Traum durch die Dämmerung', to a text by Otto Julius Bierbaum, is moving gently to his love through broad meadows in the 'grey of twilight' – his very slowness caught in the repeating falling phrase to which the words that Warner quoted are sung. His arrival is lovingly postponed, his progress is as slow as the fading of the light into the blue of latest evening:

> *durch Dämmergrau in der Liebe Land,*
> *in ein blaues, mildes Licht.*[14]

through the grey twilight to the land of love, into a mild blue light.

A party lingering in the timeless summer evening led the Scottish writer Robert Louis Stevenson to his future wife. The account from family tradition was recounted by Fanny Stevenson's sister:

> One evening in the summer of 1876 the little party of guests of the old inn sat at dinner about the long table in the centre of the salle-à-manger . . . it was a soft, sweet evening, and the doors and windows were open; dusk drew near and the lamps had just been lit. Suddenly a young man approached from the outside. It was Robert Louis Stevenson, who afterwards admitted that he had fallen in love with his wife at first sight when he saw her in the lamplight through the open window.[15]

Quasi-magical suspensions of light and time are also found in Sean O'Brien's prose-poem of sleep, summer evenings and railways: 'I am lying in bed when the train goes by – on summer nights, that blue sound, like remembering an unlived life.'[16] The sequence of trains and evenings then shows us these unlived lives of the imagined past – a woman who was an adult when the poet was a child:

> A woman draws the curtains, turns from the window and leaves the room but comes back to peer out again at the line that runs at the end of the garden. It is a long evening in late summer, the heavy blueness hanging everywhere, and visible among the branches, the one green eye.[17]

The poet dreams of her in his 'English reverie', drowsing in the smell of rotting grass-clippings from the garden, 'sent to bed at summer's end, in the last thick light'. Eventually he sleeps as the summer stars come out, leaving his reader haunted by the warm evenings of the past and the fading rattle of the trains that carry the imagination between provinces and decades.

It is as quotidian and mysterious as Wordsworth's poem of the glow-worm carried secretly at night into the orchard of his beloved's house, left until the next nightfall, rediscovered together:

> The whole next day, I hoped, and hoped with fear;
> At night the Glow-worm shone beneath the Tree.[18]

Again, in Eric Rohmer's film *Le Rayon vert* (The Green Ray, 1986), the quotidian – a young office worker's spoiled and disappointing holidays – is transformed at the last minute by the light of the summer evening. Delphine's overhearing of an exposition of the 'green flash' of the last rays of the setting sun, and the memory of the lovers hunting the green flash in Jules Verne's novel of the same name, linger through the resolution of the film. Walking through an ordinary seaside resort with the gentle young cabinetmaker she has just met at the station, they come upon a scruffy general shop called *Le Rayon vert*, the first sign of hope before they watch the evening over the sea together. In the last moments of the sunset the young man dries her tears in a gesture of beautiful, clumsy tenderness and the appearance of the green flash draws from her a half-articulated 'yes' – a yes to his tentative plans for their future, to his hope that the green flash will bring them luck together.

A more mysterious meeting of lovers in the summer evening is the subject of American poet Theodore Roethke's verse 'The Visitant', with its benign apparition out of the long twilight of summer:

> A voice said:
> Stay. Stay by the slip-ooze. Stay.
> . . .
> She came without sound,
> Without brushing the wet stones,

In the soft dark of early evening,
She came,
The wind in her hair,
The moon beginning.[19]

A feeling of the inevitability of the otherworldly – that credibility of
the supernatural in the white nights observed by William Maxwell –
is expressed by the near-rhymes of 'evening' and 'beginning', words
which enclose the apparition who has manifested herself out of the
deserted frontier between day and night, between earth and water –
an apparition who has departed, inevitably, by morning.

There is another aspect of the summer evenings that might be
expressed as the male pastorals of the summer term, the long school
or college evenings of the nineteenth and twentieth centuries, times
of apparently unlimited leisure and light. One such is Auden's very
early poem, one of those hand-set by his friend Stephen Spender,
which evokes a Corinthian arcadia at the end of the cricket match
in its four lines:

The sprinkler on the lawn
Weaves a cool vertigo, and stumps are drawn;
The last boy vanishes,
A blazer half-on, through the rigid trees.[20]

This is answered by the early Victorian undergraduate arcadia of
Edward Fitzgerald's *Euphranor*, an account of a river excursion with a
group of friends on a summer day, with much discussion of 'the good
life' in a rather archaic sense whose relevance and interest has perhaps
faded with time. But the book is memorable for the felicitous recording of incidental details of the Cambridge of the 1840s – the white
doves fluttering about the roofs of Trinity College, the lilacs in the
bowling alley at Chesterton. But for the contemporary reader, the
book comes to life in its close: as the protagonists walk home along
the river where a boat race has just been rowed, the description of the
great trees and the coming of evening is beautiful and memorable:

We walk'd along the fields by the Church, . . . cross'd the Ferry,
and mingled with the crowd upon the opposite bank . . . all these,
conversing on all sorts of topics, from the slang of Bell's Life to the
last new German Revelation, and moving in ever-changing groups
down the shore of the river, at whose farther bend was a little knot
of Ladies gathered up on a green knoll faced and illuminated by
the beams of the setting sun . . . Then, waiting a little while to
hear how the winner had won, and the loser lost, and watching
Phidippus engaged in eager conversation with his defeated
brethren, I took Euphranor and Lexilogus under either arm . . .
and walk'd home with them across the meadow leading to the
town, whither the dusky troops of Gownsmen with all their confused voices seemed as it were evaporating in the twilight, while
a Nightingale began to be heard among the flowering Chestnuts
of Jesus.[21]

An extraordinary moment when the evocation is so vivid that the
reader almost inhabits a world now lost, passed almost without regret.

Once midsummer is over, the twilight shadows us. In a month,
even in the north, the prodigal evening light will already be dwindling.
In the resplendently miserable words of A. E. Housman:

> . . . the subterranean dark
Has crossed the nadir, and begins to climb.[22]

The dark shadows the light: Sara Maitland points out that Norse
mythology is the exception among European mythologies. In pre-
Christian Scandinavia the victory of the light at the last day is not
assumed. It remains wholly possible in minds used to the black
trough of the dead year, a fortnight and more either side of the
winter solstice, that the dark will win the last battle:

Norse mythology is the only theistic theology I know of where the issue
remains in serious peril. The gods will go out to fight at Ragnarok. They
will do their best for themselves, for humans, and for the light; but

Baldur the Beautiful is dead and we do not know if they or the forces of the dark will triumph.²³

Grim hints in the Poetic Eddas suggest that both the sun and the father of the gods will be devoured by the wolf Fenrir at the last battle. It has been suggested that the mitigating prophecy that Odin will be avenged and the sun may have a daughter to shine on the unimaginable world of the future are retrospective interpolations by a Christian editor of pre-Christian material. What this medieval editor is doing is trying to show that his own northern people were natural Christians, whose chthonic mythology held seeds of the truth, and thus he makes of their pagan last battle something of a parallel to the sun darkened at the Crucifixion, darkness as prologue to triumphal light.

It is possible that this parallelism of the last battle of dark and light in Norse mythology with the Crucifixion and Resurrection form the subject of what might be called the seminal work of northern English art (although it would perhaps be more accurate to describe it as southern Scandinavian): the relief-sculptured cross, dating from about 940, still in the churchyard at Gosforth in Cumbria. This northern work of art inevitably concerns itself with the light and the dark. The Gosforth Cross is one of those absolutely compelling works of hybrid art that can embody two sets of meanings, two world-views, at the same time, and interpretation depends entirely on the mental positioning of the beholder.

At Gosforth there is a battle, with one warrior, as it might be 'the champion Christ' menaced by the jaws of Hell-mouth or fighting Fenrir who will devour Odin himself and consume the sun. There is also a carving of a radiant young man with outstretched arms who is Baldur reborn or Christ resurrected. Perhaps it is more accurate to say that he is *both* Baldur reborn *and* Christ resurrected.

The shadows of the relief carving on the Gosforth Cross have grown shallower with a millennium of wind, rain and pollution, but it remains today a work about the light and the dark, about the battle of the unconquered sun with the winter, even if we know (in this instance) better than Wagner that Ragnarök means the 'judgement' or 'ordeal' rather than the 'twilight' of the gods.

In the evenings of the later summer, the water at the end of our grass comes into its own, a mirror for the lingering brightness of the sky. Standing on the bank on a late July night, Andrew Marvell's evening lines come to mind, the closing movement of his celebration of a day in the 1650s lived thoughtfully and quietly in and around a secluded house amidst the northern fields:

> So when the *Shadows* laid asleep
> From underneath these Banks do creep;
> And on the River as it flows
> With Ebon *Shuts* begin to close;
> The modest *Halcyon* comes in sight,
> Flying betwixt the Day and Night . . .[24]

The descending stillness is remarkably clear in these images: the drowsy shadows of the river banks spreading as the sun goes off the water, until they turn to sluice gates of ebony – bars of darkness across the water. Then the flight of the kingfisher brings not only the stillness associated with the bird in classical mythology, but a visual epitome of the fading colours of the day, giving way to the night that has been biding its time all through the summer day.

But, so far north as this, the night which has been lurking in the depths of the pond only comes forth for a few hours around the midnight of these unshadowed days. When I walk by the evening water, the light is hardly dimmed, the sound of the falling stream is the only sound in the still valley, except for the rare splash and ripple of a leaping fish. This is as calm, as unchangingly changing as the midsummer sea seen from the windows of the northbound evening train out of Edinburgh: streaks of colour on the waters that are almost monochromes, shifting and alternating in layers of stillness out to the horizon.

This is the very stillness of the shadowed waters in Poussin's *A Roman Road* of 1648, the cistern or canal by the roadside with the swan motionless on the mirror of its surface. It is a depiction of the paradise of evening, rich with the discovery of the possibilities of the realistic transcription of early evening light (well into the seventeenth century evening paintings, especially portraits, are often lit by a fictitious frontal light source), the scrupulous rendering of the low angle of the sunlight combed by the row of trees to the left of the road, the mountains and orange trees moulded in gold from the west. The exact travel of the light is recorded: only the tops of the bushes and the hills are still illuminated, the two women with a child in the middle distance are watching the western sky, which illuminates them through a gap in the trees; the two reclining figures on the far side of the water also inhabit a long ray of light cast between the trees.

Nicolas Poussin, *Landscape with Travellers Resting* (known as *A Roman Road*), 1648, oil on canvas.

There are many paradisal aspects to this still place: the travellers resting in the foreground have laid a full basket of peaches on the squared stone by the road, one of the trees is heavy with golden fruit in golden light. But there is also an undertone of very quietly stated remembrance of transience: the road is outside a town, the place where classical sepulchres are found, indeed there is a roadside column with an urn in the distance. In the foreground, flowers grow over ruins and the substantial structure to the left, into which the man crouching in the shadows peers, appears to be the ruin of a Roman tomb, as the canal seems to be contained by the fragments of ancient masonry. So, as elsewhere in Poussin's work, death and time claim a place in an Arcadian landscape. There is 'sadness and tranquillity' in the evening.

Virgil's vision of slow evening, warm air in the lengthening shade of great mountains, has influenced two millennia of the European arts working in the shadow of 'the ancients':

> Aspice, aratra iugo referunt suspensa iuvenci,
> Et sol crescentis decedens duplicat umbras.[25]

> Look, oxen now bring home their yoke-suspended ploughs, and the sun, going down, doubles the growing shadows.

Erwin Panofsky identifies precisely the new feeling that Virgil brought into all the arts of Europe: 'a discrepancy felt between the supernatural perfection of an imaginary environment and the natural limitations of human life as it is'.[26] So much so that at one point in the *Eclogues* he says that the gods themselves are reluctant (but powerless) that evening should come and the singing cease:

> Ille canit, pulsae referunt ad sidera valles;
> Cogere donec ovis stabulis numerumque referre
> Iussit et invito processit Vesper Olympo.[27]

> He sings, the echoing alleys tell it to the stars, till Vesper came to view, the gods themselves not wishing it thus, and bade the flock be folded and their number counted.

As Panofsky analyses this new apprehension of evening in the arts:

> In Virgil's ideal Arcady human suffering and superhumanly perfect
> surroundings create a dissonance. This dissonance, once felt, had to
> be resolved, and it was resolved in that vespertinal mixture of sadness
> and tranquillity which is perhaps Virgil's most personal contribution
> to poetry. With only slight exaggeration one might say that he
> 'discovered' the evening. When Theocritus' shepherds conclude
> their melodious converse at nightfall, they like to part with a little
> joke about the behaviour of nannies and billy goats. At the end of
> Virgil's *Eclogues*, we feel evening silently settle over the world: 'Ite
> domum saturae, venit Hesperus, ite, capellae' or 'Majoresque
> cadunt altis de montibus umbrae.'[28]

It is this 'discovery' of evening that is celebrated in *A Shaded Path*,
Ian Hamilton Finlay's work from the late 1980s, made with David
Ballantyne. This consists of 76 bricks, each one of which is stamped
(in the place where a maker's name might usually be impressed)
with the name 'Virgil'. These can then be arranged as a narrow path
in a garden, leading from sunlight into the shadow of trees, and thus
leading metaphorically from the daylit garden through the dappled
evening, which Virgil discovered for Europe, and into the green
night under the leaves.

Perhaps the most apprehensible dissonance in Virgil's pastorals
comes at the end of the first *Eclogue*: in one sense it is novel to juxta-
pose humble foodstuffs with the grandeur of the shadow of the great
mountain, pastoral with epic; but the real dissonance is that between
reality and the ideal. One of the shepherds, or rather small farmers,
has been turned off his land with his flocks to make way for an
army veteran, and is facing a future of hardship and uncertainty.
This is the contemporary political reality that intrudes into the ideal,
summer-evening world of the poem. Leisure in the shade contrasts
with real deprivation. Thus the often quoted and celebrated feast of
the shepherds at the end of the poem exists, as it were, only in a
grievously circumscribed present tense.

Hic tamen hanc mecum poteras requiescere noctem
Fronde super viridi: sunt nobis mitia poma
Castaneae molles et pressi copia lactis,
Et iam summa procul villarum culmina fumant
Maioresque cadunt altis de montibus umbrae.[29]

However for tonight you could rest here with me, upon green leafage:
I can offer you ripe fruit and mealy chestnuts and abundance of milk
cheese. Far off the roof-tops of the farms already smoke and down
from the high mountains greater shadows fall.

The disjunction is very real: the few lines about ripe fruit and white
cheese have haunted the memory of Europe as the quintessence of
fortunate simplicity. To this day they come to mind in Italy when
such ancient rustic dishes appear on the table in traditional house-
holds or country restaurants: a flat tart of bread dough and white
cheese, a cake of chestnuts, rosemary and olive oil. All of these
recall the shepherds' supper, darkened by the twin shadows of
the mountains and the future.

In later life, after many disappointments, Samuel Palmer turned
to the translation and illustration of Virgil's pastoral poems, which
were to be his last work, left unfinished at his death in 1881.[30] When
he began this work in 1872 everything had gone wrong for him,
the sympathetic eldest son of his profoundly unhappy marriage was
dead. Virgil's pastoral poems had become his last place of retreat
from a hostile present. Four etchings of Virgilian subjects were at
the stage of preliminary proofs in 1879. The plate that returns most
palpably to his early vision, the vision of his young manhood, the
years of wandering the summer fields all evening long, is his illustration to the last lines of *Eclogue* I.

Palmer turns away from the shadows, perhaps because he was
himself working on the other side of decades of personal unhappiness. Although his plate illustrates the smoke from the chimneys,
and the darkening mountains faithfully enough, there is no sense
of the loss that awaits with the morning. Everything is serene: the
shepherds' rustic table is enfolded and protected by the overhanging

branches of one of Palmer's magical apple trees. This laden tree almost seems part of the structure of the lighted shepherd's cabin, an invention reminiscent of the tree-soft cottages of Palmer's earliest drawings. In this northern European translation of pastoral, olive groves become orchards, the paradisal apple garden of the nineteenth- and twentieth-century British imagination. For Samuel Palmer, those orchards at evening are regions of a happiness as fugitive as, in the south, is the late winter scent of orange flowers in the courtyard of the Palazzo Spada. And as in Palmer's earliest evening works, the sky is illuminated by the crescent moon and the evening star. He inscribed his own free imitation of the close of the first Eclogue underneath the etched plate.

> See, glimmering in the West, the homeward star,
> And from the crest of upland towns afar,
> The hearth-smoke rise . . .

This is deliberately not exact: he has conflated the penultimate line of the first *Eclogue*, '*Et iam summa procul villarum culmina fumant*',

Samuel Palmer (completed by Herbert Palmer), *The Homeward Star*, *c.* 1880–83, etching.

with the last line of the tenth, '*ite domum saturae, venit Hesperus, ite capellae*', in the interest of eliding Virgil's disjunctions into a vision of repose under the evening sky, a continuation of Sappho's vision of the evening star drawing all scattered and lost things and people to their true homes. Palmer's last Virgilian etchings turn the apples of remembered Kentish orchards to gold, reaching back to the twilight paradises between worlds that he described in words and pictures in his first sketchbook.

One more of his last etched works also evokes what Panofsky called 'the feeling of evening silently settling over the world'. *The Bellman* (1879) is an illustration of part of the evocation of night and stillness in Milton's *Il Penseroso*, where among the noises of night come the voice and bell of the town watchman:

> Or the Bellman's drowsy charm,
> To bless the doors from nightly harm . . .

Palmer does not imagine this scene in Milton's quiet and solitude, but in a tranquil pastoral England, with many reminiscences of the Virgilian evening of his other works of the same year. The figure of the Bellman walks at moonrise through a little town of half-timbered houses, folded into the high mountains that Palmer remembered from his Italian travels. The moon is rising, casting reflections into the nearest mullioned windows. A scatter of lights is coming on in the timber houses, and a few lamps shine out from distant cottages on the slopes of the hills. The soft forms of the thatched roofs, as in Palmer's early drawings, are sinking into the contours of the landscape and the folded beasts amongst the apple orchards of the foreground are part of the pastoral that is a constant in his work. But the group of people eating at a little table under an arbour in the foreground, softly lit from the open door of the house, associates inevitably with the shepherds' supper in the first Eclogue and with Palmer's *Homeward Star*. So *The Bellman* is a personal act of intense synthesis: Milton's precociously crepuscular poem echoes across to Virgil, and Palmer brings them together

Samuel Palmer, *The Bellman, from* [Milton's] *'Il Penseroso'*, 1879, etching and drypoint.

visually in his imagined world. Echoes of Virgil through the centuries
are one of the strands that give form to European apprehensions
of evening, of places of transient serenity in the drawing-down of
the twilight. In this tradition, Palmer made his last art out of the
Virgilian evening.

MANY CENTURIES BEFORE, Leonardo da Vinci had noticed the
transformation of contour and countenance as the autumn and
winter evenings settled over Italy: 'note the faces of men and
women in the streets as evening falls and when the weather is dull,
what softness and delicacy you may perceive in them.'[31] Evening
transformations also marked the works of the last great virtuoso of
the Italian school, Giambattista Tiepolo (1696–1770). His mytho-
logical frescoes in the Villa Valmarana, near Vicenza, immerse
whole rooms in the cobalt, dust and lavender of imagined evening
skies.[32] His simulacrum of a serene and palpably nostalgic light on

his Venetian painted ceilings, with their cloudscapes of washed yellow and purple-grey, go beyond the after-sunset paradises of the Renaissance, themselves conscious shadows of the past glories of antiquity.

Perhaps his greatest (and most inscrutable) work is the great ceiling fresco of the continents above the staircase of the Residenz at Würzburg in Franconia. This culminating work is dominated, especially on the viewer's first approach to it up the staircase, by the sadness of evening. The dusk cloud overshadowing the figures who represent *America* on the ceiling is a prodigious, disquieting invention. As Svetlana Alpers and Michael Baxandall point out in their remarkable study of Tiepolo, this element of the design is born of pragmatic adaptation to the fall and movement and reflection of the light in the space under the enormous vault. The part of the coved ceiling on which *America* is depicted receives no direct and little reflected light, and it is further darkened by contrast with the bright double rank of windows in the wall below it. Thus the first part of the ceiling that any visitor sees is inevitably almost in twilight, certainly by contrast with the brilliance of light elsewhere in the staircase hall. As Alpers and Baxandall identify Tiepolo's problem and his extraordinary solution to it:

> The key to the solution is the tree-tethered cloud on which Mars and Venus lounge, immediately over the figure of America herself . . . it naturalises the relative lack of light in the (real) frieze area into the (fictive) universe of the representation by shutting off the light of Sun-Apollo . . . This cast shadow justifies bold dark silhouettes, able to register in the difficult light conditions.[33]

This cloud, grey with evening however bright the sky above it may be, identifies America as a new Hesperia, an evening land, perhaps a place of refuge as Italy had been for Aeneas, and certainly as the westerly destination of the retreating sun. The cloud also plays a large part in the creation of the atmosphere of the vast fresco, especially when viewed directly from below, where the sharp curvature of the cove seems to hold the plumed figure of America down in the area of the cornice. Seen from this point of view, the cloud moment-arily flows outwards and dominates the otherwise bright sky.

On the opposite cove of the ceiling the shadow of the velvet drapery surrounding the portrait of Tiepolo's patron, as cherubs bear it towards the Zenith, casts the heavy-eyed, disturbingly languorous figure of Europa into deep shadow. This is another troubling and beautiful invention: Europe is dreaming into stasis at the dusty end of her afternoon. She is heavy-eyed, listless, sicken-ing, ill. Her long fingers falter in their grasp of the sceptre. She has drawn a coverlet, coloured with the turquoise and rose of a frozen sunset, over her knees.

In Tiepolo's first sketch for the ceiling, it was this representation of Europe that was going to be placed on the shadowed north vault, under the great cloud, which would have created a more explicit, yet more troubling, climate of shadow, questioning, decline.[34]

There is no doubt of the effect of the evening cloud at Würzburg – it spreads its influence over the whole composition, and is essential in the creation of the elusive sense of disquiet that Alpers and Baxandall identify as characteristic of Tiepolo even at his most virtuosic – his indifference, his hints that the apotheosis depicted is no longer simple or true in a world, as Alpers and Baxandall phrase it, 'containing Frederick the Great'.[35] Nothing is made explicit, but there is an eroding undercurrent of disbelief in the whole grand invention, a sense that the allegorical and mytho-logical figures, and the earthly powers that they glorify, are themselves in their evening. As with Tiepolo's paintings at the Villa Valmarana, which were discussed in the introduction to this book, little of this is made explicit – urgent dissent is voiced in a whisper. Tiepolo's clear-eyed and uncommitted awareness of the state of things, even as he makes wonderful divertissements with light in the twilight of his world, cannot but read, if only in retrospect, as prophetic.

The fresco still sends the attentive viewer out into the scented lime *allées* of the Hofgarten beguiled but profoundly unsettled – the whole great, dancing wind-blown world of Tiepolo's invention has been laid open to view, but the last thing to remain in the memory is the first thing seen in the ascent of the great staircase: the twilight of the overshadowing western cloud, the sorrow of the Hesperides.

These images from the end of the Venetian republic, from the last decades of the Europe before the revolutions, are prefigured in the celebrated speech on the sunset clouds from Shakespeare's *Antony and Cleopatra*. Like Tiepolo's painted palaces, these make the equivalence between the fluid, labile clouds of evening and the instability of all earthly authority and power. Power and control – castles and heraldic beasts, war horses – dissolve in the fluid beauty of the sky, wonderful hints and simulacra flicker and go, but in the end all certainty dissolves in the approaching night.

> Sometime we see a clowd that's Dragonish,
> A vapour sometime, like a Beare, or Lyon,
> A toward Cittadell, a pendant Rocke,
> A forked Mountaine, or blew Promontorie
> With Trees upon't, that nodde unto the world,
> And mocke our eyes with ayre.
> Thou hast seene these Signes,
> They are blacke Vesper's Pageants.[36]

So the twilight clouds become a precise equivalent for the dissolving identity of the labile ruler defeated by the countrymen he betrayed:

> That which is now a Horse, even with a thoght,
> The Racke dislimes and makes it indistinct,
> As water is in water.

His selfhood dissolves and, with his passing, comes a characteristic Shakespearean moment of apprehension that all certainties of rule and hierarchy are brought into question by every such instance of fallen greatness going into the dark. Starker and more direct than Tiepolo, but expressing the same conclusion that the painter hid in

Giambattista Tiepolo, 'America' (detail from *The Four Continents*), 1752–3, fresco in the Residenz, Würzburg.

the cloud-borne pageants he devised for the apotheosis of an undistinguished minor prince, the same terrible clarity about the relation between their fictions and reality.

All his life, Ruskin sought refuge in the skies of evening, as if their unstable glories could somehow instruct or console him. In his youth, he studied the evening sky as intensely as ever did Goethe, but with narrower intention – his passionate impulse to verify the representations of nature made by contemporary painters, to test his own abilities to paint verbal Turners:

> the whole sky from the zenith to the horizon becomes one molten mantling sea of colour and fire; every black bar turns into massy gold, every ripple and wave into unsullied shadowless crimson, and purple, and scarlet, and colours for which there are no words in language . . . the upper sky . . . modulated by the filmy, formless body of the transparent vapour, till it is lost imperceptibly in its crimson and gold.[37]

It is at twilight that Ruskin enters his otherworld of sky and mountains: as with his description of the first overwhelming sight of the Alps. He saw them first at Schaffhausen, touring with his parents, walking out from the streets of the town in the early evening:

> it was drawing towards sunset when we got to some sort of garden-promenade – west of the town and high above the Rhine, so as to command the open country across it to south and west, far into blue . . . suddenly – behold – beyond!
>
> There was no thought in any of us for a moment of their being clouds. They were clear as crystal, sharp on the pure horizon sky, and already tinged with rose by the sinking sun. Infinitely beyond all that we had ever thought or dreamed, – the seen walls of lost Eden could not have been more beautiful to us; not more awful, round heaven, the walls of sacred death.
>
> It is not possible to imagine, in any time of the world, a more blessed entrance into life, for a child of such a temperament as mine.[38]

Such a beginning, such intensity of observation, remains entangled with a wholly personal reading of allegories into natural phenomena, not unlike those of Friedrich and Palmer before him. But the very intensity with which Ruskin reads moral qualities into the skies that he observes carries its own dangers:

> Here is a light which the eye inevitably seeks with a deeper feeling of the beautiful – the light of the declining day, and the flakes of scarlet cloud burning like watchfires in the green sky of the horizon; a deeper feeling, I say, not perhaps more acute, but having more of spiritual hope and longing . . . all that is dazzling in colour and perfect in form [is evanescent and shallow] when compared with the still small voice of the level twilight behind purple hills.[39]

So focused and troubled was the gaze he directed to the skies that the darkening skies of the 1870s and the carbon-spoiled skies of the 1880s were the prelude to the breakdown that consumed the last decades of Ruskin's life. His failures as art critic and social reformer had begun with visionary hopes in the twilight over the fields to the south of London. The last pages he managed to set down before his final breakdown were about a bird's elusive cry at dusk, about his mother's remembered garden, about an Italian evening of fireflies and lightning. In this moment of evening quiet, his projects in ruins, his selfhood shattered by mental illness, he follows a bird's cry to the otherworld through the fields above Brantwood:

> The hayfield . . . where the grass in spring still grew fresh and deep. There used to be always a corncrake or two in it. Twilight after twilight I have hunted that bird, and never once got glimpse of it: the voice was always at the other side of the field, or in the inscrutable air or earth.[40]

His moment of recovery in memory is not unlike Samuel Palmer's partial recovery in his Virgilian etchings, displaying some of the quality of his study of twilight over the southern suburbs of London when they were still half amongst fields. Parallel lives of wrong decisions, with a moment of recovery and recollection at the close. Palmer recovered his intense apprehension of the rising crescent moon and evening star, Ruskin the recollection of his mother's Dulwich garden: 'and I have been sorrowful enough for myself, since ever I lost sight of that peach-blossom avenue'.[41] So the very last words that Ruskin published about himself were an intense recollection of an Italian twilight, fireflies and thunder, and the Virgilian sense of evening settling over the world:

> Fonte Branda I last saw with Charles Norton, under the same arches where Dante saw it. We drank of it together and walked together that evening on the hills above, where the fireflies among the scented thickets shone fitfully in the still undarkened air. *How* they shone! moving like fine-broken starlight through the purple leaves. How

they shone! through the sunset that faded into thunderous night as
I entered Siena three days before, the white edges of the mountainous
clouds still lighted from the west, and the openly golden sky calm
behind the Gate of Siena's heart, with its still golden words, *Cor
magis tibi Sena pandit*, and the fireflies everywhere in sky and cloud
rising and falling, mixed with the lightning and more intense than
the stars.[42]

Day passes westwards and the evening follows, as harvest follows
summer and the long days. August passing, the white nights over.
August passing: the death of the summer in lengthening twilight.
This is a grave month in the north: the evenings shorten so fast,
the dark comes down from the pole day by day and the lack of light
contrasts sharply with the prodigality of midsummer. August passing:
the days still warm but the barley bending heavy ears in the fields,
gold going over to white as the stalks begin to show.

All the retrospection and self-examination, all the vows of
improvement and industry that attend most people at the end
of December, attack in force on 15 August, the midpoint between
academic years, when the crocosmia comes into flower and the
Scottish summer goes over into the harvest. In the garden, white
windflowers, for all their beauty, offer little pleasure with their
opening each year: they are too much an index of the passing of
time towards the week of partings at the end of August. Soon the
machines will begin the harvest in the silent fields. Soon the chill
will lie on the valley in the morning and the season of dusks and
departures will begin.

And so we are come to the last room of the summer.[43] Far-
travelled friends come to stay the last night of August with us.
When they arrive in the afternoon, potatoes have already been lifted
for dinner; salmon is cooling with dill and lemon and the last wild
raspberries from the wood are setting into that red berry gruel eaten
with cream all through Scandinavia. Harvest-coloured light slants
across grass and water and we wander by the pond, and sit and talk
on short, dry grass until the light begins to fail.

But there is a sudden turn of warm air as the hour grows late and a showing-forth of the late summer stars. Our guests begin to drift out onto the lawns again as we light a few candle lanterns in the trees. These shine out, as though their candle flames were very far away, and eyes growing used to the dimness are dazzled by the stars in the zenith. The house, like any house at nightfall, with light from its uncurtained windows seen from a distance, moves us almost to tears, contemplating those long rays of light that lie on grass like midwinter light on the floors of cold rooms. The talk goes on, with the lights above and the flames in the leaves below, stolen from the cold days to come and the partings that will come with the morning. For one last hour, one hour more.

Peter Levi, in his fine late poem 'He Considers the Closing Day', remembers solitary expeditions of his youth on winter evenings, when he had explored the furthest regions of twilight, as Hopkins did, when he too was a young Jesuit staying out late, making meticulous observations of clouds and weathers:

Coming home late shoes soaking feet frozen
Waiting to see the last light really go[44]

And comprehends the passage of time in his (now, greatly changed) life with contentment, an old poet reconciled and at peace *im Abendrot* on a flawless summer evening:

I am pleased to be crumbling and aged,
and stalking among long shadows of trees:
and think when like a swallow I shall sleep
in the rough greenness and the rough darkness.[45]

At the very end of his life, in the very last twilight of the musical tradition into which he had been born, Richard Strauss ended his *Four Last Songs* with a setting of Eichendorff's 'Im Abendrot', a poem of fidelity and love, as two people, like the figures in Friedrich's *Der Abend*, advance together deep into the twilight,

Wir sind durch Not und Freude
gegangen Hand in Hand;
vom Wandern ruhen wir
nun überm stillen Land.

Through sorrow and joy we have gone hand in hand,
now we rest from our travels in this quiet country.

All troubles are over, the larks sing in the stillness of dusk, darkness
and rest lie ahead.

O weiter, stiller Friede!
So tief im Abendrot . . .

O vast, tranquil peace! so deep into the evening's glow . . .

The slow-moving music is extraordinary, rich and haunting – always
shifting texture, opening downwards to ever-deeper sonorities.
The texture is darkened by the edge of the oboe cutting through the
orchestra, is drawn back into the European past by horns calling in
the distance, is sweetened in passing by mimetic trills on the flutes as
the larks pass through the song. But the most extraordinary invention
is the music after the voice has led the faithful lovers to the contemplation of death and fallen silent: it is music of the very end, in the
same way that some of the music of William Lawes is music of the
ends of things (see chapter Two). Textures and harmonies shift in
the deep twilight, slow moving, regretful and half-allusive to the
theme of Strauss's earlier *Death and Transfiguration*. The bird trills
sound again, somehow further removed, fixed in the heights, as slow
chords move, almost like a chorale, to a final flooding, metamorphic,
fading, resolving major chord, after which the larks sing one last time,
devastatingly, out of the dark.

   As we walked away from that late summer party towards the trees
at the edge of the grass and into the noise of the water, the two of us
looked back at our friends under the glow-worm lanterns. All three of
them are fifteen or twenty years younger than us. And there are those
who hate those who will survive them for that reason alone, and then

there are those who are indifferent, accepting the passage of time and what it brings. This scene in a twilight garden, far to the north, at the far end of summer is almost an allegory of that. We are looking back towards them from the shadow of the trees, from the region where it is already night, to where they sit under the firefly lanterns in the last of the light. We are hearing the fall of water that they cannot yet hear.

We begin to walk further away, across the clearing at the edge of the wood. Remembering a visit earlier in the year from a French poet, in her distinguished and productive old age, who had spoken all evening in the beautiful and precise English of the mid-twentieth century. Remembering, acutely, one of the poems in her book, a poem of white flowers at evening – white flowers at evening and the ashes of the fading sky. A sombre poem, written by a poet conscious of belatedness, of the long past years of her own career:

> La mort est ce pays que j'ouvre avec mes pas quand la mer se retire, laissant sur la grève les bateaux immobiles. Et les fleurs blanches du soir cueillent sur leurs visages aveugles, les restes du ciel.[46]

Death is this land which I open pace by pace when the tide falls abandoning boats on the sands. And white flowers of evening gather, on their blind faces, the ashes of the sky.

Walking away into the deeper shade of the wood and the noise of the stream was like walking into another realm, shadowed by memories of otherworlds in failing light. To look back across the dark garden at the very end of the summer towards that company in the lantern-light was to feel the progression of things, of all that passes with the passing light.

So we came into the dim wood and into the water loud in the air, looking back at the scatter of lit windows, at the figures of our friends moving among shadows and glimmerings and lanterns and leaves. Now that the evening has given way, so quietly, and after such long twilight, to the dark. Ferns at our feet and stars in the cobalt above, we live together in this moment of lastness, with all of our night to come.

J. D. Fergusson, *Dieppe, 14 July 1905: Night*, 1905, oil on canvas.

Epilogue: Fireworks and Reflected Lights

Fireworks and lanterns in the deepening dusk before true nightfall: coloured lights in trees, shining globes along white esplanades at the frontiers of the dark. There is an otherworldly quality to these things, these attempts to draw out and prolong the fading evenings beyond the frontiers of the summer. In Japan, a cloud of fireflies was released at the culmination of an evening party.[1] Candle lanterns, paper lanterns hung in the trees: planets and glow-worms. There is an inevitable poignancy attending the fireworks and candles that attempt to draw out and prolong the long evenings of high summer when they are already shortening and fading. Even though it is described almost entirely in terms of the visual arts of the day, how sad this early twentieth-century evening party now seems:

> Below, on the water, lanterns were coming alight, faint ghosts of warm flame floating in the pallor of the first twilight. The earth was spread with darkness, like lacquer, overhead was a pale sky, all primrose, and the lake was pale as milk in one part . . . All round, shadow was gathering from the trees.[2]

John Singer Sargent's famous picture of children lighting lanterns in a garden, *Carnation, Lily, Lily, Rose*, had its origin in just such a moment observed in August 1885 on the upper reaches of the Thames, where Sargent was boating with an American friend: 'I am trying to paint a charming thing I saw the other evening. Two little girls in a garden at twilight lighting paper lanterns from rose-tree to rose-tree. I shall be a long time about it if I don't give up in despair.'[3] Part of the purpose of the whole lies in the very belatedness that is

235

crucial to the painting and its atmosphere (indeed in a letter to R. L. Stevenson, in which he also identifies the way in which the sight of the children and the lantern had become entwined in his imagination with the phrase that eventually gave the picture its title, Sargent remembers the month as September rather than August).[4] Yet this is balanced by a sense of celebration – the lanterns amongst the flowers are able to prolong the gathering in the garden beyond the daylight and lucid twilight to the threshold of the night. Sargent lamented that he had seen his 'most paradisic sight' so late in the year, that it had come too late for him to capture the extraordinary effect of falling light that had first moved him, seeing the lanterns in the garden across the water.

The process by which the finished painting came into being is chronicled by Sargent's letters, and by the survival of numerous sketches and discarded versions, as well as by the intensity of working and reworking on the finished canvas.[5] Sargent painted on in the shortening autumn dusks of 1885, asserting that by November he was reduced to tying artificial flowers to withered rose-trees. *Carnation, Lily, Lily, Rose* was not finished until the October of the following year, after much careful advance planting of lilies and equally careful timing of the few minutes in any day when the light was right: diffused, slightly purpled twilight to make the flowers, clothes and lanterns stand forward from their green background. He would place his easel and paints beforehand, and pose his models in anticipation of the few moments when he could paint in the right light: 'Paints are not bright enough and then the effects only last ten minutes.'[6]

This is an extreme attempt at the old task of painting the moment as though in a moment, but in this case it took years and endless stopwatch-timings of shifting twilights to achieve. Yet the finished painting is little haunted by the feeling of fugacity that usually attends such images captured from changing light; a sense pervades it rather of quiet illumination and of darkness and autumn held at bay.

The title cites a line from a song from the 1800s that seems to have remained popular through to the end of the nineteenth century.[7]

It appears, for example, in 1870 as one moment of illumination in the crepuscular second chapter of Dickens's last novel, *The Mystery of Edwin Drood*, where the benign Mr Crisparkle claims the song for the light that is ciphered by his name, singing it as he moves innocently out of the shadowy lodgings of the dark choirmaster, through the oppressive autumn twilight that haunts and shapes the novel. The song is also mentioned as intensely and widely popular in an 1877 letter by Stevenson,[8] and it was reprinted as late as 1892, six years after Sargent's picture was finished. Yet in content and musical style, the song (or, more precisely, glee) looks backward to the eighteenth century. The flowers compose a wreath worn by Flora as she passes through a pastoral landscape and their beauties are seen as reflections of her own. So the verbal and musical phrase that Sargent expected to echo in the viewer's mind as they contemplated his picture in the 1880s would have been one shaped by the decorum of the previous century, an echo from a world growing remote, a parallel effect of old-world distancing to the removed twilight garden glimpsed across the river.

H. D.'s poem 'Evening' also isolates and commemorates the moment when civil twilight gives way to nautical twilight in a summer garden. Pale flowers fade into shadow as though the petals were folding in upon themselves and thus vanishing from sight – until a wash of dimness consumes all in the astronomical twilight that ushers in the night:

> Shadow seeks shadow
> Then both leaf
> And leaf-shadow are lost.[9]

The slow leaf-drift of the lines is itself expressive of the drawn-out, suspended movement of the summer evening.

Baudelaire's twilight place in 'Harmonie du soir' evokes a pleasure garden with a dance floor, high summer and the overpowering scent of lilies, a melancholy waltz on the evening air. And yet, as the imagery of the poem insists in troubled counterpoint, this place of summer pleasure is paralleled with the desolate liturgy of Maundy Thursday, the removal of the Host from the tabernacle, enacted desecrations, the stripping of the altars. Fear of the dark opposes the desire to retain every glimmer of the past day. Melancholy and pleasure and twilight are haunted by sombre, sacred enactments.

> Voici venir les temps où vibrant sur sa tige
> Chaque fleur s'évapore ainsi qu'un encensoir;
> Les sons et les parfums tournent dans l'air du soir;
> Valse mélancolique et langoureux vertige![10]

> See the hours come when quivering on its stalk, each flower gives
> forth its scent like a censer; the sounds and the perfumes turn in
> the evening air, melancholy waltz and languorous vertigo.

Even amongst the sensual beauties of the moment, the slow turns of the waltz and the outpouring of scent from the twilight flowers, fear and loss and regret are present. The final lines recall lost love and the sun setting red on the horizon, memory glimmering like the Host in the monstrance.

> Un coeur tendre, qui hait le néant vaste et noir,
> Du passé lumineux recueille tout vestige!
> Le soleil s'est noyé dans son sang qui se fige . . .
> Ton souvenir en moi luit comme un ostensoir![11]

> A tender heart which hates the great dark emptiness,
> recalling every trace of the brightness now gone; the sun drowns
> in its clotting blood, your memory flames in me like a monstrance.

The dance hall is transfigured and solemnized, the sacred and the profane coexist in air thick with the incense of the flowers.

The summer twilights of the Europe before the Great War are an imaginative territory that returns continually to haunt contemporary poets in English, as in Sean O'Brien's thoughtful cento of Rilke, 'Abendmusik'. The poet is present at a musical gathering in the drawing-room of a great house by the water:

> . . . You promise an angel
> To meet us, here in this room – let it be now –
> In the stars, in the dusk-heavy pier-glass
> Containing the river . . . [12]

But the angel never materializes, and an atmosphere of waiting,
repetition, even entrapment, grows slowly as stars come out
but the evening never moves into night. Very much the same
feeling is evoked by John Ash's 'Without Being Evening': the
elegant society of an empire reaching its end is in a city with
views out to seas and mountains, inhabiting a world of stasis and
languor, with natural and supernatural dangers waiting just out
of sight. The poem works within the tension between belle époque
Europe, and the slow fall of the empires of the ancient world,
city and shadow:

> From café terraces it is pleasant to watch
> the changing colours of the mountains
> as evening approaches, to conjure
> images of those near places it would be
> too troubling actually to visit –
>
> places where, at this hour, a deer steps down
> to a blue pool like an eye . . . [13]

Both of these poets are, more or less directly, paying homage to
Rainer Maria Rilke, himself a twilight figure inhabiting the end of
an empire, of a European order, but poised in the shadows between
multiple worlds, two of which might be identified as aristocratic
and modernist.

THE MANY BOOKSHOPS of Trieste all display piles of bilingual
editions of the *Elegie duinesi*. Rilke's great *Duino Elegies* were begun
a few miles to the west of the city, on a night of black wind blowing
over the clifftop castle at Duino, and in the wind he thought he

heard the celebrated first line of supplication to the unheeding orders of angels. The rich ambiguities of the *Elegies* fit them for local adoption, naturalization. (The city was Austrian when Rilke began them, Italian by the time they were finished.)

These *Elegies* are shot through with evening, as in the lovers in the *First Elegy* 'speaking wondrously in the night air'[14] ('*in der Nachtluft wunderlich reden*') and the overflowing calendar of affirmations of the *Seventh Elegy*:

> *nicht nur die Wege, nicht nur die Wiesen im Abend,*
> *nicht nur, nach spätem Gewitter, das atmende Klarsein,*
>
> . . .
>
> *sondern die Nächte! Sondern die hohen, des Sommers,*
> *Nächte, sondern die Sterne, die Sterne der Erde.*[15]

Not only the paths, not only the meadows at twilight, not that breathing at dusk, not that brightness which follows the storm . . . but the nights, the nights too, those tall nights of Summer, but the stars too, the stars of our Earth.

And it is by such evening paths through abruptly remote country that Rilke's last shape-shifting protagonist – the '*jungen* Toten' – the young man who has just died in the *Tenth Elegy* – follows a mature woman who is the personification of Grief, who is Grief itself, guardian of a starlit mountain landscape of authentic sorrow, into which the dead boy makes his way under blazing summer heavens. Their place of departure has been from one of Rilke's most disconcerting and elusive constructions, a raucous fairground on the outskirts of the City of Mourning (or, rather, the City of False Consolation). Beyond this fairground, beyond the hoardings that advertise an extra-bitter beer called 'Deathless', is a twilight place (time of day is not precisely defined, but the pursuit of Grief that begins here passes in seven lines to the night valleys and the starlit mountains) and the region lies in dusk as a place of transition, its reality ('*ists wirklich*') as a place lying between imaginary and expressive worlds:

. . . O aber gleich darüber hinaus,
Hinter den letzten Planke . . .

. . .

Kinder spielen, und Liebende halten einander, – abseits,
ernst, im ärmlichen Gras, und Hunde haben Natur.[16]

. . . Just opposite, only just after the last of the hoardings . . .
Children are playing, and lovers, a little apart, Hold one another on
thin, threadbare grass, and dogs will be dogs.

This whole imagined borderland of fairground and back-lot
resonates with a letter of Sylvia Townsend Warner's describing the
work of an unidentified young poet of the 1940s, a letter which is
itself almost a prose poem about urban high summer: 'He has got
the emotion of vulgarity, the overtone of fairs and bank holidays and
crowded summer parks, and people coming back in the evening
from their day out . . . this particular smell of bruised public grass.'[17]

LOOKING SEAWARD from the Piazza Grande and crowded esplanades
of Trieste on an evening of high summer, into the myriad colours of
the Adriatic clouds at nautical twilight (their roses and yellows
beginning to fade into uniform tones of grey and blue) brings another
line of Rilke's to mind, from one of his matchless poems on autumn:
'*Als welkten in den Himmeln ferne Gärten*' (As farthest gardens dwindle
in the skies). This image immediately recalls one of the forgotten
translations that I edited as a student (an example of that crepuscular
phenomenon, English baroque), a momentary interpolation in a
masque, a three-line improvisation on the evening sky:

> . . . Like Summer's Clouds
> When the Day feels a light'ning before Death,
> Or Gardens in the Air.[18]

Evening draws the high-summer crowds to walk on the esplanade
and out into the Adriatic on the great stone jetties, the *Mole*, which

reach westward into the waters, out towards the Habsburg palace of Miramare and the distant castle at Duino. It is inevitable that this book should find its end at Trieste, if a place can be (in a positive sense) a twilight place, then this frontier city, which I prefer to think of as a 'hinge city', is that place. It is also a haven at the turn of the Adriatic that offers an unrivalled point of vantage for the observation of the progress of twilight over water. Its great contemporary topographer, Claudio Magris, defines the gulf that stretches between the last Venetian outpost of Grado and the former Habsburg territories on the mainland: 'Those eleven kilometres mark the passage from the airy marine ethos of Venice to a continental and problematic *Mitteleuropa*, grand, morose laboratory of a civilisation's discontents, expert in emptiness and death.'[19]

Trieste is a place of twilights in itself – between languages, between western and central Europe. Culturally, the city is beguilingly 'transitional Europe', with Catholic, Greek and Serbian Orthodox cathedrals (S Giusto, S Nicolò, S Spiridione), as well as a fine synagogue: a cosmopolitan, pragmatically tolerant city, with considerable future potential as a place of convergence and discovery. Architecturally and linguistically it is hybrid: Italian, Slav, German. Indeed, all those languages were used at one point or another one evening at our table in the Caffè Tommaseo (as well as the new, inescapable *lingua franca*, English). A place of exile, perhaps disproportionately so in the imaginations of scholars of Anglo-Irish literature. From one perspective it is a city at the end of a line, the eastern terminus of the railway from Venice and Rome, from the familiar cities. And beyond it are territories coming to focus in the western imagination. Indistinct kingdoms – Istria, Illyria – are lost to the south beyond the capes and the sea haze.

As evening comes on the city blazes with light, brighter than any liner seen across the waters: floodlight and lamplight, refracted and reflected. One of the most complete and elegant ensembles created between the 1870s and 1930s is the great sea-square, the Piazza Unità d'Italia, with its flanking white stucco esplanades – the Savoia Excelsior hotel, great palaces of commerce and marine insurance.

Tall clusters of lights on magnificent standards in the Piazza. Globes of yellowish light all along the esplanades and some way along the Molo Audace, the chief pier and promenade thrown out into the waters. Glimpses up into the hills, to the floodlit citadel of ancient Cathedral and Roman forum; the lights of distant villas amongst trees. Pale stucco grandeurs along the esplanade: S Nicolò 'dei Greci' with its pediment and flanking towers; a great domed insurance building with statues flickering on the skyline. Cafés, hotels, restaurants. Music coming and going with the soft onshore wind.

The whole ensemble is a realization of all the nineteenth-century fantasies of the city radiant with electricity, of the city of light. On the Molo dei Bersaglieri the shallow arches of the art deco Stazione Marittima are lit with a greenish radiance, as though the lights shone through the aqueous etched glass of that epoch. This is the pier where great liners still dock. It can be seen at the end of the view down from high windows in the old town, with a liner the size of a cathedral at its end, under a late afternoon sky that turns (at this season) early to grey and rose with the airborne dust from the uplands behind the city.

Turning away from that brilliance, from the belle époque ensemble of white stucco and high, blazing streetlights, turning onto the Molo Audace, you see twilight prolonged to the west in all the rich subtleties of advancing evening – the depths of colour in the sea and sky, which are not yet night, not yet even astronomical twilight, but profoundest nautical twilight greatly prolonged. Lucent blues – aquamarine below, lapis lazuli above – still shine from the west, with subtler refractions of madder red and light-shot azure on the water below. The sun may seem far below the horizon, but there is still moving light in the sky. Time seems suspended, nightfall postponed.

There are piercing blue lights let into the paving of the great piazza; lights of the same intense blue are set into the bollards along the esplanade. These combine to form a poetic evocation of the frontier of the retreated sea, the old shoreline before the great engineering works of the nineteenth century. There is a vendor moving through the piazza selling balls that sparkle with blue light when they are moved or thrown – magically it is exactly the same intense blue as the lights in the paving. The effect of these blue lights thrown up into the dark is haunting, as they flash and shine against the darkening inland sky above the gleaming stucco buildings. It is as though the blue lights in the paving have become animated, soaring at random into the evening above the city. Slow in their descent, the effect is like a continuous, measured firework display, like the regular and irregular play of vast, glimmering fountains.

Walking out onto the Molo beyond the lamps, into the high-summer night and the sound and breath of the sea, is to move into the summer festivals painted in the belle époque, something more intricate than Sargent's lanterns in a country garden, complex in feeling like Baudelaire's pleasure garden, more of the urbane order of J. D. Fergusson's evocation of fireworks over the esplanade at Dieppe.

This work, *Dieppe, 14 July 1905: Night* (National Galleries of Scotland; see p. 234) was painted relatively early in Fergusson's long career, when he was in his early thirties. It is dominated by a profound blue sky, under which elegant figures in white summer clothes or evening dress stroll on a promenade by grey water. A great avenue of streetlights curves away towards lit buildings in the distance. The whole is dominated by a great incandescent blaze of fireworks on the far side of the water, from which great rockets have shot up on stems of fire to explode in white, yellow and pink light in the heights of the sky.

The influence of Whistler's famous *Nocturne in Black and Gold: The Falling Rocket* (1875) is palpable, but compared to Whistler's sombre colouration, only partially relieved by yellow light on the ground and in the sky, Fergusson's painting is shaped and illuminated by the brilliance of the fireworks. The rendering of both the direct and reflected light of these is achieved with great economy of means, as it modifies the deep hue of the sky and throws a border of rose-coloured light onto the white shawl of a woman in the foreground, catches a gleam from the paving of the promenade.

The chief impression of the picture, apart from the sensuous profundity of the cobalt night, as offset against white clothes and resplendent fire, is of immediacy – like Sargent's work it is an attempt at the old illusion of a moment caught in a moment – the fireworks fixed in their curving, branching descents; the choreography of the two crossing groups of elegant strollers; the fleeting stillness of the man in a white suit who has turned his back, his hands in his pockets, his whole attention absorbed by the coloured fires rising from the other side of the water. Warm season and slow moment are powerfully conveyed by airy and rapid brushwork, light figures varnished onto depths of sky.

That moment is described as 'night' in the title, but what the painting conveys is the cobalt of the very end of nautical twilight: the clear outlines of the distant buildings hint that there is still a little ambient light as well as artificial light, light subordinate to the fireworks that are the picture's chief focus. From the pure brightness of the fireworks themselves come subtle flickerings of colour that draw the composition together: touches of red on the white clothes of the women in the foreground picking up the pure red blaze of the falling rockets. In the grey water, the reflections of their falls are perfectly rendered as a vestigial constellation of specks of yellow.

Fergusson's picture remains in the mind walking further out to sea along the Molo Audace, with the blue lights that soar through the sky above the piazza glimmering against the inland evening. After the streetlamps give out in the warm dark, there are benches, groups in quiet conversation. A young man, sitting alone, is playing his guitar to himself, to the Adriatic – soft alternations of major and minor chords. Looking back, lights from the city and the Stazione Marittima mingle on the surface of the waters at his feet, like a glimmering carpet of jade green and Naples yellow.

Turning, moving away to seawards. I moved away from the light thus, decades ago, leaving the fair on Midsummer Common in Cambridge, walking with my oldest friend. Booths and lights and the noise of people growing distant. Fading shouts from the Sky Skimmer; a panache of Lucozade-coloured light bulbs rotating, flickering in the distance against a backdrop of chestnut leaves, and the two of us moving away into the darkness under the trees, both finding ourselves unaccountably moved by the long shadows of the crowds thrown outwards onto the grass, as though we were leaving behind something infinitely more wonderful than a transitory constellation of coloured lights and mechanical music.

THERE IS A SINGLE PILOT BOAT riding on the sombre cobalt of the Adriatic, its white lights casting long streamers of reflection across the waves. Exactly above it, the evening star – so late – is riding in clear sky above the stroke of purple-grey cloud lingering on the western horizon.

Walking on, facing out to the west, further out into the waters. Through crowds that move softly in the dark, dressed in their pale summer clothes. Then further out into the smell of salt and the steady, soft percussion of the little waves, and the colours come clearer to the west, the colours of the last of the light. And to walk thus, warm air stirring white linen, amidst the flow and counterflow of people strolling through this festal high summer, through this always lingering, endless end of twilight, is to move westward under glimmers fading rose and aquamarine, strolling on the still-warm flagstones, music coming and going on the water, as if there were no night, nor morning, nor death.

REFERENCES

INTRODUCTION

1 John Ruskin, *Praeterita*, vol. xxxv of *The Works of John Ruskin*, ed. E. T. Cook and Alexander Wedderburn (London, 1903–12), p. 286. A popular version of this perception is cited by Aden and Marjorie Meinel in their *Sunsets, Twilights and Evening Skies* (Cambridge, 1983), p. 1: 'as in Bing Crosby's theme song of Big Radio days "the blue of the night meets the gold of the day"'.

2 Angela Carter, *Black Venus* (London, 1985), p. 9.

3 Lawrence Durrell, *Bitter Lemons* (London, 1957), p. 19.

4 *Beowulf*, ll. 642–51.

5 Seamus Heaney, trans., *Beowulf* (London, 1999), p. 22.

6 'Te lucis ante terminum', in *Early Latin Hymns*, ed. A. S. Walpole (Cambridge, 1922), p. 299.

7 *The Works of John Ruskin*, ed. E. T. Cook and Alexander Wedderburn (London, 1908), xxxiv, pp. 28–9.

8 Sappho, fragment xc.

9 Nigel Lewis, *The Book of Babel: Words and the Way We See Things* (London, 1994), p. 199.

10 Ibid., p. 200.

11 For detailed consideration of the metaphorical shadows of British 'dark corners', in the historian's phrase, see chapter Four in this volume.

12 For a fuller discussion of these, see chapter Two.

13 Vladimir Nabokov, *Pale Fire* (Harmondsworth, 1973), p. 29.

14 T. S. Eliot, *The Complete Poems and Plays* (London, 1969), p. 173.

15 Donald Ritchie, *A Tractate on Japanese Aesthetics* (Berkeley, CA, 2007), pp. 47–8.

16 Aden and Marjorie Meinel, *Sunsets, Twilights and Evening Skies* (Cambridge, 1983), see especially pp. 11–12, 25–6.

17 Emily Winterburn, 'Twilight for Astronomers and Physicists', in *Twilight: Photography in the Magic Hour*, ed. Martin Barnes and Kate Best, exh. cat., Victoria & Albert Museum, London (London, 2006), p. 25.

18 For these, see chapter Two.

19 Peter Wright, *The Language of British Industry* (London, 1974), pp. 141–2.

20 Definition from Lester V. Berrey and Melvin van der Bank,
   The American Thesaurus of Slang (London, 1954).

21 Barnes and Best, eds, *Twilight: Photography in the Magic Hour*.

22 W. H. Auden, *Collected Poems*, ed. Edward Mendelson (London,
   1991), p. 493.

23 Ibid., p. 459.

24 Lawrence Smith, *The Japanese Print since 1900* (London, 1983),
   pp. 23–4.

25 Victor Hugo, *Les Chants du crépuscule*, vol. XVI of *Oeuvres
   Complètes* (Paris, 1909), p. 178: 'Tout aujourd'hui, dans les idées
   comme dans les choses, dans la société comme dans l'individu, est
   à l'état de crépuscule. De quelle nature est ce crépuscule? de quoi
   sera-t-il suivi? . . . c'est cet étrange état crépusculaire de l'âme et de
   la société dans le siècle où nous vivons; c'est cette brume au dehors,
   cette incertitude au dedans; c'est ce je ne sais quoi d'à demi éclairé
   qui nous environne.'

26 Paul Verlaine, *Selected Poems* [bilingual edn], trans. C. F.
   MacIntyre (Berkeley, Los Angeles and London, 1948), p. 28.

1 ABOUT SHADOWS AND GARDENS

1 Federico García Lorca, 'Romance de la Guardia Civil española',
  Selected Poems, ed. and trans. Merryn Williams (Newcastle, 1992),
  p. 108. Before the Civil War, about the time in the 1920s when
  Lorca was composing his *Romancero gitano*, my grandfather served
  as Consul or Honorary Consul for the Anglo-Spanish community
  of sherry merchants at Cádiz. Thus I have often speculated as to
  whether he could be the *'cónsul de los Ingleses'* who offers warm
  milk and gin to the gypsy woman Preciosa in her flight from the
  importunities of the wind (ibid., p. 70).

2 Ibid., 'Prendimiento de Antoñito el Camborio en el camino del
  Sevilla', p. 98.

3 Ibid.

4 Ronald Firbank, 'Concerning the Eccentricities of Cardinal Pirelli',
  in *The Complete Ronald Firbank* (London, 1961), p. 648.

5 Ibid.

6 Ibid., p. 650

7 Ibid., p. 669.

8 Guido Gozzano, *The Man I Pretend to Be*, ed. and trans. Michael
  Palma (Princeton, NJ, 1981), p. 148.

9 Ibid., p. 150. The prose translations are my own.

10 The term, applied to a loose group of poets who never constituted a formal school or movement, was first used in *La Stampa* (1 September 1910) by the critic Giuseppe Antonio Borghese.

11 Gozzano, *The Man I Pretend to Be*, p. 66.

12 Ibid., p. 108.

13 Ibid., p. 68.

14 Ibid., p. 82.

15 Ibid., p. 96.

16 Ibid.

17 See the Introduction in this volume.

18 *Odyssey*, x.507–9; Richmond Lattimore, trans., *The Odyssey of Homer* (New York, 1991), p. 165.

19 *Odyssey*, xi.11–16; Lattimore, trans., p. 168.

20 *Aeneid*, vi.238; H. Rushton Fairclough, ed. and trans. (Cambridge, MA, and London, 1974), i, p. 522.

21 *Aeneid* vi.264–6; Lattimore, trans., p. 524.

22 *Aeneid* vi.390; Lattimore, trans., p. 532.

23 *Aeneid* vi.444; Lattimore, trans., p. 536.

24 *Aeneid* vi.452–3; Lattimore, trans., p. 536.

25 'Virgil's evening' will be discussed in chapter Five of this volume.

26 *Ausonius*, ed. and trans. Hugh Evelyn White (Cambridge, MA, and London, repr. 1951), vol. i, p. 208.

27 A. S. Walpole, ed., *Early Latin Hymns* (Cambridge, 1922), p. 299.

28 Ibid., pp. 134–5.

29 *The Towneley Mysteries*, Surtees Society (London, 1836), p. 196 ('The Buffeting', ll. 253–4).

30 Adrian Fortescue, J. B. O'Connell and Alcuin Reid, *The Ceremonies of the Roman Rite Described* (London, 2009), pp. 335–6.

31 *Threni, id est Lamentationes* i:1–2.

32 Evelyn Waugh, *Brideshead Revisited* (Harmondsworth, 1975), p. 331.

33 Marc-Antoine Charpentier, *Leçons de ténèbres de Jeudi Sainct*, Concerto Vocale, René Jacobs; Harmonia Mundi, HMA 1951006, 2001.

34 Théophile Gautier, *Voyage en Espagne* (1840), quoted in William T. O'Dea, *The Social History of Lighting* (London, 1958), p. 150.

35 Stephen Orgel and Roy Strong, *Inigo Jones: The Theatre of the Stuart Court* (London and Berkeley, CA, 1973), vol. ii, p. 481.

36 Andrew Gurr, *The Shakespearean Stage* (Cambridge, 1992), pp. 202–4.

37 John Ash, 'Portraits ii', *Casino, The Branching Stairs* (Manchester, 1984), p. 13.

38 Ibid.
39 Joseph Conrad, *Heart of Darkness and Other Stories* (Ware, 1995), p. 102.
40 Ibid., p. 103.
41 Ibid., pp. 104–5.
42 In the Allen Memorial Art Museum, Oberlin College, Ohio. Cf. Guido Jansen and Peter C. Sutton, *Michael Sweerts, 1618–1664* (Zwolle, 2002), pp. 164–5.
43 Ibid., pp. 161–3.
44 Ibid., pp. 130–32.
45 Ibid., p. 108, where the resemblance of the theme to works by Teniers is emphasized.
46 Ibid., pp. 106–7.
47 Ibid., p. 106, citing Rolf Kultzen.

2 ENGLISH MELANCHOLY

1 Christopher Isherwood, *Lions and Shadows* (Norfolk, CT, 1947), p. 23.
2 Lethbridge's typescript 'Observations upon Unusual Phenomena noted in the Cambridge District, June–August, 1940', published by Tim Brennan as part of his artist's book *English Anxieties* (Brighton and Cardiff, 2009).
3 Isherwood, *Lions and Shadows*, p. 67.
4 Ibid., p. 68.
5 This extraordinary, terrifying series of paranoid deductions is preserved in the Mass Observation archive, now at the University of Sussex, although it appears that they were originally offered in all seriousness to the security services. The document has been republished with commentary by Tim Brennan in his artist's book *English Anxieties*.
6 Michael Innes was a pseudonym of the novelist J.I.M. Stewart (1906–1994). He published many crime and mystery fiction books under this alias.
7 Michael Innes, *The Bloody Wood* (Harmondsworth, 1968), pp. 11, 155. These passages are testimony to support Philip Larkin's appreciative characterization of Innes's genre fiction: 'I don't know why there has never been a serious study of him: he's a beautifully sophisticated writer, very funny, and, now and then, very moving.' Philip Larkin, *Required Writing* (London, 1983), p. 53.
8 C. S. Lewis, *The Magician's Nephew* (London, 1955), p. 61.

9   Frances Cornford, RCM *Magazine* (Easter 1959), quoted in Ursula
    Vaughan Williams, *R.V.W.: A Biography of Ralph Vaughan
    Williams* (London, 1964), p. 35.
10 Louis MacNeice, 'Valediction', *Collected Poems*, ed. E. R. Dodds
    (London, 1979), p. 52.
11 Peter Levi, *Agenda*, XXIV/3 (Autumn 1986), p. 6 [Peter Levi special
    issue].
12 Emily Dickinson, 'There's a certain Slant of light', quoted in *The
    Rattle Bag*, ed. Seamus Heaney and Ted Hughes (London, 1982),
    pp. 418–19.
13 Robert Louis Stevenson, *A Child's Garden of Verses* (New York,
    1906), p. 31.
14 Matthew Arnold, 'The Scholar Gypsy', *Poetical Works of Matthew
    Arnold* (London, 1898), p. 277.
15 T. S. Eliot, *The Complete Poems and Plays* (London, 1969), p. 21.
16 Sean O'Brien, 'Grimshaw', *The Drowned Book* (London, 2007), p. 66.
17 All this section owes much to discussions with Mark Gibson. The
    most comprehensive work on Grimshaw to date is *Atkinson
    Grimshaw, Painter of Moonlight*, ed. Jane Sellars, exh. cat., Mercer
    Art Gallery, Harrogate and Guildhall Art Gallery, London (London,
    2011), especially pp. 87–112.
18 All quotations that follow are from Sean O'Brien's poem 'Grimshaw'
    in his collection *The Drowned Book* (London, 2007), p. 66.
19 Notes from Mark Gibson, Esq.
20 Alfred, Lord Tennyson, *Poetical Works* (London, 1899), p. 7.
21 Mercer Art Gallery, Harrogate.
22 John Ruskin, *Modern Painters* in *The Works of John Ruskin*, vol. III,
    ed. E. T. Cook and Alexander Wedderburn (London, 1903), p. 275.
23 Ibid., p. 274.
24 John Ruskin, 'The Storm Cloud of the Nineteenth Century', lecture
    delivered 4 February 1884 at the London Institution, in *The Works
    of John Ruskin*, vol. XXXIV, ed. E. T. Cook and Alexander Wedder-
    burn (London, 1908), p. 40.
25 Ibid., p. 10.
26 Ibid., p. 63.
27 Ibid., p. 35, describing the evening of Sunday 25 June 1876.
28 Ibid., p. 36.
29 John Ruskin, *Academy Notes* for 1856, in *The Works of John Ruskin*,
    vol. XIV, ed. E. T. Cook and Alexander Wedderburn (London,
    1904), pp. 66–7. All of the effects that Ruskin praises could have
    been found in the works of the north German painters of the early

nineteenth century, then virtually unknown in Britain. *Autumn Leaves* was in fact painted in Perth, although there seems to be an element of freedom in the rendering of the distant landscape, and the treatment of the town-smoke in the valley brings it close in atmosphere to the works which Millais painted in England.

30 Steven Connor, 'A Certain Slant of Light', in *Twilight, Photography in the Magic Hour*, ed. Martin Barnes and Kate Best, exh. cat., Victoria & Albert Museum, London (London, 2006), p. 26.

31 Ruskin, 'Storm Cloud of the Nineteenth Century', p. 34.

32 John Batchelor, *John Ruskin, No Wealth but Life* (London, 2000), p. 288. On p. 289 Batchelor observes the degree to which Ruskin's mental collapse manifested itself in obsession with the weather.

33 Ruskin, 'Storm Cloud of the Nineteenth Century', p. 36.

34 Ibid., p. 37, describing 17 August 1879. For the evening observations of the poet Gerard Manley Hopkins, and for the observations on carbon pollution and 'black rain' of his colleague S. J. Perry of the Stonyhurst observatory, see chapter Four. It is a haunting thought that Hopkins and Ruskin, 60 miles apart in the Lancashire of the early 1880s, were observing the same twilights and evening skies. I know of no record of their meeting or correspondence.

35 Ibid., pp. 38–9.

36 Ibid., p. 40.

37 Ibid., p. 63.

38 Aden and Marjorie Meinel, *Sunsets, Twilights and Evening Skies* (Cambridge, 1983), p. 51.

39 Ruskin, 'Storm Cloud of the Nineteenth Century', p. 78.

40 G. J. Symons, ed., *The Eruption of Krakatoa and Subsequent Phenomena* (London, 1887), p. iii.

41 Ibid., p. 49.

42 Ibid., pp. 152–78. For a full discussion of the observations, published by the Royal Society at pp. 222–3, made by 'Gerard Hopkins, Stonyhurst', see chapter Four.

43 Ibid., p. 153.

44 Ibid., p. 167.

45 Ibid., p. 171.

46 Alfred, Lord Tennyson, *The Poetical Works* (London, 1899), p. 55.

47 Ibid., p. 80.

48 Ibid., p. 81.

49 Ibid., p. 97.

50 Ibid., p. 281; Hopkins could quote this stanza from memory.

51 Ibid., p. 282.

52 'Crossing the Bar', ibid., p. 636.
53 The poem dates from 1857 but the present chapel by Butterfield, with its wildly inventive tower, dates from 1872.
54 Matthew Arnold, 'Rugby Chapel', *Poetical Works* (London, 1898), p. 304.
55 John Ash, 'Bespalko's Devotions', *The Branching Stairs* (Manchester, 1984), p. 107.
56 Sylvia Townsend Warner, *Lolly Willowes; or, the Loving Huntsman* (London, 1926), p. 76.
57 Ibid., p. 77.
58 Ibid., p. 128.
59 Mark Cocker, *Crow Country* (London, 2008), pp. 137–8.
60 Ibid., p. 139.
61 Ibid.
62 John Meade Falkner, *Poems* (London, 1933), pp. 60–61.
63 Ibid., p. 30.
64 A hauntingly close equivalent of those lost, misty places can be found in the landscape photographs of the contemporary Robert Davies; www.robertdavies.uk.com, accessed 15 October 2014.
65 Sean O'Brien, 'The Island', *November* (London, 2011), p. 41.
66 Alan Powers, *Eric Ravilious, Artist and Designer* (Farnham, 2013).
67 O'Brien, 'The Island'.
68 Peter Levi, *The Flutes of Autumn* (London, 1983), p. 82.
69 Levi, *Agenda* [Peter Levi Special Issue], p. 5.
70 Levi, *The Flutes of Autumn*, p. 135.
71 Dodie Smith, *Stories of the Hundred and One Dalmatians* (London, 1989), pp. 88, 91–2.
72 Sylvia Townsend Warner, 'Memories of Laurel Lodge, Moth Hall and Fineshade Priory', in *With the Hunted: Selected Writings*, ed. Peter Tolhurst (Norwich, 2012), pp. 22–3.
73 In the *Shell Guide to Oxfordshire* (London, 1938); see also David Heathcote, *A Shell Eye on England* (Faringdon, Oxfordshire, 2011), p. 58.
74 Laurence Whistler, *The Laughter and the Urn: The Life of Rex Whistler* (London, 1985), p. 66.
75 Peter Scupham, 'Hauntings: Walter de la Mare', *Collected Poems* (Manchester, 2002), p. 189.
76 T. S. Eliot, 'To Walter de la Mare', *Complete Poems and Plays*, p. 204.
77 Walter de la Mare, 'The Children of Stare', *Collected Poems* (London, 1979), p. 21.

78 Ibid., p. 179.

79 Ibid., p. 5.

80 Ibid., p. 205.

81 Walter de la Mare, 'Crewe', in *The Faber Book of Ghost Stories*, ed. Anne Ridler (London, 1945), p. 261.

82 A part of the sheer horror of James's story, a story based on a narrative told to him as truth, is the nightmarish passivity of the governess narrator, who remains imprisoned in the isolated country house with its revenants, never seeking the assistance of the local clergyman, despite being described as herself a cleric's daughter. Jane Stevenson's fascinating suggestion is that the original oral narration would have made complete and terrible sense if set in an ascendancy house in Ireland, rather than in England. It would seem that James was told the story as originating from Yorkshire, although it is uncertain if it is meant to have happened there.

83 De la Mare, *Collected Poems*, pp. 265, 268.

84 Harold Owen, *Journey from Obscurity* (London, 1963), pp. 79–84.

85 Ibid., p. 80.

86 Ibid., pp. 80–81.

87 Ibid., p. 81.

88 Ibid., p. 82.

89 The authorship seems certain: there is also a fine verse on her brother's tomb at Hambleden in Buckinghamshire. See also Peter Davidson, *Poetry and Revolution* (Oxford, 1998), p. 18.

90 Ibid.

91 The reticent Pevsner is moved to describe it as 'a work of great importance and exceptional beauty'; Nikolaus Pevsner, *The Buildings of England: Leicestershire and Rutland* (Harmondsworth, 1960), p. 297.

92 Davidson, *Poetry and Revolution*, pp. 413–15.

93 I cannot now recover an assertion made unreferenced in a nineteenth-century history that one defeated Royalist had his windows varnished during the interregnum, so as to live out the Cavalier winter in a perpetual twilight of mourning. It may be an antiquarian urban myth based on the real 'mourning chamber' of Thomas Bushell, described by John Aubrey.

94 See also Malcolm Rogers, *William Dobson, 1611–46*, exh. cat., National Portrait Gallery, London (London, 1983).

95 Ibid., no. 23.

96 Ibid., no. 33.

97 Ibid., no. 19.

98 'Concord is conquer'd: In this urne there lies / The Master of great Musick's mysteries, / And in it is a riddle like the *cause: Will. Lawes* was slain by such whose *wills* were *laws*.' Thomas Jordan's quatrain quoted in Geoffrey Hill, *Broken Hierarchies: Poems, 1952–2012*, ed. Kenneth Haynes (Oxford, 2013), p. 789.

99 I am much indebted to Prof. Stephen Orgel for this phrase, personal communication, February 2014.

100 Recorded by Phantasm for Lynn Records. I am indebted to Laurence Dreyfus's programme notes for the adjective 'Elysian' applied to the first movement of the *Set a6 in B flat*.

101 Harold Love, 'The Religious Traditions of the North and l'Estrange Families', in *Writing and Religion in England, 1558–1689*, ed. Roger D. Sell and Anthony W. Johnson (Farnham, 2009), pp. 411–27.

102 Ibid., p. 418.

103 Ibid., pp. 419–20.

104 Geoffrey Hill, *Clavics* (London, 2011), p. 15.

105 Ibid., p. 19.

106 Geoffrey Hill, 'Damon's Lament for his Clorinda, Yorkshire 1654', *Tenebrae* (London, 1978), p. 23.

107 'Vocations', *Tenebrae*, p. 29.

108 Ibid., p. 33.

109 Geoffrey Hill, *Broken Hierarchies: Poems, 1952–2012*, ed. Kenneth Haynes (Oxford, 2013), p. 382.

110 Ibid., p. 435.

111 A. E. Housman, *A Shropshire Lad and Other Poems*, ed. Archie Burnett (London, 2010), p. 37.

112 Ibid., p. 130.

113 Ibid., p. 85.

114 Ibid., p. 154.

115 Ibid., p. 173.

116 Personal communication from the late Sir Geoffrey Keynes, early 1980s.

117 Charles Dickens, *The Mystery of Edwin Drood* (London, 1870), p. 6.

118 Ibid., p. 4.

119 Thomas Hardy, *Collected Poems* (London, 1930), p. 137.

120 Ibid.

121 There is a watercolour version of *Pegwell Bay* (perhaps a preparatory sketch for it) in Aberdeen Art Gallery, in which none of the foreground figures are present – only two working women in the middle distance gathering shellfish. It emphasizes how much

of the emotional charge of the picture is carried by the foreground group of figures in the oil version.

122 Paul Wheatley, *The Pivot of the Four Quartets* (Edinburgh, 1971), p. 435, quoting (without reference) Nelson Wu on things evoked by colour associated with autumn.

123 MacNeice, 'Birmingham', *Collected Poems*, p. 47.

124 W. H. Auden, *The English Auden*, ed. Edward Mendelson (London, 1986), p. 100.

125 O'Brien, 'Five Railway Poems for Birtley Aris', *The Drowned Book*, p. 61.

126 Sean O'Brien, 'Sunday in a Station of the Metro', *November* (London, 2011), p. 36.

127 Ibid., p. 31. The coinage echoes the Decembrists and Octobrists of Russian Revolutions, and there are, or have been, in North America, bands both Novembrist and Decembrist.

128 Simon Armitage, *Tyrannosaurus Rex versus the Corduroy Kid* (London, 2006), p. 40.

129 'Thomas Kerrich', Oxford Dictionary of National Biography, accessed 23 August 2013.

130 Private Collection, London. See Paul Spencer-Longhurst, *Moonrise over Europe* (London, 2006), p. 110.

131 William T. O'Dea, *The Social History of Lighting* (London, 1958), p. 49.

132 Arnaud Maillet, *Le Miroir noir* (Paris, 2005).

133 Donald Ritchie, *A Tractate on Japanese Aesthetics* (Berkeley, CA, 2007), pp. 54–5.

134 William Collins, 'Ode to Evening', *The Longman Anthology of Poetry*, ed. Lynne McMahon and Averill Curdy (New York, 2006); available at www.poetryfoundation.org, accessed 12 December 2014.

135 *Designs by Mr R. Bentley for six poems by Mr T. Gray* (London 1789), p. 29.

136 Samuel Taylor Coleridge, *The Works in Prose and Verse* (Philadelphia, PA, 1840), p. 58.

137 Ibid.

138 Dorothy Wordsworth, *Journals*, ed. William Knight (London and New York, 1904), vol. I, p. 4.

139 Ibid., p. 83.

140 A matchless account of Cotman's formative painting tours in northern England is given in David Hill, *Cotman in the North: Watercolours of Durham and Yorkshire* (New Haven, CT, and London, 2005).

141 For a discussion of some of the earliest attempts to photograph the twilight of evening, see chapter Three.

142 John Ruskin, *The Stones of Venice* (Orpington and London, 1894), p. 1.

3 CITIES OF EVENING

1 Quoted by Derek Hudson, *James Pryde* (London, 1949), p. 90, and by Louise Welsh, 'James Pryde: The Edgar Allen Poe of Painting', *The Bottle Imp*, 6 (November 2009), available at www.arts.gla.ac.uk, accessed 30 July 2014; the other chief published source for Pryde's paintings is Ann Simpson, *James Pryde*, exh. cat., National Galleries of Scotland, Edinburgh (1992).

2 Hudson, *James Pryde*, p. 64.

3 Ibid., p. 81, identifies two unfinished paintings in Pryde's studio for more than a decade: *The Untouchables* and *The Death of the Great Bed*.

4 Augustus John, quoted in Hudson, *James Pryde*, p. 82.

5 Simpson, *James Pryde*, no. 25.

6 'Claud Lovat Fraser's Set Design for *The Beggar's Opera*', www.vam.ac.uk, accessed 7 August 2014.

7 Technically, Pryde's mature figure painting owes a good deal to English baroque sketches in general, but there is particularly close resemblance between the figures in *The Human Comedy* and Thornhill's sketches *Time, Truth and Justice* and *Time, Prudence and Vigilance* in Manchester Art Gallery.

8 Ann Simpson, *James Pryde*, cat. no. 71.

9 Government Art Collection.

10 'D'hyacinthe et d'or', 'L'Invitation au Voyage', *Les Fleurs du mal* (Paris, 1972), p. 84.

11 G. K. Chesterton, 'A Defence of Detective Stories', *The Defendant* (London, 1901), pp. 118–23; available at www.chesterton.org, accessed 12 August 2014.

12 Ibid.

13 Parts of his series *Les Vampires* (1915) use hand tinting on the film to indicate night with blue and twilight and dim interiors with lavender colour.

14 T. S. Eliot, *The Complete Poems and Plays* (London, 1969), p. 22. Of course, Eliot's city is inevitably a compound of Boston and London.

15 G. K. Chesterton, *The Penguin Complete Father Brown* (Harmondsworth, 1981). pp. 54, 64, 424, 634.

16 Eliot, *Complete Poems and Plays*, p. 22.

17 Charles Dickens, *Bleak House* (London, 1948), p. 1.

18 Ibid., p. 9.

19 Ibid., p. 795.

20 George Eliot, *Daniel Deronda* (Edinburgh and London, n.d.), p. 127 [Book II, Chapter 27].

21 Ibid., p. 140.

22 Michael Steinman, ed., *The Element of Lavishness: Letters of Sylvia Townsend Warner and William Maxwell* (Washington, DC, 2001), p. 50.

23 Virginia Woolf, 'Street Haunting: A London Adventure' (1930), in *Selected Essays*, ed. David Bradshaw (London, 2008), pp. 177–87.

24 Ibid.

25 James McNeill Whistler, 'Mr Whistler's Ten O'Clock Public Lecture, Prince's Hall, Piccadilly, 20 February 1885', available at www.whistler.arts.gla.ac.uk, accessed 30 August 2013.

26 Anna Whistler, the artist's mother, in a letter to Julia and Kate Palmer, 3 November 1871; quoted in Richard Dorment and Margaret F. MacDonald, *James McNeill Whistler*, exh. cat., Tate Gallery, London (London, 1994), pp. 122–3, no. 46.

27 Dorment and MacDonald, *James McNeill Whistler*, p. 122. This purely visual assertion is to some degree at odds with the narrative of transformation and enchantment attributed to twilight in the lecture.

28 The other is a sunset painting that he titled *Variations in Violet and Green*: the extreme colouration suggested by the title, at this date, presumably was due simply to pollution.

29 Eliot, *Complete Poems and Plays,* pp. 21, 18.

30 '*nous plongerons*', Charles Baudelaire, 'Chant d'Automne', *Les Fleurs du mal* (Paris, 1972), p. 87; '*Voici le soir*', 'Le Crépuscule du Soir', ibid., p. 128; 'as the air-frost comes down', '*Et sur qui dès longtemps descendent les frimas . . . vos pâles ténèbres*', 'Brumes et Pluies', ibid., p. 135.

31 Eliot, *Complete Poems and Plays*, p. 68.

32 Ibid., p. 74.

33 For a superb history of photography in the twilight, and of Silvy's place within that tradition, see Martin Barnes and Kate Best, eds, *Twilight: Photography in the Magic Hour*, exh. cat., Victoria & Albert Museum, London (London, 2006), especially pp. 10–23.

34 Mark Haworth-Booth, *Camille Silvy, Photographer of Modern Life* (London, 2010), pp. 34–8, 142–3.

35 The eponymous *Evening Star* in Friedrich's view of Dresden so titled is equally hard to pinpoint.

36 Haworth-Booth, *Camille Silvy*, pp. 48–59.

37 This comprehensive analysis is that of Weston Naef, published in *Photographers of Genius at the Getty* (Los Angeles, CA, 2004), p. 40; quoted in Haworth-Booth, *Camille Silvy*, p. 59.

38 A remarkable series of stereoscopic photographs of the progress of a sunset on Loch of Park, taken by the Aberdeen photographer George Washington Wilson (1823–93), date from 1859 and appear to be successful captures of sunset and dusk taken with very short exposures.

39 All the following information about twilight in the cinema was kindly supplied by Dr Jonathan Key, who has taken notable trouble to collect material for this book.

40 Jules Laforgue, 'L'hiver qui vient', in *The Penguin Book of French Poetry, 1820–1950*, ed. William Rees (London, 1990), p. 349.

41 This would be particularly true of the deep shadows in his unusually densely furnished *Interior Strandgade 30* in the Kunsthalle, Hamburg.

42 *Dust in Sunbeams, Strandgade 30*, cf. Poul Ved, *Hammershøi, vaerk og liv* (Copenhagen, 2003), p. 227.

43 Felix Krämer, Naoki Sato and Anne-Birgitte Fonsmark, *Hammershøi*, exh. cat., Royal Academy of Arts, London (London, 2008), pp. 25, 39.

44 Tiroler Landesmuseum Ferdinandeum, Innsbruck.

45 W. G. Sebald, *Austerlitz*, trans. Anthea Bell (London, 2011), p. 188.

46 Ibid., pp. 190–91.

47 Ibid., p. 192.

48 Ibid., p. 205.

49 Ibid., p. 221.

50 Ibid., p. 222.

51 Ibid., p. 415.

52 Angela Carter, *Black Venus* (London, 1985), p. 9.

53 Victor Hugo, *Les Chants du crépuscule*, vol. XVI of *Oeuvres Complètes* (Paris, 1909), p. 181.

54 Jules Laforgue, *Poésies complètes*, ed. Pascal Pia (Paris, 1979), II, p. 181.

55 Ibid., p. 157.

56 Ibid., p. 106.

57 Georges Rodenbach, *Bruges-la-Morte*, trans. Mike Mitchell and Will Stone, intro. Alan Hollinghurst (Sawtry, 2005).

58 Ibid., p. 25.

59 Ibid., p. 30.

60 Ibid., p. 131.

61 Frances Fowle, 'Silent Cities', *Van Gogh to Kandinsky: Symbolist Landscape in Europe, 1880–1910*, ed. Richard Thomson and Rodolph Rapetti, exh. cat., Scottish National Gallery, Edinburgh (2012), pp. 105–25.

62 The classic discussion of this is in Joseph Leo Koerner, *Caspar David Friedrich and the Subject of Landscape* (London, 2009), especially pp. 194–5.

63 Ibid., p. 269.

64 Ibid., p. 291.

65 Johann Wolfgang von Goethe, *Werke, Briefe und Gespräche* (Zurich, 1949), vol. XVI, p. 47. '*Auf einer Harzreise im Winter stieg ich gegen Abend vom Brocken herunter. . . die Sonne senkte sich eben gegen die Oderteiche hinunter. Waren den Tag über, bei dem gelblichen Ton des Schnees, schon leise violette Schatten bemerklich gewesen, so musste man sie nun für hochblau ansprechen, als ein gesteigertes Gelb von den beleuchteten Teilen widerschien. Als aber die Sonne sich endlich ihrem Niedergang näherte und ihr durch die stärkeren Dünste höchst gemässigter Strahl die ganze mich umgebende Welt mit der schönsten Purpurfarbe überzog, da verwandelte sich die Schattenfarbe in ein Grün, das nach seiner Klarheit einem Meergrün, nach seiner Schönheit einem Smaragdgrün verglichen werden konnte. Die Erscheinung ward immer lebhafter, man glaubte sich in einer Feenwelt zu befinden, denn alles hatte sich in die zwei lebhaften und so schön übereinstimmenden Farben gekleidet, bis endlich mit dem Sonnenuntergang die Prachterscheinung sich in eine graue Dämmerung, und nach und nach in eine mond – und sternhelle Nacht verlor.*' This passage has been kindly translated for this book by Dr Hugh Salvesen.

66 Victoria Crowe, *Real and Reflected*, exh. cat., Scottish Gallery, Edinburgh, 1–30 August 2014; available at www.scottish-gallery.co.uk, accessed 4 March 2015.

67 Helen Tookey, *Missel-Child* (Manchester, 2014), p. 68.

68 Ibid.

4 Dark Corners

1 Henry Foley SJ, *Records of the English Province of the Society of Jesus* (London, 1875) , vol. II, p. 230.

2 Peter Levi, *The Flutes of Autumn* (London, 1983), p. 99.

3 John Henry Newman, 'Sermon 10: The Second Spring' ['Sermon preached July 13, 1852, in St Mary's, Oscott, in the first Provincial Synod of Westminster'], in *Sermons Preached on Various Occasions* (London, 1908), p. 168; available at www.newmanreader.org, accessed 2 July 2013.

4 Ibid., pp. 171–2.

5 Ibid., pp. 172–3.

6 For a full academic discussion of these and many other 'dissident spaces', see Peter Davidson, 'Recusant Catholic Spaces in Early Modern England', *Catholic Culture in Early Modern England*, ed. Ronald Corthell and others (Notre Dame, IN, 2007), pp. 19–51.

7 I have written a full academic discussion of this topic in 'Pope's Recusancy', *Studies in the Literary Imagination*, XXXVIII/1 (Spring 2005), pp. 63–76.

8 'The Second Satire of Dr John Donne', revision of 1735, ll. 11–12, quoted with excellent contextual discussion in Paul Gabriner, 'The Papist's House, the Papist's Horse', *Centennial Hauntings*, ed. C. C. Barfoot and Theo D'haen (Amsterdam and Atlanta, GA, 1990), p. 33.

9 The most extensive accounts of the subject are found in Gabriner, 'The Papist's House', pp. 13–64, and Maynard Mack, *Alexander Pope: A Life* (New Haven, CT, 1985), especially pp. 336–9. Gabriner, 'The Papist's House', p. 47, quoting George Sherburn, ed., *The Correspondence of Alexander Pope*, IV (Oxford, 1956), pp. 504–5.

10 Gabriner, 'The Papist's House', p. 30.

11 George Sherburn, ed., *The Correspondence of Alexander Pope*, vol. IV (Oxford, 1956), p. 454.

12 Alexander Pope, 'Windsor Forest', *The Works of Mr Alexander Pope* (London, 1717), pp. 50–51.

13 Alexander Pope, 'Ethic Epistles', *The Works of Mr Alexander Pope* (London, 1735), p. 51.

14 Ibid., p. 18.

15 Ibid., pp. 42–3.

16 Maynard Mack, *The Garden and the City* (Toronto, Buffalo and London, 1969), pp. 41–77.

17 Ironically, or appositely, the structure that the era of the Grand Tour identified as the grotto of Egeria was in fact a garden building, the Nymphaeum of the Villa of Herodes Atticus, lying between the Via Appia Antica and the Via Appia Nuova.

18 These verses are first found in a letter to Bolingbroke of 3 September 1740; Sherburn, ed., *Correspondence of Alexander Pope*, vol. IV, p. 262.

19 See Peter Davidson, *The Universal Baroque* (Manchester, 2007), pp. 161–6.

20 Much the same would be true *mutatis mutandis* of the gay community in the mid-twentieth century, who were themselves often fascinated with their resonances with the overshadowed people of history, those who followed the road not taken, as with Firbank's obsession with deposed sovereigns, disgraced prelates.

21 A full discussion of the known stages of the evolution of Pope's grotto can be found in Anthony Beckles Willson, *Alexander Pope's Grotto in Twickenham* (London and Twickenham, 1998).

22 The register of listed buildings in England and Wales and the information held at the National Monuments Record at Swindon (a division of English Heritage) does not even conjecture dates for any of the elements of the grotto as now surviving. In the light of this, my paragraph about the reused recusant stones must be read with caution. They could have been imported after Pope's death: the statues now in the grotto certainly were.

23 See Mack, *The Garden and the City*, pp. 63–5.

24 On 'Green Grow the Rushes': Dr Alison Shell, University College, London, generously communicated this idea; on Triangular Lodge, see Nikolaus Pevsner and Bridget Cherry, *Northamptonshire*, The Buildings of England (London, 1973), p. 400.

25 Sara Stevenson and Duncan Thomson, *John Michael Wright, the King's Painter*, exh. cat., Scottish National Portrait Gallery (Edinburgh, 1982), cat. 36.

26 This perception was generously communicated by Professor Hugh Cheape of Sabhal Mòr Ostaig, University of the Highlands and Islands; in fact, Mungo died young in a small war in central America, fighting for Scotland's doomed colony in Panama.

27 John Michael Wright, *An Account of His Excellence Roger Earl of Castlemaine's Embassy, from . . . James the IId . . . to His Holiness Innocent XI* (London, 1688). The publication of an engraving of a banquet decoration depicting the subjugation of Protestantism was well-nigh inexplicable in a publication addressed to a Protestant nation increasingly suspicious of the intentions of its Catholic king.

28 John Fleming, *Robert Adam and his Circle in Edinburgh and Rome* (London, 1962), pp. 146–7.

29 Edward Gibbon, *Memoirs of My Life*, ed. Betty Radice (Harmondsworth, 1984), p. 142.

30 For Byres's career, see Peter Davidson, 'James Byres of Tonley: Jacobites and Etruscans', *Recusant History* (October 2010),

pp. 261–74. For Wynnstay, see Timothy Mowl, 'A Roman Palace for a Welsh Prince: Byres' Designs for Sir Watkyn Williams-Wynn', *Apollo* (November 1995), p. 33.

31 James Byres, *Hypogaei; or, Sepulchral Caverns of Tarquinia* (London, 1842).

32 Gibbon, *Memoirs of My Life*, p. 143. Anatole France locates the conversation that forms the substance of his philosophical novel *Sur la Pierre blanche* in the same place and light as that which gave Gibbon the idea for his history: '*Le soleil, descendu derrière le Capitole, frappait de ses dernières flèches l'arc triomphal de Titus sur la haute Vélia. Le ciel, où nageait à l'occident la lune blanche, restait bleu comme au milieu du jour. Une ombre égale, tranquille et claire emplissait le Forum silencieux*'. Anatole France, *Sur la Pierre blanche* (Paris, 1905), p. 6.

33 John Wilton-Ely, *The Mind and Art of Giovanni Battista Piranesi* (London, 1978), p. 113.

34 These plates depict the Piranesi Vase, now in the British Museum, and one of the Newdigate Candelabra, now in the Ashmolean Museum, Oxford. It is possible that Byres may have played some part in the process of 'restoration', or more precisely 're-invention', of these excavated fragments.

35 Wilton-Ely, *Mind and Art*, pl. 73.

36 Ibid., pl. 93.

37 Ibid., pl. 132.

38 A phenomenon attested by generation after generation of visitors disappointed, on arrival at the real Rome, by the modesty of its scale compared to the scale implied by Piranesi; see Wilton-Ely, *Mind and Art*, p. 44.

39 See chapter Two.

40 For an extensive discussion see chapter Five.

41 Jerrold Northrop Moore, *F. L. Griggs, the Architecture of Dreams* (Oxford, 1999), p. 103.

42 In my book *The Idea of North* (London, 2005), p. 226, I wrote of Griggs's etching *The Almonry* as a last glimpse of a pre-Reformation England, in which deepening winter acts as a metaphor for imminent catastrophe.

43 Moore, *F. L. Griggs*, p. 109.

44 Ibid., p. 127.

45 Ibid., p. 175.

46 Ibid., p. 194.

47 Ibid., pp. 166–7.

48 Griggs changed the sky once more, in the 1920s, in a moment of recollection of what he then considered the pristine England of the pre-war years. He altered the sky to a Palmerish scene of early morning, with wood smoke drifting up into the rays of the rising sun.

49 Gerard Manley Hopkins, *The Notebooks and Papers*, ed. Humphry House (Oxford, 1937), p. 213.

50 See chapter Two. Hopkins's 1884 letter to *Nature*, quoted below, is reprinted in part in G. J. Symons, ed., *The Eruption of Krakatoa and Subsequent Phenomena* (London, 1887), p. 172. For a thoughtful and comprehensive treatment of Hopkins as scientist, see Tom Zaniello, *Hopkins in the Age of Darwin* (Iowa City, 1988), especially pp. 79–129, to which the following pages are much indebted.

51 Hopkins, *Notebooks and Papers*, p. 129.

52 Ibid., p. 181.

53 Ibid., p. 186.

54 Ibid., p. 203; see also Zaniello, *Hopkins in the Age of Darwin*, pp. 81–4.

55 Zaniello, *Hopkins in the Age of Darwin*, pp. 82–3.

56 Gerard Hopkins, 'A Curious Halo', *Nature*, XXVII/681 (16 November 1882), p. 53.

57 Ibid.

58 Gerard Hopkins, 'Shadow-beams in the East at Sunset', *Nature*, XXIX/733 (15 November 1883), p. 55.

59 See chapter Two.

60 Zaniello, *Hopkins in the Age of Darwin*, p. 125.

61 All the following quotations are from *Nature*, XXX (3 January 1884), pp. 222–3; this letter is reprinted in part in Symons, ed., *The Eruption of Krakatoa*.

62 See chapter Two.

63 Gerard Hopkins, 'The Remarkable Sunsets', *Nature*, XXIX/740 (3 January 1884), p. 223.

64 Zaniello, *Hopkins in the Age of Darwin*, p. 61.

65 S. J. Perry, 'Extraordinary Darkness at Midday', *Nature*, XXX/757 (1 May 1884), p. 6.

66 John Ruskin, 'The Storm Cloud of the Nineteenth Century', lecture delivered 4 February 1884 at the London Institution, in *The Works of John Ruskin*, vol. XXXIV, ed. E. T. Cook and Alexander Wedderburn (London, 1908), p. 38.

67 Geoffrey Hill, 'The Orchards of Syon', *Broken Hierarchies: Poems, 1952–2012*, ed. Kenneth Haynes (Oxford, 2013), p. 370.

5 HESPERIDES

1 Immanuel Kant, *Beobachtungen über das Gefühl des Schönen und des Erhabenen* (Riga, 1771), p. 5.

2 William Wordsworth, *Poems*, ed. John O. Hayden (Harmondsworth, 1977), vol. i, p. 85.

3 Ibid., p. 87.

4 Martin Butlin, ed., Samuel Palmer's *Sketch-book, 1824* (Clairvaux, 1962) [facsimile edn], p. 7.

5 Ibid., pp. 74–82.

6 Letter to John Linnell, December 1828, quoted in Jerrold Northrop Moore, *The Green Fuse: Pastoral Vision in English Art, 1820–2000.* (Woodbridge, 2007), p. 49.

7 A comprehensive account of these tours is found in David Hill, *Cotman in the North* (New Haven, CT, and London, 2005).

8 Ibid., pp. 155–64.

9 Gerard Manley Hopkins, *The Notebooks and Papers*, ed. Humphry House (Oxford, 1937), p. 124.

10 Ibid., p. 213.

11 Johann Wolfgang Goethe, *Briefe und Gespräche, Naturwissenschaftliche Schriften*, Part 1, vol. xiv of *Gedenkausgabe der Werke* (Zurich, 1949), p. 9. I am much indebted to Dr Hugh Salvesen for much advice on Goethe and his contemporaries.

12 Michael Steinman, ed., *The Element of Lavishness: Letters of Sylvia Townsend Warner and William Maxwell* (Washington, DC, 2001), pp. 189–90.

13 Ibid., p. 222.

14 Otto Julius Bierbaum, 'Traum durch die Dämmerung', *Erlebte Gedichte* (Berlin, 1892); available at http://gutenberg.spiegel.de, accessed 29 June 2014.

15 *Selected Letters of Robert Louis Stevenson*, ed. Ernest Mehew (New Haven, CT, 2001), p. 121.

16 Sean O'Brien, 'The Railway Sleeper', *Downriver* (London, 2001), p. 75.

17 Ibid., p. 76.

18 William Wordsworth, 'Among all lovely things my love had been', *The Collected Poems of William Wordsworth* (Ware, 1994), p. 739.

19 Theodore Roethke, 'The Visitant', quoted in Seamus Heaney and Ted Hughes, eds, *The Rattle Bag* (London, 1982), pp. 450–51.

20 W. H. Auden, *Juvenilia: Poems, 1922–1928*, ed. Katherine Bucknell (London, 1994), p. 205.

21 Edward Fitzgerald, 'Euphranor, a dialogue on youth', *Selected*

Works (London, 1962), p. 94.

22 A. E. Housman, 'Revolution', *A Shropshire Lad and Other Poems*,
ed. Archie Burnett (London, 2010), p. 104.

23 Sara Maitland, *The Book of Silence* (London, 2009), p. 129.

24 Andrew Marvell, *Miscellaneous Poems* (London, 1681), pp. 99–100.

25 Virgil, *Eclogues*, II.66–7.

26 Erwin Panofsky, 'Et in Arcadia ego', in *Meaning in the Visual Arts*
(London, 1993), p. 345.

27 *Eclogues*, VI.84–6.

28 Panofsky, 'Et in Arcadia ego', p. 346; 'Go home little goats, you
are fed now, go home', 'And the lengthening shadows fall from
the high mountains.'

29 *Eclogues*, I.79–83.

30 Samuel Palmer, *An English Version of the Eclogues of Virgil by
Samuel Palmer, with Illustrations by the Author*, ed. A. H. Palmer
(London, 1883). As many commentators have observed, these late
works regain something of the strange authority of Palmer's earliest
pastoral work, looking back as they do to his teacher William Blake's
1821 wood engravings for Thornton's imitation of the first Eclogue.

31 Leonardo da Vinci, *Notebooks*, ed. Irma A. Richter (Oxford, 2008),
p. 210.

32 See the Introduction to this book.

33 Svetlana Alpers and Michael Baxandall, *Tiepolo and the Pictorial
Intelligence* (New Haven, CT, and London, 1994), pp. 118–27.

34 Ibid., p. 153.

35 'at his most virtuosic', ibid., p. 166; 'containing Frederick the Great',
ibid., p. 164.

36 *Antony and Cleopatra*, IV.xiii.12–24. *The First Folio of Shakespeare,
the Norton Facsimile*, ed. Charlton Hinman (London and New
York, 1968), vol. III, p. 362 [editorial pagination, p. 870].

37 John Ruskin, *Modern Painters*, vol. III of *The Works of John Ruskin*, ed.
E. T. Cook and Alexander Wedderburn (London, 1903), pp. 285–6.

38 John Ruskin, *Praeterita* (Oxford, 1978), p. 103.

39 Ruskin, *Modern Painters*, pp. 79–80. Yet, as quoted above, he denied
that such a twilight had ever been painted until the late 1850s: even
from comparatively early in his career, the expectations he places on
the visual arts have elements of his later undirected vehemence.

40 Ruskin, *Praeterita*, p. 525.

41 Ibid., p. 526.

42 Ibid., p. 527.

43 The line is in imitation of Yves Bonnefoy's superb 'Et maintenant

tu es Douve dans la dernière chambre d'été', 'La Salamandre' in *Du Mouvement et de l'immobilité de Douve* (Newcastle upon Tyne, 1992), p. 124.

44 Peter Levi, *Shadow and Bone* (London, 1989), p. 22.

45 Ibid., p. 23.

46 Heather Dohollau, *La Venelle des portes* (Bédée, 1996), p. 48.

EPILOGUE: FIREWORKS AND REFLECTED LIGHTS

1   William T. O'Dea, *The Social History of Lighting* (London, 1958), p. 181.

2   D. H. Lawrence, *Women in Love* (London, 1995), p. 171.

3   Letter to Edwin Russell, 10 September 1885, Tate Gallery Archives, cited in Elaine Kilmurray and Richard Ormond, *John Singer Sargent* (London, 1998), p. 114.

4   Undated letter in the Stevenson papers, Beinecke Library, Yale University, cited in Kilmurray and Ormond, *John Singer Sargent*, p. 114.

5   Ibid., pp. 114–15.

6   Ibid., p. 114.

7   'Ye Shepherds Tell Me' by Joseph Mazzinghi (1765–1844): London publications with frequent reprints run from 1800 to the 1830s; the first New York publication of the glee was in 1832.

8   *Selected Letters of Robert Louis Stevenson*, ed. Ernest Mehew (New Haven, CT, 2001), p. 127.

9   H.D. [Hilda Doolittle], 'Evening', *Collected Poems, 1912–1944*, ed. Louis L. Martz (New York, 1986), p. 18.

10 Charles Baudelaire, *Les Fleurs du mal* (Paris, 1972), p. 77.

11 Ibid.

12 Sean O'Brien, *The Drowned Book* (London, 2007), p. 71.

13 John Ash, 'Without Being Evening', *The Branching Stairs* (Manchester, 1984), p. 119.

14 Rainer Maria Rilke, *Duino Elegies*, trans. Stephen Cohn (Manchester, 1989), pp. 28–9.

15 Ibid., pp. 58–9.

16 Ibid., pp. 80–81.

17 Sylvia Townsend Warner, *Letters*, ed. William Maxwell (New York, 1983), p. 81.

18 Richard Fanshawe, *The Poems and Translations*, ed. Peter Davidson (Oxford, 1997–9), II, p. 528.

19 Claudio Magris, *Microcosms*, trans. Iain Halliday (London, 1999), p. 71.

ACKNOWLEDGEMENTS

This book has been eight years in the making, and has its origin in travels which began more than twenty years before that. I am much indebted to Clémence and Ralph O'Connor, Robert Macfarlane, Peter Scupham, Margaret Steward, Jane Stevenson and Jill and Stephen Wolfe for the conversations that defined it.

I owe a great deal to Daniel MacCannell for his enviable dexterity as research assistant, prose stylist and picture researcher. Harry Gilonis at Reaktion Books has offered an exceptional and creative contribution to the final choice of images and to the shaping of the whole book. I would like also to acknowledge the exceptional help of my editor Aimee Selby and the creative and thoughtful contribution made by Simon McFadden's design.

I am grateful to those who have invited me to give parts of the book as conference papers or public lectures: the University of Oulu and Prof. Anthony Johnson; the National Galleries of Scotland; the universities of Newcastle and York; Gresham College and the City of London Festival.

This book touches on works in many languages and I am grateful, as ever, to those whose knowledge of them is greater than my own: to Jane Stevenson for the ancient languages; Hugh Salvesen, Daniel Höhr and Sophie Dietrich for German; Winifred Stevenson for Old Norse and Old English; Laura Tosi, Loredana Polezzi and Susan Bassnett for Italian; Clémence O'Connor and Alison Saunders for French; my beloved cousins Nicola and Paula for Spanish and for their corroborative recollections of our grandparents' crepuscular household.

I am most grateful to those who have made the crucial suggestions which have given the book its present form: to Jane Stevenson, as always; to Robert Macfarlane, who has selflessly fostered and encouraged the whole and who wrenched a wandering project back onto course at an early stage and read it in its entirety at a late one; to Laura Tosi for an introduction to Gozzano and the *crepuscolari*; to Jelena Todorovič for hospitality in

Trieste and for extraordinary illuminations in the discussion of Baroque twilights and the lighting of twilight baroque paintings; to Janet Graffius, who brought the nineteenth-century element of the book to focus around the figure of Hopkins as poet and scientist; to Mark Gibson, who guided me to Ruskin's later writings and who has been endlessly willing to discuss ghost stories, Tenebrae psalms, Pope's grotto and lighted windows; John Morrison, who guided me to an apprehension of the convergences of Scottish and Low Countries landscape painting in the nineteenth century; Andrew Biswell and Tim Brennan, whose *English Anxieties* project generated a whole series of thoughts and conversations about Cambridge in the twilight.

Alexandra Harris has, with great generosity and friendship, read the completed text, to its vast improvement. This book moves, like one of the double oratorios or operas of Pietro Raimondi (1786–1853), in counterpoint with her own remarkable *Weatherland*. This harmony, this fugue of two texts on related themes, written at the same time, is atmospheric and instinctive: she did not read this book until her own was finished, nor I hers.

The chapter on 'Dark Corners' could not have been written without the extraordinary kindness of scholars and custodians of the heritage of recusant Catholicism in Britain: Maurice Whitehead, Thomas McCoog sj, Alison Shell, Anne Dillon and Janet Graffius, whose generosity in granting access to the collections in her care at Stonyhurst is matched only by her profound knowledge of those collections and by her hospitality and that of her family. I am most grateful to Catriona Graffius for a defining conversation about the nature of 'dark corners of the land', which stretched through the whole of one lucid midsummer day in the valley of the Hodder.

I have also cause to extend warm thanks to Giles Connacher osb, Victoria Crowe, Sophie Dietrich, Rt Rev. Hugh Gilbert osb, Jane Griffiths, Patricia Hanley, Michael Leaman, Paul Mealor, Duncan Rice, Malachy Tallack, Adriaan van der Weel and Bill Zachs.

I cannot find words to thank two of my former colleagues at the University of Aberdeen, Mary Pryor and John Morrison, both of whom have gone far beyond any plausible call of duty or friendship to help me to finish this book, sometimes by actions which can only be described as *providing covering fire.*

I am lastingly in the debt of those companions on crepuscular excursions through the cities and landscapes of the 1970s and early 1980s who have become the friends and teachers of a lifetime: Edward Coulson, Mark Gibson, Alan and Susanna Powers, James Stourton.

Jonathan Key has offered me unstinting help with every aspect of film and photography discussed in this book. A long conversation with him about cricket and slowly dimming summer evenings was vital to the beginning of work on this project. His sheer courage in adversity and his long-during friendship have respectively merited the epigraph and more than earned the dedication.

PHOTO
ACKNOWLEDGEMENTS

The author and publishers wish to express their thanks to the below sources of illustrative material and/or permission to reproduce it. Some locations of artworks are also given below, in the interests of brevity.

AROS Århus Kunstmuseum: p. 154; reproduced by permission of the artist (Tim Brennan): p. 6; reproduced courtesy of the artist (Victoria Crowe) and The Scottish Gallery, Edinburgh: p. 167; British Museum, London: p. 121; photos © The Trustees of the British Museum, London: pp. 121, 200; Ca' Rezzonico – Museo del Settecento Veneziano, Venice: p. 15; City Art Centre, Edinburgh: p. 131; Dulwich Picture Gallery, London: p. 217; reproduced courtesy of The Fergusson Gallery, Perth & Kinross Council, Scotland: p. 235; Freies Deutches Hochstift/Goethe Museum, Frankfurt: p. 166; photo © Harrogate Museums and Arts/Bridgeman Images: p. 64; from the Krakatoa committee of the Royal Society (ed. G. J. Symons), *The Eruption of Krakatoa, and Subsequent Phenomena: Report of the Krakatoa committee of the Royal Society* (London, 1888): p. 82; McManus Art Gallery and Museum, Dundee (photo © Dundee Art Galleries and Museums): p. 19; Mercer Art Gallery, Harrogate: p. 64; National Galleries Scotland, Edinburgh: p. 180; Niedersächsiches Landesmuseum, Hannover: p. 206; Ny Carlsberg Glyptotek, Copenhagen: p. 151; private collections: pp. 107, 145, 167, 187; from [Samuel Palmer], *An English Version of the Eclogues of Virgil by S. Palmer, with Illustr[ations] by the Author* (London, 1883): p. 200; Rijksmuseum Amsterdam: p. 163; photo courtesy The Royal Commission on the Ancient and Historical Monuments of Wales, Aberystwyth: p. 121; Scottish National Gallery of Modern Art, Edinburgh: p. 235; photo Sir Duncan Rice Library, University of Aberdeen: p. 82; Staatsgalerie, Würzburg: p. 45; photo Jane Stevenson, reproduced by kind permission of the Governors of Stonyhurst College: p. 199; Tate, London: pp. 116 (purchase, 1894), 143 (bequeathed by

273

Miss Rachel and Miss Jean Alexander, 1972); Worcester Art Museum,
Worcester, Massachusetts: p. 61; photos Yale Center for British Art,
New Haven, Connecticut: pp. 190, 221, 223.

INDEX